Medical Practice Transformation with Information Technology

Charles M. Kilo, MD, MPH

Mark Leavitt, MD, PhD, FHIMSS

With a Foreword by

Donald M. Berwick, MD, MPP, FRCP

HIMSS

INSTITUTE FOR
HEALTHCARE
IMPROVEMENT

HIMSS Mission

To lead change in the healthcare information and management systems field through knowledge sharing, advocacy, collaboration, innovation, and community affiliations.

IHI Mission

The Institute for Healthcare Improvement (IHI) is a not-for-profit organization driving the improvement of health by advancing the quality and value of health care. Founded in 1991 and based in Cambridge, Massachusetts, IHI offers comprehensive products and services. IHI is a reliable source of energy, knowledge, and support for a never-ending campaign to improve health care worldwide. The Institute helps accelerate change in health care by cultivating promising concepts for improving patient care and turning those ideas into action. For more information about IHI, please visit www.IHI.org.

Printed in the U.S.A. 5 4 3 2 1

Requests for permission to reproduce any part of this work should be sent to

Permissions Editor
HIMSS
230 E. Ohio St., Suite 500
Chicago, IL 60611-3269
nvitucci@himss.org

ISBN: 0-9761277-0-9

For more information about HIMSS, please visit www.himss.org.

About the Authors

Charles M. Kilo, MD, MPH, FACP, is the CEO of GreenField Health, an internal medicine practice focused on developing innovative ways of delivering care to patients, and The GreenField Group, a consulting group serving clinical organizations and healthcare-focused technology companies interested in medical practice performance improvement and redesign. He is a fellow of the Institute for Healthcare Improvement (IHI) where he was previously Vice President. At IHI, he developed and led the international Idealized Design of Clinical Office Practices initiative. Dr. Kilo works regularly with IHI, the American Academy of Family Physicians (AAFP), the American College of Physicians (ACP), and others on issues pertinent to healthcare quality and medical practice performance improvement.

He serves on the Board of Directors of Kryptiq Corporation, a provider of secure messaging and workflow solutions to enhance connectivity in healthcare, the Practice Resource Center, an AAFP subsidiary, and The Foundation for Medical Excellence. He serves on advisory boards for the Association of American Medical Colleges' Institute for Improving Clinical Care, Lifecom Incorporated, a software company developing advanced healthcare decision-support and knowledge management tools, and Wired. MD, a provider of online patient education resources.

Dr. Kilo is actively engaged in many national initiatives focused on healthcare quality, safety and reliability, health system design, healthcare information technology, and medical practice performance improvement. He is a practicing internist with subspecialty training in infectious diseases. He attended Washington University School of Medicine in St. Louis where he also completed his internal medicine training. He subsequently completed an infectious diseases fellowship and Master of Public Health at Harvard.

Mark Leavitt, MD, PhD, FHIMSS, joined the HIMSS management team in December, 2003 and now serves as Chief Medical Officer. Considered one of the pioneers of electronic health records, he is actively engaged in a number of national initiatives to accelerate their adoption and enhance their interoperability. He currently chairs the Certification Commission for Healthcare Information Technology. Dr. Leavitt is a Fellow of HIMSS as well as a Clinical Assistant Professor in the Department of Medical Informatics at Oregon Health and Science University. Originally trained in Electronic Engineering at the University of Arizona and Stanford University, he transitioned to medicine at mid-career, receiving his MD from the University of Miami followed by post-graduate training in Internal Medicine at Oregon Health and Sciences University. After practicing full-time for 10 years, he led a project to launch the implementation of system-wide electronic records at Providence Health System in Oregon. In 1985 he founded MedicaLogic, leading the company as its CEO and Chairman for 15 years. Following the acquisition of MedicaLogic by GE Healthcare in 2002, Dr. Leavitt served as GE's Vice President of Clinical Initiatives.

Contributors

Jill K. Arena, FACMPE, is the Chief Operations Officer for GreenField Health System. She has worked within clinic operations in a variety of settings for more than 13 years, and has been involved in more than 15 different implementations of electronic health record (EHR) products within the physician office setting. Ms. Arena is a Fellow of the American College of Medical Practice Executives, and is a member of the Oregon Health Policy Commission Subcommittee on EHR Connectivity. As a result of her work with GreenField, she is frequently called upon to speak on EHR and other technology issues across the country.

Bruce Bagley, MD, is the Medical Director for Quality Improvement for the American Academy of Family Physicians. In this new role, he serves as the Academy's liaison with other state and national organizations working in physician practice improvement and performance measurement. Dr. Bagley also provides clinical oversight for quality improvement programs developed by the Academy such as METRIC, the Practice Enhancement Program and the Performance Measures Training Course. Dr. Bagley has spoken extensively on the topics of quality improvement, office redesign, electronic medical records and leadership. He also serves as a 2005 Malcolm Baldrige Quality Award examiner.

Scott A. Decker is the Vice President of Operational Innovation and Quality for ThedaCare, a nationally recognized Northeastern Wisconsin-based integrated healthcare delivery system. Scott has a career history of utilizing innovative and proven improvement methodologies including lean manufacturing to better the clinical and service processes in both rural and suburban healthcare settings. For the past four years, he has also served as faculty for the Institute for Healthcare Improvement.

Susan Edgman-Levitan, PA, is Executive Director of the John D. Stoeckle Center for Primary Care Innovation at Massachusetts General Hospital. She is a Lecturer in the Department of Medicine, Massachusetts General Hospital, and Associate in Health Policy, Harvard Medical School. Prior to coming to MGH, Ms. Edgman-Levitan was the founding President of the Picker Institute. Ms. Edgman-Levitan has been the co-principal investigator on the Harvard Consumer Assessment of Health Plans Study (CAHPS) study from 1995 to the present. She has served as Chair of the Institute for Healthcare Improvement (IHI) Breakthrough Series Collaborative on Improving Service Quality, and is the IHI Fellow for Patient and Family-Centered Care. She is an editor of *Through the Patient's Eyes*, a book on creating and sustaining patient-centered care and *The CAHPS Improvement Guide* and has authored many papers and other publications on patient-centered care.

James L. Holly, MD, is in the private practice of medicine in Beaumont, Texas. He is the CEO of Southeast Texas Medical Associates, LLP (www.setma.com), a multispecialty group which has used electronic medical records since 1999. Dr. Holly's practice and disease-management-development effort has focused on metabolic disorders including diabetes, lipids, metabolic syndrome and hypertension, as well as heart failure, renal disease and weight management. For the past ten years, Dr. Holly has worked toward the design and implementation of a "systems approach" to healthcare delivery similar to the business model advocated by Dr. Peter Senge in *The Fifth Discipline.*

Jeffrey L. Kegarise, OD, is a graduate of the Ohio State University College of Optometry. Since his residency at the University of Alabama at Birmingham, he has been involved in the management of physician referral networks. He has lectured nationally on eye disease treatment and quality in healthcare for more than 12 years. Dr. Kegarise was a design team member for IHI's Idealized Design of Clinical Office Practices initiative. He specializes in creating dynamic office practices through a focus on leadership, innovation, and staff performance. In addition, he was the author of a chapter in the *Lippincott Manual of Primary Eyecare* on the use of eye medications. Before becoming a partner in Cool Springs Eyecare in Franklin, Tennessee four years ago, Dr. Kegarise was the managing director of an ophthalmic referral center in Nashville and ran operations for 13 eyecare clinics. He has spent his clinical career specializing in the treatment of complex eye disorders.

Tom Landholt, MD, is a physician and healthcare consultant. His area of expertise is office workflow engineering, work he puts into practical use every day as a practicing family doctor. He has been using electronic medical records for over ten years and is at the forefront of helping practicing physicians understand and adopt the "digital workflows" he has helped to develop through lectures, publications and demonstrations. He is an in-house consultant for Kryptiq Corporation and participates in the Missouri DOQ-IT initiative.

David Lansky, PhD, is Director of the Health Program for the Markle Foundation. His work focuses on accelerating the adoption of interoperable health information technology throughout U.S. healthcare, with a particular emphasis on ensuring that patients and consumers have access to and control over their information and can participate fully in the redesign of the healthcare system. For more than 20 years, Dr. Lansky has been a proponent of a more responsive and accountable healthcare system, most recently serving as President of the Foundation for Accountability (FACCT) from 1995 to 2004. A nationally-recognized expert in accountability and quality measurement, Dr. Lansky has served as a board member or advisor to numerous healthcare projects and programs, including the National Quality Forum, the Joint Commission on Accreditation of Healthcare Organizations, the National Patient Safety Foundation, the Leapfrog Group, and President Bush's 2002 Economic Summit.

Thomas M. Leary, MALA, is the Director of Federal Affairs for HIMSS. Mr. Leary is the Society's public policy advocate to the U.S. government healthcare agencies, working to improve the federal government's response to healthcare information technology issues. Much of Mr. Leary's career in Washington has focused on federal healthcare policy and regulation development. His experience includes work both inside and outside of government. As a Division Manager for Science Applications International

Corporation's TRICARE Division, he helped to coordinate healthcare administrative outsourcing solutions for the Military Health System. He has also served as a political appointee at the Defense Department where he spent four years as the Special Assistant to the Assistant Secretary of Defense for Health Affairs, serving on the Assistant Secretary's senior management team that addressed medical readiness and peacetime healthcare delivery for the Military Health System. Mr. Leary obtained his bachelors degree in History/Political Science from Rutgers University and his masters in Legislative Affairs from The George Washington University.

Keith MacDonald has over 20 years of experience in strategic planning, operations improvement, and research in ambulatory healthcare delivery. As a member of FCG's Emerging Practices applied research group, Mr. MacDonald tracks and reports on operational best practices and the optimal use and benefits of information technology to support the ambulatory physician setting. He has broad expertise in clinical operations and the clinical information systems that support an ambulatory practice through extensive consulting and market research experience in this arena. He has authored or co-authored a number of industry reports, including E-Encounters, Online Patient-Provider Communication Tools, Achieving Tangible IT Benefits in Small Physician Practices and Clinical Decision Support for the Independent Physician Practice (all for the California HealthCare Foundation), and has consulted for many of the country's leading ambulatory group practices.

Jane B. Metzger is a Research Director in Emerging Practices, the applied research arm of First Consulting. She came to First in 1996 following 23 years of research and consulting on IT support to patient care processes at Arthur D. Little, Inc., Cambridge, MA. At First, Ms. Metzger is part of a team responsible for watching industry trends and innovations in applying IT to healthcare delivery, as well as conducting original research. Much of her work has addressed IT for direct care, especially for physicians, and rules-based clinical decision support that can be used to assist clinicians in delivering safe, high-quality care more consistently. She is part of the FCG team that advises the Leapfrog Group on its IT-related standards and is currently developing an evaluation methodology for safety- and quality-related decision support in electronic health records for the physician office. She was recently appointed to serve on the 14-member Certification Commission for Health Information Technology, which is setting up a certification process for physician office EHRs.

Blackford Middleton, MD, MPH, MSc, is Corporate Director of Clinical Informatics Research & Development, and Chairman of the Center for Information Technology Leadership at the Partners Healthcare System, and Assistant Professor of Medicine at Brigham and Women's Hospital, Harvard Medical School. Dr. Middleton's work focuses on the design and implementation of integrated clinical information systems, with special focus on electronic health records, technology assessment, and patient-centered informatics, in both commercial and academic settings. He has over 150 publications and presentations on computer-based patient records, the Internet in healthcare, and related policy and technical issues. Dr. Middleton is the Chair of the Board of Directors of HIMSS, a member of the Board of Directors for the e-Health Initiative, and a member of the HealthTech IT Working Group.

Arnold Milstein, MD, MPH, is the Medical Director of the Pacific Business Group on Health (PBGH) and a Worldwide Partner at Mercer Human Resource Consulting. PBGH is the largest healthcare purchasers' coalition in the U.S. His work and publications focus on healthcare purchasing strategy, clinical performance measurement, and the psychology of clinical performance improvement. Dr. Milstein co-founded both the Leapfrog Group and the Consumer-Purchaser Disclosure Project. He heads performance measurement activities for both initiatives and is a MedPAC commissioner. Previously a Rosenthal Lecturer at the Institute of Medicine, the *New England Journal of Medicine's* series on employer-sponsored health insurance described him as a "pioneer" in efforts to advance quality of care. Dr. Milstein is an Associate Clinical Professor at the University of California at San Francisco.

Sally Podoski is the Quality Manager supporting Physician Services, Senior Services, and the Behavioral Health divisions at ThedaCare™, a healthcare system in northeast Wisconsin. Her role includes a focus on publicly reported measures, performance improvement, and achieving the divisional outcomes for quality and safety. With over 25 years of experience in a variety of inpatient and outpatient settings and 15 years of management experience, Ms. Podoski brings a depth and breadth of experience to quality. This experience is further complemented by recent work as a facilitator with the ThedaCare™ Improvement System implementing Toyota Production System Lean principles in various divisional initiatives.

David W. Roberts, MPA, FHIMSS, is Vice President of Government Relations for HIMSS. Formerly a professional staff member for both the U.S. House Appropriations Committee and the U.S. Senate Health Subcommittee on the Handicapped, and a civilian financial analyst for the U.S. Air Force, Roberts now resides with his family in Solana Beach, California, where he is an elected member of the City Council, and maintains a HIMSS office in Alexandria, Virginia.

Joseph E. Scherger, MD, MPH, is Clinical Professor of Family Medicine at the University of California, San Diego. Dr. Scherger has a long interest in the redesign of primary care and quality improvement through the use of new health information technology. Dr. Scherger served on the Institute of Medicine Committee on the Quality of Health Care in America, which wrote *Too Err is Human* (1999) and *Crossing the Quality Chasm*. He was an early adopter of the use of e-mail with patients. He has written and presented extensively on the redesign of primary care and teaches often for the Institute for Healthcare Improvement.

Edward H. Wagner, MD, MPH, FACP, is a general internist/epidemiologist and Director of the MacColl Institute for Healthcare Innovation at the Center for Health Studies (CHS) Group Health Cooperative. His research and quality improvement work focus on improving the care of seniors and others with chronic illness. Since 1998, he has directed "Improving Chronic Illness Care," a national program of The Robert Wood Johnson Foundation. He and his MacColl Institute colleagues developed the Chronic Care Model, which has now been used in quality improvement programs worldwide. He also is Principle Investigator of the Cancer Research Network, a National Cancer Institute-funded cancer research consortium of 12 HMO-based research programs. He has written two books and more than 200 publications. He serves on the editorial boards of *Health Services Research, BMJ-USA*, and the *Journal of Clinical Epidemiology*.

John H. Wasson, MD, is Professor of Community and Family Medicine and Medicine, and Herman O. West Professor of Geriatrics at Dartmouth Medical School. He is Director of the Center for Aging and Research Director of the Dartmouth Northern New England Primary Care Research Network (COOP). Dr. Wasson is faculty for the Institute for Healthcare Improvement's Idealized Design of Clinical Office Practices, IMPACT, and Planned Care programs and for Lumetra's DOQIT Program.

Contents

Foreword

Donald M. Berwick, MD, MPP, FRCP
President and CEO
Institute for Healthcare Improvement

"Transformation" is a big word. Often, sneers and yawns follow. Who can really believe that American healthcare—entrenched, gargantuan, tightly connected to massive economic forces and self-interests, and bound in centuries of belief, ritual, and dogma—can ever be a fit target for fundamental change? Technological change—yes. Our industry avidly soaks up new machines and medicines. But deep cultural change? Basic reconfigurations of "relationship, service, and reliability," as this book categorizes the challenges in Section II? "Don't hold your breath," says the skeptic who recalls the apparent overreaching of the Clinton healthcare reform effort, the ungracious trashing of managed care, and the turtle pace of growth of electronic health records in the past quarter-century. "Ho-hum," yawns the day-to-day doctor, who has heard big talk too many times from "Big Hat–No Cattle" people who don't understand practice, and who can see clearly at ground level that little ever really seems to change.

Of all the bastions of the healthcare *status quo*, office-based medical practice—the main subject of this book—may have remained the farthest from transformation of any sector of healthcare, save possibly nursing homes. American hospitals have become sleek star-ships over the past few decades, as new imaging machines, audacious surgery, and—much more than in offices—computer-based systems have taken hold. Habits and cultures in hospitals have remained largely as they were, but the technological revolution in hospital care seems profound and continuing. Whether we wish to call that "transformation" or simply old tea in new pots is a matter for debate, but a physician beamed forward from a 1950 hospital to a 2005 one would have a rough time getting his (if from 1950, most probably "his") bearings.

Not so in the clinical office. A 1950 doctor would miss the typewriter and not recognize the PC on the receptionist's desk, would find the pharmacopoeia temporarily a challenge, and would most certainly need an orientation—a long orientation—to proper billing procedures, but he would do a fairly credible job seeing the next patient even within moments after stepping out of the time machine. The current processes are, pretty much, the old ones.

And, therefore, the physician would not, could not, serve that patient well. Not, at least, if "serving well" meant promising that patient without fail the benefits of current medical science, the respect now wanted and the control now feasible for generations X and Y, and (for a patient with a complex or chronic illness) coordination, safety, and efficiency across the continuum of care. The office practice unchanged, untransformed, cannot offer the 2005 doctor what that doctor needs to give the patient what the patient needs. To manage the 2005 patient well would require the memory and manipulation of far too much information for the doctor's mind to handle, the coordination of specialists and facilities too far away for the doctor to be familiar with, and an agile response to diversity of needs, ethnicity, preference, and talent in the patients that a "piecework" office could not feasibly attend to. That is the starting place for this book—the problem statement that Doctors Kilo and Leavitt are trying to tackle—as the Institute of Medicine and many of the scholars who write or are quoted herein have been trying to do for well more than a decade now.

Is the challenge really new? That is, was the physician in the 1950s in a more fortunate position, better able to recruit the resources he needed to meet the mid-century patients' needs? Was *that* office as a system adequate to *that* era's job? I don't know. My father was a general practitioner in a small Connecticut town for almost 50 years. I know the medical office of 1950 because I was in one, seeing my father work, every week of my young life. It seemed OK. He was widely respected and trusted in our town, and, though he worked very, very hard, his daily shuttles to the community hospital 17 miles away, his structured office hours, his orderly file cabinets, his house calls (day and night), and his memory seemed quite good enough. No "Quality Improvement Organization," NCQA, or Leapfrog Group was looking over his shoulder, and I do not believe that he systematically measured either his processes or outcomes; but between him and his community, there was plenty enough trust to get them both through any day.

But it doesn't really matter now. Whether the romantic view of the fine country doctor is right, or the more skeptical suggestion that neither my father nor his patients had enough information to tell for sure if quality was good enough, that day is over, and we now have bright lights shining on the office practice of today, and giving us little reason for comfort. The defect rates are phenomenal. We know that now. And they are high not because the doctor of 2005 is one whit less capable, ethical, or committed to patients than my father was, but because the game has changed.

The early chapters of this book recount effectively the nature of the changes, and the consequences for quality and cost. As systems thinkers, the authors of each chapter use these findings of problems as a jumping-off spot, not for criticizing or exhorting doctors to try harder, but for raising important, scientific questions about the proper nature of the system redesigns that can close those gaps in quality. Indeed, this is the only way out.

It will be neither comfortable nor easy for us to redesign office practices for the 21st century, nor to make those new designs true norms, everywhere available. Each chapter in this book lays out the scale of that challenge in one or more areas of system performance: reliability, patient-centeredness, cooperation, information systems, leadership, and more. Taken in one bite, this view of transformed medical practices is intimidating and seems unrealistic. But, as the authors also show, each element of needed change has now progressed far beyond theory and rhetoric. Step by step, example by example, we can now see practices somewhere that have tackled each of these changes and won. This book carries the case for transformation forward not by inventing new ideas, but by assembling them into a coherent whole—a picture of the new place and its new processes.

Sneers and yawns won't do. Critics remain welcome, but naysayers are not. The needs of our patients, the evidence of the quality chasm, the lessons from our modern health service researchers, and the beacons of early success all provide a basis for both hope and action.

When the Institute for Healthcare Improvement began to tackle radical redesign of office practice in 1997, in a project called "Idealized Design of Clinical Office Practices" (IDCOP), we were basing that effort on the example of transformation of the entire production system in another industry—automobile manufacturing—documented in a multi-year research program housed at the Massachusetts Institute of Technology, and beautifully documented for the lay public as "lean production" in the book, *The Machine That Changed the World.* The idea behind the IDCOP project, similar to that in this volume, was to try to piece together an image of the new clinical practice based on an assemblage of progressive, bold, scientifically based redesign concepts, sculpted into a coherent whole, and able to achieve unprecedented results. Guided by a host of participating scholars and practitioners, including several represented as authors in this book, as well as Tom Nolan, Richard Rockefeller, Maureen Bisognano, Ed Wagner, and many others, the collaborating IDCOP teams from three dozen practice sites, ranging from a solo practice to groups of over 100 physicians, were able to take remarkable steps forward, leaving us all not just impressed, but hopeful that, in that case, "transformation" might not, after all, be too big a word. We discovered an enormous reservoir of talent, energy, and curiosity in the participating clinical practices, and a willingness to set aside habits that good doctors of the past, my father included, might well have regarded as immutable.

In the IDCOP project, that effort centered on a phrase that we proposed as the project's call-to-arms, stating a vision, on behalf of the practices, of what they wanted to offer their patients and communities. That vision, which has remained for me an orienting compass for improvement of clinical practice, was this:

We intend that our patients will say of us, "They give me exactly the help I want and need exactly when I want and need it."

The IDCOP project participants—faculty and teams alike—never flinched from that vision, though it called upon them to reconsider the design and theory of nearly every major system and subsystem in their clinical office practices. In many of those sites, that quest continues today, and, thanks to the work of the scholars and teachers like those who Doctors Kilo and Leavitt cite in this volume, the odds of success for those medical practices willing to think big are steadily rising.

Preface

Charles M. Kilo, MD, MPH, and Mark Leavitt, MD, PhD, FHIMSS

"In its current form, habits, and environment, American healthcare is incapable of providing the public with the quality healthcare it expects and deserves."
Institute of Medicine, Crossing the Quality Chasm[1]

The opportunity is truly unprecedented. Like no time in history, we have today both the knowledge and the technology necessary to transform the medical practice. And that transformation is underway. Many barriers remain and the challenges are substantial, but the pace of change over the past five years has been remarkable.

Many of our medical colleagues do not yet see those changes, or they see only inklings of the coming transformation. At this point however, it is unstoppable. The transformation will increasingly penetrate our daily lives.

Many physicians believe that substantive change in delivery is necessary, but that they cannot change until the financing system changes first. Understanding this real life view, we are fortunate to have the opportunity to thank three groups of individuals.

First, those innovators who have not waited for the payment system to change, but rather have sought to understand the necessary modifications in medical practice design and demonstrate their value before asking others to pay for them. Second, our technology colleagues who have demonstrated consistent vision and tenacity over the past decade within a marketplace that is only now ready to appreciate their products. And third, our health insurance industry colleagues who understand that their reimbursement mechanisms must also be transformed and who have begun to make such substantive changes. We are fortunate that some of those courageous leaders are authors of chapters of this book.

It is not the purpose of this book to revisit the data that documents our ambulatory care shortcomings. That has been aptly done elsewhere, and we assume that those reading this book will already be fully cognizant of that data. If not, then we refer those individuals to other sources such as the Institute of Medicine's book *Crossing the Quality Chasm,*[1] Elizabeth McGlynn and colleagues' 2003 article published in the *New England Journal of Medicine,*[2] and many other sources.[3]

This book is intended to look forward, not backward. The future is in front of us. We seek to leverage lessons from the past into designs for the future—to use the past as a springboard toward much smarter system design that intelligently and rationally incorporates technology to produce fundamentally different outcomes.

Section I of the book, Introduction and Historical Perspective, provides a historical perspective for readers. Current efforts to redesign ambulatory systems have been well underway for over a decade, driven by a clear imperative based on data about the performance of our ambulatory practices.

Section II, Principles for Transforming Practice, focuses on the provision of three key deliverables or promises that our patients want and need, and that we are charged with delivering: deep, personal relationships, impeccable service, and high clinical reliability. We will provide information on both the system design and technology necessary to deliver on these promises.

Section III of the book, Achieving the Vision, is about implementation. We present information on both the management and information technology systems and capabilities necessary for practices to participate in the transformation.

Section IV, The Changing Environment, examines the changing external environment. We evaluate the powerful roles that our medical payment system and government will play in transforming medical practice.

Finally, we wish to express our deep appreciation to those who made this book possible: to Don Berwick for his inspiring foreword, to our chapter contributors for their substantial commitments of time and expertise, and to our case study practices for sharing their experiences. Our heartfelt thanks also go to Nancy Gorham Haiman for her steadfast assistance in developing the manuscript. We also wish to acknowledge Jane Roessner for her support for the project by the Institute for Healthcare Improvement, and to Fran Perveiler of HIMSS who skillfully managed the book from start to finish.

References

1 Institute of Medicine. *Crossing the Quality Chasm: A New Health System for the 21st Century.* Washington, DC: National Academy Press; 2001.

2 McGlynn EA, Asch SM, Adams J, et al. The quality of healthcare delivered to adults in the United States. *New Engl J Med.* 348(26): 2635-2645, June 26, 2003.

3 Wennberg JE, Cooper MM, et al. *The Dartmouth Atlas of Health Care 1999.* Washington DC: American Hospital Association; 1999.

Section I

Introduction and Historical Perspective

CHAPTER 1

A Framework for Transformation

Charles M. Kilo, MD, MPH, and Mark Leavitt, MD, PhD, FHIMSS

THE IMPERATIVE FOR TRANSFORMATION

The talk of transformation today is so present and so overwhelming as to seem vituperative to the hard working, well intended healthcare professionals who labor daily in their efforts to delivery high quality care. As we stated in the Preface, the need for transformation is supported by a considerable amount of data, but it is also supported by our collective personal experiences as healthcare professionals, as patients ourselves, and as parents of children and children of elderly parents who need care. The need to transform is not a condemnation of our hard working healthcare colleagues. Rather, it is a realistic assessment of our current state.

We know that the vast majority of our colleagues are well motivated and deeply caring. But they are stuck in a system that is broken—a system that does not support their needs as hard working healthcare professionals trying to deliver the best possible care, and it doesn't meet their personal health needs or those of their children or those of their elderly parents.

While healthcare in the United States is frequently held up as being the best in the world, a substantial amount of data fail to support this claim. We spend vastly more per capita on healthcare than other industrialized nations and we have much better access to health services than those in other countries, but that money and access have failed to deliver measurably better healthcare outcomes or overall health compared with other industrialized countries.[1] And, we should not forget that our superior access to high technology belies the fact that 40 million Americans, or about 15% of the population, have no health insurance at all—and therefore exceedingly poor access to care.

Elizabeth A. McGlynn, PhD, and colleagues recently reported that only about 56% of patients received recommended care for chronic conditions.[2] These kinds of data are abundant. Approximately 133 million Americans, or 44% of the total population, have at least one chronic illness, with half of these individuals having more than one such illness. Approximately 75% of healthcare expenditures are devoted to the treatment of chronic disease.[3]

Consider the following:

- Only 55% of individuals receive recommended care across a wide range of conditions and treatment approaches, with the doctors' ability to provide the recommended treatment varying significantly depending on the specific medical condition, ranging from 79% for senile cataracts to just 10.5% for alcohol dependence.[2]
- One in 12 older individuals (8%) is prescribed an inappropriate drug at doctor visits where inappropriate medications were defined as those that had a risk of adverse outcomes outweighing the potential benefits for most elderly patients.[4]
- Medical errors and preventable events occur in nearly 24% of primary care visits.[5]
- From the patient's perspective, 25% experience adverse drug events associated with medications prescribed in ambulatory settings of which 63% were associated with physician failure to respond to medication-related symptoms and 37% were associated with patient failure to inform the clinician.[6]

"The gap between what we know works and what is actually done is substantial enough to warrant attention," a RAND study concluded. "These deficits, which pose serious threats to the health and well-being of the U.S. public, persist despite initiatives by both the federal government and private health systems to improve care."[2]

Healthcare, particularly healthcare provided in ambulatory settings, is exceedingly and increasingly complex. Multiple practitioners in multiple care settings provide services to patients with increasingly complex conditions. Continuity of care is often problematic. Technological advances have enabled all but the most acute of care to be provided in outpatient settings. Simultaneously, reimbursement constraints have forced hospitals and physicians to discharge hospitalized patients earlier. With little additional time, and no additional funding going into primary care in particular, the demands put on our ambulatory systems have risen dramatically.

Likewise, the information explosion threatens to overwhelm all practitioners. In the 1960s, approximately 100 randomized control trial results were published yearly with that number rising to 10,000 in the 1990s. Notes David Eddy, "The complexity of modern medicine exceeds the inherent limitations of the unaided human mind."[7] Medicine can no longer be practiced safely or reliably "off the top of the doctor's head," yet almost all practitioners continue to try to do so.

The use of medications is probably the most obvious example. Modern pharmacology has made it possible to treat previously intractable conditions. More than 10,000 registered drugs are now available on the market, and more than 1,000 new prescription drugs have been introduced since 1975, with nearly 90 new drugs approved by the FDA in one recent year alone.[8] In excess of three billion prescriptions are dispensed by community pharmacists each year[9] and newly discovered drug interactions are documented daily. More than three-quarters of ambulatory office visits result in a patient having a new or refill prescription.[10] The known and clinically significant interactions of commonly used medications are now too many for any physician, nurse or pharmacist to remember at the time of caring for a patient.

Yet the pressure to be more "productive" is relentless for many, if not most, practitioners, particularly primary care physicians. In 2003, the mean number of ambulatory encounters for pediatricians in group practices was 5,051 per year; for family physicians, the mean number was more than 4,500 encounters per year.[11] Ambulatory appointment lengths for internal medicine now average approximately 18 minutes, and many are interrupted multiple times. More often than not, neither the patient's accurate medical history nor best-practice information are available to the physician during the patient visit. This means that the physician is functioning with partial information, partial knowledge, and reliance on memory. Communication about what occurred with the patient between the last and current visit must be crammed into a brief period of time.

In fact, the current system is stuck in an acute care model that relies almost exclusively on brief doctor-patient visits as the mechanism of care. The acute care model is synonymous with episodic care and it simply does not work well for prevention and chronic illness management. The care we need today is broadband care—the ability to manage multiple complex issues consistently and continuously over time. Today's brief episodic visits create a bottleneck between the skills of the clinician, available medical knowledge, and patient needs. Our dedicated primary care physicians know better than most the extent of chronic illness in the United States, and how difficult it is to manage these patients in the current paper-based, visit-based system. The end result is that we are burning out our primary care physicians at an alarming rate given the untenable expectations placed upon them.

Patients are understandably frustrated as well when they try to get timely and appropriate care, because their access to care is poor, their access is dependent upon visits in an age of universal telephone and e-mail connectivity in the rest of their lives, and their medical information is often missing, incomplete, out-of-date, or located in several different locations.

For patients with chronic illnesses, it's no wonder that their medical data can be so elusive: A recent Gallup Poll survey found that more than half are seen by three or more doctors. Care delivery is even more fragmented for patients with chronic conditions covered by Medicare, who see an average of six physicians.[12]

A FRAMEWORK FOR SYSTEM DESIGN

Many models exist that provide insight into better design of the medical office. Most of these models are useful in helping those who seek to transform the practice. The best known of these is the Chronic Care Model developed by Ed Wagner and colleagues.[13] More important than the specific model is the ability of medical practice leaders to understand the practice as a system and to develop a deep working knowledge of the medical practice system's components and how they need to work together.

In this book, instead of promoting a specific model, we focus on three critical functions that every practice—primary care or specialty, urban or rural, academic or non-academic—needs to deliver. We believe that these functions are universal in providing care—irrespective of the setting and applicable to any specific model that one may be using.

Those three critical functions are what our patients want and need, and what we, healthcare professionals, do and should seek to provide—deep, trusting relationships, impeccable service, and highly reliable clinical care. We have chosen to organize this book around these three themes. In this book, we ask the question, "What are the critical components of medical practice system design and technology that allow a practice to deliver on the promises of great relationships, impeccable service, and high clinical reliability?"

In answering this question, several items should be clear. To deliver great relationships, service, and clinical reliability, the medical practice must be specifically and thoughtfully designed to do so; it must merge information technology (IT) effectively into its work processes; and there must be in place a core set of management functions and capabilities that serve as a bedrock foundation for the practice. Without appropriate management systems, medical practices will not be able to effectively implement or sustain the changes necessary to meet these challenges. Management systems are the foundation upon which our clinical systems are built and maintained, and they require their own specific, intentional design and technology for optimal performance.

The processes that produce these results—relationship, service, and reliable care—do not exist in isolation. They interact heavily with each other. In fact, as you will appreciate in the pages ahead, the processes that produce great relationships are often critical to good service as well. This is no surprise—a system is a collection of components such as people, resources, and processes that work together to achieve a common aim. Those components work together to produce the desired outcomes. So it is natural that there is significant overlap and interaction between the processes that help us deliver these critical functions.

We also want to maintain our sobriety. We understand the challenges that still lie ahead. We understand the many barriers to practice transformation, barriers extremely palpable to the practicing clinician, particularly the primary care physician. We address many of those challenges and barriers in this book.

SYSTEM DESIGN AND INFORMATION TECHNOLOGY

The job of getting IT into medical practices has been far more difficult than anyone would have expected or desired over the past decade. As a marketplace, ambulatory care presents a harsh reality. The ambulatory arena is fragmented and dominated not by large organizations but rather by very small medical groups with the majority of physicians in this country working in private practices of fewer than eight clinicians. While not universally true, these practices traditionally have weak governance structures, poor capital structures for investment, and little time to contemplate ideal workflow and technology to assist in their work—particularly when the payment structure has not encouraged such different organizational mindfulness.

For the technology vendor, the cost of development, marketing, sales, and support in this environment has been substantial. We know the financial realities of the marketplace, and we are sympathetic to the many well intended technology companies who have helped forge the path forward. Their work is to be celebrated, not condemned. We also understand that the financial resources to drive deep and appropriate research and development into product design are highly limited in this marketplace.

One critical need that we face is a more thorough and thoughtful application of information technology into clinical processes. The customary design approach of observing existing workflows, creating product prototypes, and refining them with the help of "typical" end users produces software that supports existing practice patterns. An additional injection of input from those who wish not just to automate, but transform their practices with these tools is needed.

It is understandable and logical for technology vendors to design their products to meet the needs of today's mainstream customers. Unfortunately, today's needs emanate from concerns driven by chaotic, ineffective clinical workflows and reimbursement systems. This creates products designed to optimize coding rather than optimizing relationship, service, and reliability of care. To address this situation, we must find ways to bring together leaders in practice transformation with leaders in ambulatory care technology development.

Those of us who have been focused on driving system redesign have not sufficiently engaged with our technology colleagues to understand and help guide the technology necessary to meet our needs. The needs here are enormous—in order to achieve optimal performance, technologists and system designers must work much more closely to design and test the impact that their products have on performance.

Fortunately, this is beginning to occur. In fact, the synergy between system designers (or redesigners) and technologists is growing very rapidly. Where recently these camps existed in some isolation to each other, those walls have been very rapidly broken down. The system designer of today must understand the appropriate use of technology and design the new systems with technology in mind, and the technologist had better understand the work of ambulatory care much more deeply. Both camps need to design not for yesterday or today, but for tomorrow. Our work has to take healthcare where it needs to go, not replicate where it currently is.

MOVING FORWARD

In this time of tremendous change, we see little but opportunity. Deep change is always accompanied by stress and anxiety, particularly when the endgame is not always clear to those involved. We believe that the transformation underway will provide significant benefits to the ambulatory care setting, in particular to primary care physicians and other primarily ambulatory-based specialists. That does not reduce the stress and anxiety of implementing the necessary change, however.

Many hard working clinicians remain realistically skeptical—you cannot expect most clinicians to forge into the future when the payment system is designed to perpetuate the past. Like others, physicians will do what they get paid to do—irrespective of whether or not that service is truly necessary.

Fortunately, this situation has also changed dramatically in recent years—witness the rate of innovation in healthcare financing that we are now experiencing. Instead of well intended but large scale, relatively draconian changes in health financing, payers are, like never before, actively experimenting with a wide variety of smaller changes that seek to foster the necessary transformation.

This book addresses the transformation underway in ambulatory care. It discusses critical elements of what new systems of ambulatory care will look like, it describes the vital components of the system, it presents the technology that is and will be necessary to enable that transformation, and it addresses payment reform that is underway to support these efforts.

Synergy is the critical message—the synergy of system design, technology, and financing that is making transformation feasible.

References

1 Schoen C, Osborn R, et al. Primary care and health system performance: Adults' experiences in five countries. *Health Affairs.* October 28, 2004; W4-487-503.

2 McGlynn EA, Asch SM, Adams J, et al. The quality of healthcare delivered to adults in the United States. *New Engl J Med.* June 26, 2003; 348(26): 2635-2645.

3 Institute of Medicine. *Crossing the Quality Chasm: A New Health System for the 21st Century.* Washington, DC: National Academies Press; 2001.

4 Goulding MR. Inappropriate medication prescribing for elderly ambulatory care patients. *Arch Intern Med.* Feb 2004; 64: 305-312.

5 Elder NC, Meulen MV, Cassedy A. The identification of medical errors by family physicians during outpatient visits. *Ann Fam Med.* March/April 2004; 2:125-129.

6 Gandhi TK, Saul N. Weingart SN, Borus J, et al. Adverse drug events in ambulatory care. *New Engl J Med.* April 17, 2003; 48:1556-1564.

7 Millenson ML. *Demanding Medical Excellence: Doctors and Accountability in the Information Age.* Chicago: University of Chicago Press; 1997.

8 Proulx S, Wilfinger R, Cohen MR. Medication error prevention: Profiling one of pharmacy's foremost advocacy efforts for advice on error prevention. *Pharm Pract Manage Q.* 1997; 17(1): 1-9.

9 National Association of Chain Drug Stores. In 2001 retail pharmacies filled over 3 billion prescriptions totaling $164 billion. [News release August 12, 2002.] www.nacds.org/wmspage.cfm?parm1=2998 (accessed April 7, 2005).

10 Centers for Medicare and Medicaid Services. http://www.cms.hhs.gov/statistics/nhe/default.asp?

11 Medical Group Management Association. *Physician Compensation Production Survey: 2004 Report Based on 2003 Data.* Englewood, CO: MGMA Press; 2004, 144-145.

12 Bodenheimer T, Wagner EH, Grumbach K. Improving primary care for patients with chronic illness. *JAMA.* Oct 9, 2002; 288 (14):1775-1779.

13 The Improving Chronic Illness Care National Program of the Robert Wood Johnson Foundation. www.improvingchroniccare.org.

CHAPTER 2

The Evolution of Medical Practice Redesign

John H. Wasson, MD, and Edward H. Wagner, MD, MPH, FACP

If the purpose of this chapter was to provide historical perspective on the design or redesign of ambulatory medical practice, the chapter would be a short one indeed. *Design* most often implies a purposeful and organized process for producing something or proceeding from point A to point B. Similarly, *redesign* implies that something was designed in the first place, and that a "re-do" is needed to achieve a given objective.

Ambulatory medical practice, in fact, has not benefited from this kind of purposeful design, but instead has evolved and many would say, only slightly so at that. This chapter traces that evolution, describes efforts during recent decades to consciously bring critical design elements to ambulatory practice, and highlights promising elements of future medical practice design.

THE DESIGN OF AMBULATORY CARE IN THE 1900s

Printed by permission of the
Norman Rockwell Family Agency.

The vision of ambulatory medical practice captured by Norman Rockwell has been the standard for medical practice throughout the 20th century. In Rockwell's paintings, a physician examines a child up close, meets with an anxious family, or sits at an elderly patient's bedside. A face-to-face visit is the primary design element of this relationship and trust-based healthcare process. As the century progressed, most physicians no longer made house calls, of course, nor did they sit at the bedside of dying patients. The purpose of face-to-face visits focused on the treatment of discrete episodes of acute illness.

In the latter part of the 20th century and into the current decade, the hoped-for healthcare experience remained and remains a patient-centered one full of trust and compassion. However, new forces, such as the explosion of scientific/medical knowledge, pharmacological advances, healthcare payment systems, regulation, and technology are changing Rockwell's vision of ambulatory practice.

This notwithstanding, the key design element of office-based ambulatory care continues to be the face-to-face visit. The reality is that both the patient and physician usually conduct this visit without preparation or efficient access to critical decision support information. This has resulted in well-documented performance problems, categorized by the Institute of Medicine (IOM) as:[1]

- Underuse of evidence-based treatments known to help patients;
- Overuse of care and services, generally due to poor documentation and information exchange; and
- Misuse, which occurs when potentially valuable care or services are provided incorrectly.

Until recently, quality, outcomes, and safety problems experienced by patients while receiving healthcare were viewed primarily as practitioner performance problems. The script read like this: "The physician or other practitioner just didn't have the right training or information. Or, the practitioner had the training and information but was not using them or using them incorrectly." This led to interventions, such as educational initiatives, designed to fix cognitive "errors."

The evidence that improvement is needed in office practice, where most Americans receive their healthcare, is overwhelming.[2] Patients and providers are seldom on the same page about the issues that really matter to patients—meaningful interaction, access when and where care is needed, and provision of the right, reliable care. These problems reflect a system that lacks the correct design elements to ensure the following:

- Informed patients who are ready and able to manage health issues that come their way;
- A practice team that understands what really matters to patients and hence can provide high quality service; and
- The provision of best practice, evidence-based preventive and continuing care.

The important system design work conducted in the field of anesthesiology during the 1970s helped to refocus improvement initiatives on system and process design, which is now known to be the root cause of most healthcare quality, outcomes, and safety problems. However, the focus of much of the work has been on care provided in hospital settings, not ambulatory practices.

PIONEERING A SYSTEMS APPROACH TO AMBULATORY PRACTICE IMPROVEMENT IN THE 1960s

John W. Runyon, Jr., of the University of Tennessee, was one of the early pioneers of a systems approach to the redesign of ambulatory care. Beginning in the early 1960s, Runyan and colleagues established neighborhood-based, "decentralized" clinics in Memphis. Their goal was to meet the medical care needs of socioeconomically disadvantaged individuals with chronic illnesses, specifically diabetes, hypertension, and cardiac diseases. These individuals were heavy users of Memphis' public hospitals for outpatient care.

Runyan was unaware of the groundbreaking system design work achieved through the clinics he established. Financed by the public health department, the clinics offered the following system design elements:[3,4,5]

- ***Identification of patient populations:*** Patient lists—the precursors of patient registries—were developed and maintained.
- ***Use of a care team:*** The care team included nurse practitioners and nutritionists who staffed neighborhood clinics; physicians staffed a central referral clinic for consultations and the management of complicated problems.
- ***Emphasis on disease prevention:*** Patients received extensive education on risk reduction practices, such as weight management, salt restriction, smoking cessation, and alcohol moderation.
- ***Provision of guideline-based care:*** Clinicians used protocols or clinical guidelines to provide preventive and ongoing care.
- ***Integrated, whole-person care:*** To reduce fragmentation of care, coexisting illnesses as well as other chronic diseases were treated using protocols in the clinics or in the home.
- ***Focus on measurement:*** Patient health status, treatment outcomes, and costs were tracked longitudinally and prospectively over long periods of time (decades).
- ***Use of community resources:*** Patients were referred to community programs and resources, as needed.
- ***Outreach:*** Extensive and regular follow-up prevented individuals from falling through or between the cracks.

The results achieved in the neighborhood clinics were impressive. For example, the patients who received care in the Memphis clinics had 47% lower total hospital rates than patients treated in private medical practices and hospital clinics.[4] Total care costs were commensurately lower.

SHARPENING THE FOCUS IN AMBULATORY CARE: THE 1970s THROUGH EARLY 1990s

Health services research, and specifically major ambulatory-oriented research studies conducted by physicians, emerged with considerable rigor during the 1970s. Up to this point in time, research primarily had been conducted by sociologists and economists.

Researcher-clinicians began conducting studies to examine the effectiveness of various interventions present in Runyan's model, such as protocol-based care, structured visits, outreach to patients, organized patient education, and development and use of patient databases. Many initiatives examined the literature and experience base on treatment outcomes related to common diseases and conditions most often handled in office practice. One goal was to identify best practice (i.e., best outcome) clinical treatments for conditions such as headache, back pain, urinary tract infections, diabetes, and others, and to identify whether specific interventions made a difference. The paucity of published information that could answer physicians' simple questions, such as "What's the best treatment for a patient with a sore throat and a fever?" or "How should I treat a patient with a headache?" was striking. This led to the creation of the first clinical algorithms, which have evolved into what are now called "clinical guidelines."

In the 1980s and into the 1990s, health services researchers also started looking at how office-based practice was conducted and exploring, for example, whether other care delivery modes could be effective in providing continuity of care. Large controlled studies of selected patient populations were conducted to explore such questions as, "Do health outcomes improve if patients see the same physician over time?" and "Might telephone care be as effective as face-to-face visits for routine follow-up care?[6,7]

Other research during this period looked at the healthcare delivered in community medical practices, and specifically at the interaction between physicians and patients. The research was grounded on the fundamental belief that the quality of the patient-physician interaction has a significant impact on health outcomes. It explored how well physicians actually relate to patients and whether physicians know what is important to their patients. The results of a large study of community practices published in the early 1980s, for example, indicated that physicians were not even close to being on the "same page" as their patients.[8] This spawned considerable research on how to improve patient-physician interaction.

Access to services was also the subject of considerable research in the early 1990s. While working at Kaiser, Mark Murray and Catherine Tantau devised the Advanced (or Open) Access Scheduling system which will be described fully by Susan Edgman-Levitan in Chapter 5.

All of the research from the 1980s and very early 1990s described here focused primarily on discrete care interventions, rather than the totality of medical practice and how to achieve system-wide design or redesign. Some approaches aimed to improve patient access or enhance the efficiency of office scheduling systems, for example, but were not intended to impact an important dimension of care such as patient health outcomes.

The work of John Wennberg and colleagues in identifying and understanding the distinctive variations in clinical practice patterns in U.S. healthcare, first published in 1973,[9] overarched the research described here. Practice variations existed and continue to exist because no consensus has been achieved about clinical and care delivery approaches that should be used. A consensus on what is important to the patient and a systematic way to measure outcomes achieved in ambulatory healthcare were also lacking.

IMPROVEMENT-ORIENTED APPROACHES TO PRACTICE REDESIGN: THE MID- TO LATE 1990S

Up to the early 1990s, efforts to identify and adopt a system-wide approach to ambulatory care design continued to be quite limited. Care models from other countries, such as British "mini-clinics" run for patients with similar needs, for example, asthma or diabetic mini-clinics, existed, but were not widely studied. In such settings, physicians with responsibility for a cohort or population of patients provided high quality continuity of care for patients with chronic illnesses.[10,11] In this country, the growth of community health centers, made possible by a federal grant program funded under the Public Health Service Act, offered an organized, designed approach to primary healthcare for adults, children and families who normally experienced financial, geographic, or cultural barriers to care.

Integrated group practices operated by such giants as Kaiser Permanente and Group Health Cooperative of Puget Sound, played an early role in medical practice redesign. Preventive and guideline-based care was integral to the design of services they provided and continue to provide. Study of care interventions for patients with chronic illnesses, including diabetes and hypertension, planted the seeds for a "big picture," comprehensive practice redesign as envisioned in the Chronic Care Model described later in this chapter. The medical literature base reviewed by Wagner and his Group Health Cooperative colleagues indicated that patient outcomes could be improved by five types of interventions: [12]

- ***The use of evidence-based, planned care:*** Use of explicit guidelines for what needs to be done for patients, at what intervals, and by whom "requires the doctor to make the intellectual leap from constantly thinking and worrying about specific patients to considering all patients with specific clinical features or needs and how those needs might be met. This leap is facilitated by the use of practice protocols or guidelines based on scientific evidence of effectiveness," noted the author team.[12]
- ***Reorganization of practice systems and provider roles:*** Practice redesign requires physicians to reconsider their practices and re-plan the basic ways they do their clinical work, including the organization of the practice team and the allocation of tasks among them, the management of patient contact (appointments, follow-up), and the use of other health professionals.[12] The delegation of key tasks to appropriate members of the practice team, especially nonphysicians, was identified as a central feature of successful chronic care programs.[13] The most successful programs relied heavily on nurses.
- ***Improved patient self-management support:*** Successful protocols or chronic illness programs provide patients with the education needed to change their lifestyles and develop self-management competencies.
- ***Increased access to clinical expertise:*** The physician's specialized clinical knowledge and expertise has a significant impact on patient outcomes. Continuing medical education in various forms is the most common approach to increasing physicians' expertise. Other strategies include collaborative care, whereby specialists and generalists manage patients together in the primary care setting,[14] and computer decision support systems, whose reminder systems have proven effective in promoting recommended physician behaviors.[15]
- ***Greater availability of clinical information:*** "Information about patients, their care, and their outcomes is an essential ingredient of all population-based strategies to improve chronic illness care. Without a list of all patients with a condition—a registry—providers are forced to be responsive, waiting for patients to present for care," noted the authors.[12]

The research concluded that major improvement of health outcomes for patients with chronic illnesses required organizing these five components into an "integrated system of care."

Several years later, a systematic review of 41 controlled trials that evaluated the effectiveness of interventions to improve the management of diabetes in primary care, outpatient, and community settings indicated that improvement interventions were more potent when used in combination: multifaceted professional interventions (such as education of healthcare professionals) and organizational interventions (such as the provision of part of the care by a nurse or pharmacist) that facilitate structured and regular review of patients were effective in improving the process of care. The addition of patient education to these interventions and the enhancement of the role of nurses in diabetes care led to improvements in patient outcomes and the process of care, noted Carry M. Renders and colleagues.[16]

During the mid to late 1990s, two practice design "models," which took a more systematic approach to ambulatory practice design, emerged—the Chronic Care Model and the Idealized Design of Clinical Office Practices. Use of the term *model* is problematic with many physicians, but the planned approaches to practice design offered by these two models can bring improvements to practices of all sizes.

The Chronic Care or "Planned Care" Model

Developed by Wagner and colleagues at the Group Health Cooperative's MacColl Institute for Healthcare Innovation as part of the RWJ Foundation-supported Improving Chronic Illness Care Program, the Chronic Care Model addresses the need to care for the aging population with an increasing prevalence of chronic illness in the U.S., and changes the vision of medical practice as portrayed in Rockwell's paintings. The sidebar below outlines its six key design elements.

Key Design Elements of the Planned Care Model

(from www.improvingchroniccare.org)

- ***Linkage to community resources:*** Provision of linkages to community resources keeps patients supported and involved with care and provides cost-effective services not available inside the organization, such as nutrition counseling and smoking cessation programs.
- ***Leadership:*** The practice's leaders create the culture, organization and mechanisms that promote safe, high quality care and encourage effective care of patients with chronic illnesses. Leaders secure resources for quality improvement activities.
- ***Patient self-management support:*** Patients are empowered and prepared to manage their health and healthcare. Effective self-management support strategies include assessment, goal-setting, action planning, problem-solving and follow-up. Practices organize internal and community resources to provide ongoing self-management support to patients.
- ***Delivery system design:*** Planned visits and active follow up are central to care delivery design. The actions of care teams, whose size and composition can range widely, are coordinated. Team member roles are defined and tasks distributed to assure the delivery of effective, efficient clinical care and self-management support. Planned interactions support evidence-based care and follow up with the patient by the care team is ensured.

- ***Decision support:*** Clinical care is consistent with scientific evidence and patient preferences. Evidence-based guidelines are imbedded into daily clinical practice and shared with patients through use of proven education methods to encourage patient participation.
- ***Clinical information systems:*** Design of medical records and access to records, whether manual or electronic, facilitates efficient and effective care. It also enables timely reminders for providers and patients, the identification of relevant subpopulations for proactive care, and individual patient care planning. Information systems assure ready access to key data on individual patients as well as populations of patients. A registry or database of key information on all patients with a chronic condition is the glue that holds an effective chronic care system together.

Use of these design elements results in "productive interactions" between informed, activated patients and their prepared, proactive practice team (Figure 2-1). The evidence base shows that by redesigning delivery systems to meet the needs of chronically ill patients, these chronic disease management strategies achieve better disease control, higher patient satisfaction, and better adherence to guidelines.[18]

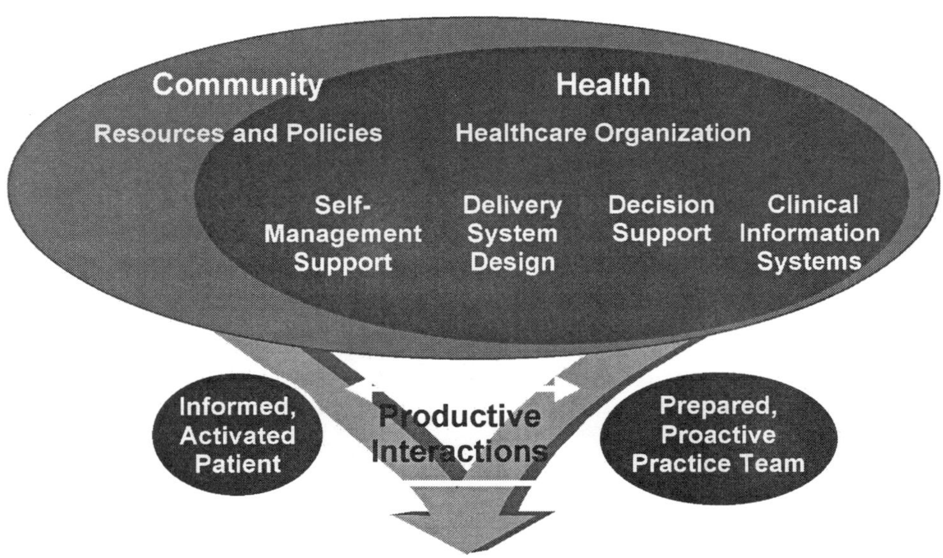

Figure 2-1: The Chronic Care Model

The applicability of the Chronic Care Model, in fact, extends beyond patients with chronic conditions. All patients and the broad medical practice can benefit from integration of the model's six design elements. Reflecting this broader scope, the model is often now called the Planned Care Model.

Up to this point, dissemination of the Chronic Care Model has occurred primarily in large health systems which have highly organized quality improvement initiatives, such as the VA, Kaiser, and the Mayo Clinic. Nonetheless, collaborative efforts are occurring nationwide, sponsored by health departments, quality improvement organizations, large medical groups, and health plans. Dissemination to smaller practices has been more limited. The Breakthrough Series Collaboratives, designed by the Institute of Healthcare Improvement (IHI) and described in the next section, have facilitated use of the approach by hundreds of practices, which have achieved significant benefits.

Concerted efforts are now being made, primarily driven by purchasers, which include some state governments, to use the model in local medical practices. Much work has been done to show how the approach can be used, but the adoption challenge remains for smaller practices. Pay for performance initiatives may provide financial incentive for adoption by solo and small group practitioners. A concerted effort is now being made to make adoption more efficient and effective for small practices.

The Idealized Design of Clinical Office Practices

Under the leadership of Donald M. Berwick, MD, MPP, President and Chief Executive Officer, IHI, which entered the healthcare scene in 1991, provided major impetus in driving the improvement of health through system-wide medical practice design in ambulatory and other care settings.

The IHI's early Breakthrough Series Collaboratives in the mid 1990s focused on discrete initiatives, such as improving asthma management and improving prescribing practices in the ambulatory environment. The results of the Collaboratives were encouraging, but because the improvements were not systemic ones, they were "not good enough" to IHI leaders. "We were coming up with great band-aid solutions that we would use to patch parts of a broken system, but not surprisingly, the whole system didn't improve. We needed to take a systematic approach and rethink the whole system of ambulatory care," comments Charles Kilo, MD, MPH, then IHI Vice President.[19]

To drive the transformation of ambulatory practice to the extent it needed to be transformed, Kilo and Wasson developed and led the international Idealized Design of Clinical Office Practices (IDCOP) initiative, launched under IHI's leadership in 1998. IDCOP pursued the question: "How good can medical practice get?" and provided a framework for present and future medical practice in office and outpatient settings. "We wiped our minds clear of any vision we already had of ambulatory care and addressed how such care could and should be designed to achieve optimal outcomes," notes Kilo. Four themes for change were key to the IDCOP design:[20]

- ***Access:*** Care is available when patients want and need it. Patients have unlimited access to the care and information they need, when they need it.
- ***Interaction:*** Every patient is the only patient. Interaction between the patient and care team is deep and personal. The care team has "memory" of the patient.
- ***Reliability:*** The system exhibits high reliability in that it provides all and only the care known to be effective and helpful.
- ***Vitality:*** The practice is sustainable and continually innovating. The practice has a happy staff, a spirit of innovation, and financial viability.

In January 1999, 34 prototype office sites in the United States and one in Sweden started testing the IDCOP model, which, over the next three years, was used in hundreds of ambulatory practices, ranging from community health centers and large primary care practices, to solo primary care practices. Significant improvements in patient satisfaction, staff satisfaction, revenues, and costs, have been achieved by practices using the IDCOP model. Other organizational players, most notably the American Academy of Family Physicians, have become fully engaged in extending the model's use.

CURRENT STATE OF REDESIGN EFFORTS AND HOPES FOR THE FUTURE

In spite of all the initiatives described here, ambulatory medical practice today is not so different from the practice that existed 50 years ago, or even 100 years ago. The design of medical office practice simply has not kept up with the changing face of medical practice.[21] It still relies heavily on the private office visit, physician memory, written medical records, and inadequate patient involvement. Developed in response to the burden of caring for individuals with acute infectious diseases and injuries, this design is in dire need of change. Obstacles that must be overcome include the following:

- Fee for service reimbursement, which creates incentives for episodic, visit-based care;
- The multiplicity of uncoordinated and competing payers, which contributes to the inertia surrounding practice change. Because most practices receive reimbursement from many different payers, it is difficult for them to envision a practice change that will be efficient for all payers;
- Academic medical centers, which continue to train physicians based on the traditional design of medical practice. Concepts of care delivery for a population of patients with chronic diseases, and the resource planning and community linkages needed to foster patient self-management fall outside most clinician education. Physician training programs continue to promote a cognitive, nonsystem view of medical practice which puts the doctor in charge of everything. Team-based training, critical to office-based practice redesign is lacking, so physicians are not being prepared to function with a team and as team players; and
- Supply-side issues, such as the number of physicians, the fragmentation of care, and the reimbursement system, which some experts argue will overwhelm almost any redesign efforts.

The multidimensional nature of the required change provides a stumbling block for many practitioners. However, there are well-tested approaches that can facilitate change and prevent already burdened and frustrated practitioners and their staffs from reinventing the wheel. "Early adopter" medical practices have made significant progress with practice redesign initiatives, which have resulted in enhanced patient-provider communication, scheduling systems, self-care by patients and families, and use of clinical guidelines, among other important advances.

When considering approaches to practice redesign, physicians are rightfully wary of "silver bullet," "plug-and-play" solutions. Adoption of some approaches may be urged "upon" medical practices by policymakers. Despite the desire for easily-implemented solutions by the entire healthcare and policymaking communities, quick, cheap fixes do not exist. In order to achieve improved patient-physician interaction, service quality, and patient outcomes, practices must make a coordinate set of system changes that involve multiple elements of the medical practice. This is a hard pill to swallow, but it's not an unswallowable one.

The use of multiple models, such as the robust IDCOP and Chronic Care models, can provide synergistic effects. Medical practice is a complex system, but good models should be complementary and can bring improvements to different aspects of the practice. Those interested in transforming ambulatory care need to view this complex system through the lens provided by different models. Unique things can be learned from each model, but no one model is right or captures everything. Every model leaves out parts of medical practice, but taken together, the models can add up to a system design that is do-able in the real world.

Success in bringing design elements to ambulatory medical practice, such as population-based care and team-based care that emphasize disease prevention and patient self-management, is attainable at all practices levels, but will take time. Academic medical schools are talking about how to respond to the IOM's call for fundamental educational reform[22] to enable physicians to deliver patient-centered care as members of an interdisciplinary team, emphasizing evidence-based practice, quality improvement approaches, and informatics.[23] Clinical curricula have not yet changed in most medical schools, but there is evidence that the medical education system is beginning to re-vision the way doctors and other health professionals are educated. The inclusion of "systems-based practice" as one of six core competencies for physicians is on the horizon.[24]

Information technology, broadly defined to include more than just electronic health records, can and will augment many of the important design functions described in the IDCOP and Chronic Care models and other redesign approaches. As both physicians and patients get better at using technologies, the effective design of healthcare practice, based on a system that does not revolve around the face-to-face visit, will become increasingly likely. Pay-for-performance reimbursement may more correctly align incentives to engage in the hard work of practice design/redesign. There is lots of work to be done, but the impetus for change remains strong, and future advances in medical practice design will be significant.

References

1 Donaldson, MS (ed). *Measuring the Quality of Health Care.* Report of the National Roundtable on Health Care Quality, Institute of Medicine. Washington, DC: National Academies Press; 1999.

2 Institute for Healthcare Improvement. Interview with John Wasson, MD. Web site: www.ihi.org/IHI/Topics/OfficePractices/officepracticesexperts.htm (accessed April 7, 2005).

3 Miller ST, Zwagg RV, Joyner MB, et al. Evaluation of a decentralized system for chronic disease care: seven years of observation. *Diabetes Care.* March/April 1980; 3(2): 382-386.

4 Runyan JW Jr, Zwagg RV, Joyner MB, et al. The Memphis diabetes continuing care program. *Med Care.* February 1980; 18(2): 147-163.

5 Mason WB, Bedwell CL, Vander Zwagg R, et al. Why people are hospitalized. A description of preventable factors leading to admission for medical illness. *J Chronic Dis.* 1980; 33(11-12): 713-720.

6 Wasson JH, Sauvigne AE, Mogielnicki RP, et al. Continuity of outpatient medical care in elderly men: a randomized trial. *JAMA.* November 2, 1984; 252(17): 2413-2417.

7 Wasson JH, Gaudette C, Whaley F, et al. Telephone care as a substitute for routine clinic follow-up. *JAMA*. April 1, 1992; 267(13): 1788-1793.

8 Nelson EC, Conger B, Douglass R, et al. Functional health status levels of primary care patients. *JAMA*. June 24, 1983; 249(24):3331-3338.

9 Wennberg JA, Gittelsohn A. Small area variations in healthcare delivery. *Science*. December 14, 1973; 82(117):1102-1108.

10 Wagner EH. The role of patient care teams in chronic disease management. *BMJ*. February 26, 2000; 320:569-572.

11 Thorn PA, Russell RG. Diabetic clinics today and tomorrow: mini-clinics in general practice. *BMJ*. June 2, 1973; (5865):534-536.

12 Wagner EH, Austin BT, Von Korff M. Organizing care for patients with chronic illness. *Milbank Q*. 1996; 74(4): 511-44, 1996.

13 Payne TH, Galvin SH, Taplin B, et al. Practicing population-based care in a health maintenance organization: evaluation after 38 months. *HMO Practice*. September 1995; 9(3):101-106.

14 Katon W, Von Korff M, Lin E, et al. Collaborative management to achieve treatment guidelines. *JAMA*. April 5, 1995; 273(13): 1026-1031.

15 Johnston ME, Langton KB, Haynes RB, et al. Effects of computer-based clinical decision support systems on clinician performance and patient outcome: a critical appraisal of research. *Ann Int Med*. January 15, 1994; 120(2):135-142.

16 Renders CM, Valk GD, Griffin SJ, et al. Interventions to improve the management of diabetes in primary care, outpatient, and community settings: a systematic review. *Diabetes Care*. October 2001; 24(10):1821-1833.

17 A detailed description of the Chronic Care Model appears at www.improvingchroniccare.org.

18 Wagner EH, Austin BT, Davis C, et al. Improving chronic illness care: translating evidence into action. *Health Aff*. November/December 2001; 20(6):64-78.

19 Personal communication with Charles M. Kilo, MD, MPH, January 3, 2005.

20 Institute for Healthcare Improvement. *Idealized Design of Clinical Office Practice*. Boston: Institute for Healthcare Improvement; 2000.

21 Wagner EH. Changing the face of chronic disease care. In *Accelerating Change Today (A.C.T.)*: The National Coalition on Healthcare and the Institute of Healthcare Improvement, May 2002. Available at www.improvingchroniccare.org/change/actreport.html (accessed April 7, 2005).

22 Institute of Medicine. *Crossing the Quality Chasm: A New Health System for the 21st Century*. Washington, DC: National Academy Press; 2001.

23 Association of American Medical Colleges. *Educating Doctors to Provide High Quality Medical Care: A Vision for Medical Education in the United States*. Washington, DC: AAMC, July 2004. Available at www.aamc.org (accessed April 7, 2005).

24 American Board of Medical Specialties. Evaluating Practice Performance for Maintenance of Certification (MOC). Web site: www.abms.org (accessed April 7, 2005).

Chapter 3

The Evolution of Information Technology in Healthcare

Blackford Middleton, MD, MPH, MSc

The purpose of this chapter—to trace the evolution of information technology in healthcare, from the beginning to the current state of affairs—is a daunting task at best. This is particularly the case if "evolution" is considered to be a linear process of gradual, peaceful, progressive change, or development, as the word is defined in *Webster's Unabridged Dictionary.*

In reviewing the decades since computers first appeared on the scene in 1945 with a machine called ENIAC (Electronic Numerical Integrator Analyzer and Computer), which consumed 1,000 square feet of floor space and weighed 30 tons,[1] major changes or metamorphoses clearly occurred at numerous points to pave the way toward healthcare IT as we know it today[2] (Table 3-1). These will be the focus of this chapter, as will a bird's-eye perspective on the current benefits, challenges, and adoption barriers associated with IT in ambulatory healthcare practice.

PHASE 1: AND IN THE BEGINNING...

The invention of the transistor in 1947 by John Bardeen, William Shockley, and Walter Brattain, scientists at the Bell Telephone Laboratories in Murray Hill, New Jersey, set the stage for modern computers. The bulky, unreliable, and power-hogging vacuum tubes used with ENIAC and other early machines could now be replaced with transistors made of semiconductors, which used less power and space. The application of the transistor to computers in 1958 enabled computers to move beyond specialized laboratories into commercial use, including healthcare.

The early use of computers in healthcare occurred almost exclusively in hospitals. In the early to mid-1960s, hospitals began to apply mainframe computer technology to manage their financial or administrative functions. Thus began the first phase of healthcare IT adoption. Hospitals installed large computer systems—both in size and in cost—for patient accounting and other fiscal operations involved in tracking the flow of revenue. Their purpose was to run the business; hospitals gave little to no consideration to clinical information management during this era. By the end of the decade, IT's dominance in the financial arena was widespread in hospitals nationwide, but practically nonexistent in ambulatory settings.

Meanwhile . . . in the Lab

Early medical informatics efforts, occurring in the 1960s, provided much of the backbone for future healthcare IT capabilities. From the beginning, medical informatics pioneers saw this technology as a potential tool to help organize, analyze, manage, and use information.[3] As early as 1960, R.S. Ledley and L.B. Lusted proposed the adoption of computers for patient data collection and storage.[4] By 1965, Lusted developed a computerized medical record system, including identification data, physical examination findings, laboratory test results, radiology reports, and disease summaries. But ironically, this primordial "electronic health record" was created to manage data on monkeys, not humans—his work occurred at the Oregon Regional Primate Research Center, not at an academic medical center. This animal-to-human lag in clinical IT application persists even today. Veterinarians' offices use more sophisticated computer technology, and do a more efficient job of reminding their patients of the need for preventive care, than do physicians' offices.

Table 3-1: Five Major Phases of Healthcare Information Technology: Application in Hospitals and Ambulatory Settings

Phase	Timeframe	Hospital IT Application	Ambulatory IT Application
Phase 1	1960s	Mainframe computers used to manage financial/administrative functions	None
Phase 2	1970s and 1980s	Mainframe and mini-computers used to manage department-based functions	Little to none; practice management systems emerging in largest practices
Phase 3	Late 1980s and early 1990s	Server-based clinical information systems integrate departmental data from "client" computers—called the "client-server" era; emergence of specialty clinical information systems	Most practices use personal computers, but almost exclusively for billing/practice management systems
Phase 4	Mid 1990s to present	"Thin-client" era: continued use of legacy systems; some adoption of Web-based and HER technologies	Low HER and Web-based IT penetration in small to medium-sized practices; higher penetration in larger practices
Phase 5	Future	Establish National Healthcare Information Infrastructure (NHII) providing seamless interoperability between hospitals	NHII providing seamless interoperability between physicians' offices, and facilitated patient access on shared online health records

From Center for Information Technology Leadership. *The Value of Computerized Provider Order Entry in Ambulatory Settings: Executive Preview.* http://www.citl.org/research/ACPOE_Executive_Preview.pdf. Used by permission.

In the human healthcare informatics arena, much of the initial research focused on expert systems and clinician decision support for patient diagnosis and treatment. Research in artificial intelligence was active, but isolated from mainstream healthcare. The practical application of IT in day-to-day care may have even been delayed due to this gap between theoretical and applied informatics. The clinical information systems to which these expert systems needed to be applied were not yet accepted.

PHASE 2: CLINICAL ANCILLARY DEPARTMENTS TAKE THE PLUNGE

During the 1970s and 1980s, hospitals were collecting lots of data but the locus was hospital clinical departments rather than the organization as a whole. Ancillary clinical departments, such as laboratory, blood bank, microbiology, and radiology, had adopted departmental information systems to manage their own business functions, including accounting, scheduling, workflow, and test ordering and results.[5] IT adoption by departments—the second phase of healthcare IT—was characterized by localized, isolated automation of clinical data through IT systems offered by several large vendors. Discrete departments were able to distribute data, but data were not yet aggregated into a centralized repository that allowed clinicians to have an integrated view of clinical information without having to go to several computer terminals.[5] Again, the use of IT in freestanding ambulatory practices was practically nonexistent.

Pioneering Integrated Clinical IT Systems

Clinical information management systems, able to integrate data across departments and systems in order to inform clinical decision making and improve patient care, started emerging in the 1970s at several major academic medical centers. Medical informatics teams focused on reducing medical errors through improved clinical information management projects.

Under the leadership of G. Octo Barnett, MD, Director of the Laboratory of Computer Science at Massachusetts General Hospital (MGH), researchers began to define the functionality of what would become an electronic health record (EHR).[6] Improved information access, and interactive data management capabilities based on a new programming language called "MUMPS" (MGH Utility Multi-Programming Systems), facilitated practitioner prompts and reminders during patient care encounters.[7] By 1975, the laboratory had developed a model EHR for ambulatory care called COSTAR (Computer-Stored Ambulatory Record), which was installed at Harvard Community Health Plan. Another ambulatory initiative was in progress through Kaiser Permanente in Northern California. COSTAR is arguably the grandfather of clinical IT systems for ambulatory care, but it also presaged the disparity in technology adoption between large and small care organizations that persists to this day.

LDS Hospital in Salt Lake City put its HELP system (Health Evaluation through Logical Processing) into operations in 1967.[8] Originally designed for a heart catheterization laboratory and a post-open heart intensive care unit, the early system stored patient data exclusively to help diagnose and treat heart disease. These early systems used mainframe or mini-computers located in a centralized location with terminals placed in clinical areas around the hospital.[9] Physicians were able to access data captured from clinical departments, such as radiology, pathology, and laboratory, but they rarely input data.

Entering the Provider Order Entry Era

The COSTAR designers were well aware of the resistance clinicians can put up if computer systems slow them down, so the implementation allowed for physicians to record their encounter on paper forms, and the data was then keyed in by clerical personnel. Getting physicians to actually enter data on the computer would prove difficult. That challenge was first tackled at the El Camino Hospital, a not-for-profit community hospital in Mountain View, California. Through a joint-venture project with Lockheed, the hospital pioneered the use of computer-based provider order entry (CPOE), which went live in the hospital in 1971.

Incentives from Above

The use of computers in hospitals for purely administrative functions continued up through the early 1980s when the shift from retrospective reimbursement to prospective payment catapulted cost management to the center of hospital radar screens. Under the retrospective fee-for-service system, national health expenditures had grown from $27 billion and 5.1% of the gross domestic product (GDP) in 1960 to $246 billion and 12% share of GDP in 1980.[10] Medicare adopted the Prospective Payment System (PPS) in 1983 with state Medicaid programs and private insurers following in 1986 and beyond. PPS used diagnosis-related groups (DRGs) to prospectively approve costs incurred by beneficiaries.

In addition to PPS and government payers, managed care and prepaid capitated healthcare offered by employers also drove health cost reductions in the late 1970s and 1980s. Hospitals were pressured and highly motivated to reduce costs and demonstrate outcomes. To win contracts, they had to be able to identify costs of specific care processes and the patient outcomes associated with that care. In order to tell purchasers, public payers, and managed care payers, "Our cardiovascular disease management services cost X and our outcomes are Y—which is Z percent better than the competitor hospital down the street," data residing in cost accounting systems needed to be integrated with clinical data. Clinical information now had to flow seamlessly between hospital departments, and getting systems to talk to one another required some common standards. The pioneering data exchange specification work in this area was done by Donald Simborg, MD, who in 1987 founded Health Level Seven (HL7) to develop messaging standards for interoperability among healthcare applications.

PHASE 3: SMALLER, FASTER, CHEAPER – MAYBE

The appearance of the personal computer in the 1980s, followed by Xerox's development of the networking standards and technology now known as Ethernet, ushered in the third phase of healthcare IT adoption—the client-server era. Individual "client" computers that performed their own functions and processing could now send data or processing requests to one or more "server" computers that could receive and handle requests from many client computers, while networking technology enabled the linking of client and server computers over local area networks (LANs) or wide area networks

(WANs). The server housed the big computing capability, while the client generally housed the interface and less intensive processing capabilities.

The plummeting cost of data storage, along with the development of relational database technologies spurred hospitals to begin gathering data, then housed in disparate department- or ancillary-based systems, into a centralized database that would give users an integrated and comprehensive view of the care provided to patients, its costs, and outcomes. Integrated clinical data repositories, accessible organizationwide through client computer terminals, enabled clinicians to begin tracking and trending in order to identify clinical performance improvement opportunities. Jack Wennberg and Alan Gittelsohn's landmark paper on practice variation published in *Science* in 1973[11] indicated huge room for process and outcomes improvement nationwide.

During the late 1980s and early 1990s, specialty clinical information systems such as PACS (Picture Archiving and Communication System), which creates digital archives for radiology-related medical images, and laboratory information systems, were also emerging. This facilitated the growth of rich clinical data repositories.

Ambulatory Care Still Plods Behind

In the ambulatory world, physicians continued to be reimbursed for services on a fee-for-service (FFS). Incentives to contain healthcare costs were entirely absent, as was automation of office or clinical functions. Paper-based records and billing systems were adequately meeting practice needs.

This changed gradually during the late 1980s and early 1990s as the proliferation of payers made it increasingly difficult for the average practice to generate bills and get them out the door on time. Many smaller ambulatory practices turned to local mom-and-pop billing support service bureaus to meet billing needs, while large practices started purchasing and implementing billing/practice management systems available from a growing number of commercial vendors. As the software matured and the cost of computers dropped, vendors were increasingly able to offer affordable practice management products to small and medium-sized practices.

Clinical information systems offered by IT vendors to hospitals and health systems remained far beyond the financial and technical means of all but the largest ambulatory practices. Both capital to purchase systems and the know-how to maintain the systems were lacking—a situation that continues to this day, as described later.

Phase 4: The Thin-Client and Web Era

The "thin-client" era began in the mid 1990s. It was a reaction to the high cost of maintaining desktop PCs, especially during this period when desktop operating systems were relatively immature and fragile. In a way, it represented a return to an older computing paradigm with powerful servers and relatively "dumb" terminals.

The Internet and World Wide Web technologies, launched by Tim Berners-Lee at Centre Européen de Recherche Nucléaire (CERN) in Switzerland, built on the WAN work conducted by the U.S. Defense Advanced Research Project Agency (ARPANET) in the late 1960s and 1970s. Berners-Lee created a hypertext system that ran across the Internet on different operating systems thereby making possible widespread connectivity to a veritable treasure trove of research information.

The development of the first Internet browser—Mosaic—by 23-year-old graduate student Marc Andreesen at the University of Illinois, Champaign-Urbana, and his subsequent development of Netscape and the development of other browsers by other individuals made possible the true World Wide Web revolution. Browser software made it easy to connect to, search, and download information from anywhere on the Internet. Development of Intranets, which use data-exchange protocols and browsers like the Internet but are access-controlled, quickly followed.[12]

The growth of Internet browsers facilitated access to the scientific and medical literature by clinicians. Then, in 1997, the National Library of Medicine made available to the public its premier bibliographic database MEDLINE® (Medical Literature, Analysis, and Retrieval System Online), which now contains more than 12 million references to journal articles in life sciences with a concentration on biomedicine, dating back to 1966. Web-based usage amounts to tens of millions of searches each year.

The thin-client and Web-based era challenged (and continues to challenge) the healthcare world to integrate legacy applications with desktop systems becoming widely available throughout healthcare organizations.

PHASE 5: NATIONAL HEALTHCARE INFORMATION INFRASTRUCTURE—SHAKING UP THE SYSTEM

Publication in 1991 of the Institute of Medicine's (IOM) report titled *The Computer-based Patient Record: An Essential Technology for Health Care*[13] focused widespread industry attention on computer-based patient records (CPRs) and their potential. The need for CPR's use was described in no uncertain terms. The report indicated that industry's failure to manage health information in a way that would control costs, reduce practice variability, and improve overall care quality and outcomes could be overcome by EHRs. Concerns about confidentiality and security systems predominated during the subsequent years, and as noted by Eta S. Berner, EdD, Don E. Detmer, MD, and Donald Simborg, MD:

> (O)nly a few major private sector organizations like the Kaiser health system picked up the challenge of implementing large-scale electronic health records. At the national level in the U.S., it was apparent that without confidentiality and security protections, CPRs would not move into widespread use.[2]

The IOM's Committee on Quality of Health Care in America published its first report, *To Err is Human: Building a Safer Health System*,[14] in December of 1999, and its second report, *Crossing the Quality Chasm: A New Health System for the 21st Century*,[15] in 2001. Both reverberated strongly in the consumer, healthcare, and policy making communities. The message was clear: Up to 98,000 deaths occur each year as a result of medical errors in healthcare settings; national commitment to and financial support of a health information infrastructure are critical to health quality and patient safety.

President George W. Bush called for widespread adoption of EHRs in his State of the Union address January 20, 2004. Such a commitment at this level in this country was unprecedented and was a direct result of the IOM reports. Through an Executive Order, President Bush created the Office of the National Coordinator for Healthcare Information Technology. Noting that "health information technology has the potential to greatly improve health care even as it yields huge savings,"[16] HHS Secretary Tommy

G. Thompson announced on May 6, 2004 the appointment of David J. Brailer, MD, PhD, to serve as National Health Information Technology Coordinator. In the absence of innovation and transformation of the healthcare industry with IT, many experts believe that double-digit cost increases and system failures that result in patient deaths will continue unabated into the future.

Dr. Brailer now calls for the widespread adoption of "interoperable" healthcare information technology, which when achieved will represent Phase 5 of healthcare information technology adoption. Interoperability implies that an authorized physician may obtain access, with permission, to the healthcare data from a system remote to his or her own system, and that hospital clinical information systems can readily exchange clinical data when authorized. In addition, it implies that clinical information exchange occurs seamlessly not only between doctors and hospitals, but also between the pharmacy, radiology centers, laboratory centers, and public health agencies. Lastly, it may imply that patients have access to and control of a shared online health record, or personal health record, which represents a life-time repository of their personal health data.

Where Are We Now?

The data related to current clinical IT penetration in hospital and ambulatory settings are somewhat inconsistent. Part of the consistency challenge is created by differing definitions of what is to be measured—practice management systems, the use of true EHRs, computer-based provider order entry (CPOE), and other components of ambulatory IT systems, or combined pieces of IT systems?[17] Definitions aside, adoption rates for all systems are low in both environments.

An extensive study conducted for the California HealthCare Foundation by David Brailer, then with the Health Technology Center, and Emi L. Terasawa,[18] indicates that in the *inpatient arena*, current CPOE adoption rates are anywhere from 3% to 21%. Many experts conclude that the adoption rate in the inpatient setting is less than 10%.[17] According to Brailer's study, rates of adoption of CPRs in *physician offices* range from approximately 14% to 39% of practices. The 2004 HIMSS Ambulatory Technology Survey[19] studied penetration of desktop, laptop, and handheld computers, software, EHR, and Internet connectivity in outpatient clinical settings. Thirty-eight percent of respondents indicated that an EHR system was in place in their facility, up from 28% in the 2002 survey. One-third of respondents reported using a desktop, laptop, or handheld computer with every patient encounter. EHR adoption rates vary significantly by type of practice, with pediatric and specialty practices having a lower penetration than internal medicine practices.

An assessment conducted by the Center for Information Technology Leadership[20] indicated a much lower use rate of 1% to 10% for any kind of CPOE by practicing outpatient physicians.

The data are all over the board, but the current status of clinical information management in inpatient and ambulatory care may best be characterized as variable. In addition, there often is a huge gap between implementing IT, such as EHRs, and really leveraging that technology to achieve quality of care. The national fervor to adopt technology assumes that better quality and cost efficiency will result from IT adoption, but many other industries have found this not to be the case.

Adoption Barriers

In a recent article published in the *Journal of the American Medical Informatics Association*,[21] this author and colleagues suggested that healthcare information technology (HIT) in the United States is stymied by a fundamental market failure due to the following:

- ***Misaligned incentives:*** The benefits of HIT—the patient safety and quality effects of EHRs that reduce healthcare costs—do not accrue to the providers that must incur the cost of purchasing the technology.
- ***Inability to achieve broad standards adoption:*** Given the absence of a clear business case for HIT, progress in stimulating adoption of standards addressing HIT functionality, interoperability, content representation, and messaging have been slow.
- ***Rapid turnover of HIT companies:*** The market has a few large vendors and a large number of small, highly unstable vendors.
- ***Lack of definition of basic product features:*** Given the marketplace characteristics, hundreds of vendors are providing products that pay little attention to basic product features and interoperability standards.

Interoperability

Within organizations, interoperability is being addressed on an organization-by-organization basis as each organization builds integrated clinical data repositories containing data from legacy and departmental systems using HL7 and other standards-setting models.

Between organizations: Given the lack of data standardization, physicians' offices or even hospitals and health systems are typically unable to electronically exchange clinical information.[22] Why? There is simply no financial incentive to do so, and in fact, there is a disincentive from a marketing standpoint. Because financial incentives for interoperability between clinical enterprises are lacking, two hospitals each with sophisticated clinical information systems located across the street from each other cannot and do not exchange data electronically. Messaging standards exist, but robust standards that allow seamless interoperability between organizations do not. Regulatory, legal, and political issues abound. One line of thinking is this: "If I'm hospital X and I share my data with hospital Y, and my data turn out to show that I'm not as good a provider, will this be used against me?" HIPAA now at least provides a framework within which to address security and confidentiality issues between organizations.

Time and Money

The two key barriers to IT adoption for physician practices are time and money. Although the financial effects of EHRs in ambulatory practices have not been well documented, a recent study[23] indicates that system costs per provider of \$1,600 for software, \$3,400 for implementation, \$1,500 for support and maintenance, and \$6,600 for hardware, totaling \$13,100 per provider are not unreasonable estimates, but may be low compared to commercial offerings. Add to this sum "induced costs" reflecting temporary productivity loss of $11,200, and the total cost per provider is $25,300. A study of EMR implementation in small practices indicates not so disparate initial costs of $15,000 to $50,000 per physician, with a median cost of $30,000, "plus revenue losses due to fewer than normal patient visits for weeks or months after the EMR implementation."[24]

Other barriers abound, including lack of management support, lack of support by medical staff, inability to achieve end-user acceptance, and difficulty migrating from paper to electronic records. Brailer and Terasawa survey and summarize the extent of the barriers.[18] In the current environment, physicians appear to be reluctant to incur the costs, and as noted by Joan Ash, PhD, and David W. Bates, MD, MSc, "to adopt new ways of doing things that interfere with their workflow and which they perceive take time away from their patient care work."[17]

Benefits in 3D

Although a full discussion of the benefits of IT in ambulatory practice is beyond this chapter's scope, suffice it to say that the evidence-base on the benefits of IT in ambulatory healthcare has been studied extensively and carefully documented.

In one such recent effort, the Center for Information Technology Leadership reviewed nearly 2,000 academic, commercial, and other studies related to computerized order entry in outpatient settings, and identified three major types of IT value: financial, clinical, and organizational.[25] Nationwide adoption of advanced ambulatory CPOE systems was estimated by CITL to be able to accomplish the following:

- Eliminate more than 2 million adverse drug events (ADEs) and more than 190,000 hospitalizations each year (improved patient outcomes);
- Save the U.S. healthcare system approximately $44 billion per year in reduced medication, radiology, laboratory, and ADE-related expenditures (improved cost savings); and
- Eliminate for providers more than $10 in rejected claims per outpatient visit (provider revenue enhancement).

The sidebar on page 30 summarizes key benefits in each dimension.

Similarly, this author has studied the literature related to EHRs in ambulatory care and assessed the value of EHRs to the clinical, financial, and organizational dimensions.[26] In the *clinical* arena, the following benefits are noteworthy:

- ***Information access:*** Simply having clinical data available in the EHR, even without clinical decision support, improves clinical decision making, reduces test utilization, and improves patient outcomes.
- ***Clinical decision support:*** The provision of clinical decision support at the point of care, through alerts and reminders and decision support for test ordering and medications, represents the most profound positive impact of EHRs.
- ***Workflow:*** EHRs are designed to improve workflow, completing tasks such as writing a prescription, ordering tests, or documenting a visit.

Benefits vary widely based on how the technology is designed and used by the organization.

In the *financial* arena, benefits include improved utilization of laboratory tests, medications, and radiology procedures, and improved coding and charge capture.

IT Value Dimensions[25]

Financial

- Cost reductions from decreased administrative, clinical staffing, and resource requirements (i.e., elimination of paper chart pulls and transcription services)
- Revenue enhancements from improved charge capture and charge entry to billing times
- Productivity gains from increased procedure volume, reductions in average length of stay, and increased transaction processing rates

Clinical

- Care process advances from better adherence to clinical protocols and improvements in the stages of clinical decision making (i.e., initiation, diagnostics, monitoring and tracking, and acting)
- Improved patient outcomes from reductions in medical errors, decreases in morbidity and mortality, and expedited recovery times

Organizational

- Stakeholder satisfaction improvements from improved access to healthcare information, decreased wait times, and more positive perceptions of care quality and clinician efficiency
- Risk mitigation from decreases in malpractice litigation and increased adherence to federal, state, and accreditation organization standards

Annual financial benefits from savings associated with chart pulls, transcriptions, ADE prevention, drugs, laboratory tests, and radiology tests, as well as savings from charge capture improvement and a reduction in billing errors are estimated to total $155,000 per physician over a five-year period.[23] In the *organizational* arena, the benefits include improved organizational efficiency and service delivery, and an improved competitive position in a medical marketplace increasingly focused on service and convenience as well as quality.

GETTING FROM HERE TO THERE

Although the data and studies related to the benefits of IT use in ambulatory care are encouraging, the most profound of the benefits can be achieved only when clinicians are directly using the technology. If a nurse or medical assistant is the person entering the drug order and receiving the alert about a potential adverse drug interaction, he or she must contact the physician to change the order. If the physician is using the technology and receives the alert, he or she can change the order before it's even dispatched by the system. Physicians and other providers must embrace the technology. As noted by Berner, Detmer, and Simborg, "While there is concern nationally about the need to improve the quality of care, it is not clear that these concerns are sufficient motivation for individual physicians to rush to adopt systems that not only may cost them large sums of money, but also could be perceived as markedly less convenient and more time-consuming than the current system."[2]

In order to get from where we are to where we need to go, this author and colleagues have recommended four broad areas for action:[21]

1. Creating financial incentives to stimulate the EHR marketplace, such as establishing financial incentives for the use of the EHR and other IT in practice, and establishing low interest loans or a grant program to facilitate hardware and software adoption in healthcare settings;
2. Setting and adopting functional and related informatics standards, such as coordinating existing efforts to specify essential standards for basic EHR functionality, and specifying a minimal clinical data set and functional standards for HIT systems;
3. Promulgating enabling policy for IT adoption, such as establishing a federal policy on clinical data ownership and stewardship; and
4. Developing educational, marketing, and supporting activities, such as campaigns to increase consumers' and health professionals' awareness and knowledge about the value of healthcare IT.

Healthcare IT is a required component for the transformation of the U.S. healthcare delivery system into the modern age with respect to information management. Healthcare IT has come of age, but making it a reality in ambulatory care, as well as in hospital care, is an imperative for patients, their physicians and other care providers, and the purchasing community at large.

References

1 Computer History Museum. www.computerhistory.org (accessed April 7, 2005).

2 Berner ES, Detmer DE, and Simborg D. Will the wave finally break? A brief view of the adoption of electronic medical records in the U.S. *JAMIA*. www.jamia.org/preprints.shtml (accessed November 10, 2004).

3 American Medical Informatics Association. History of Informatics. www.amia.org/history/what.html (accessed April 7, 2005).

4 Ledley RS, Lusted LB. The use of electronic computers in medical data processing: aids in diagnosis, current information retrieval, and medical record keeping. *IRE Transactions in Biomedical Electronics.* January 1960; 7:31-47.

5 Maviglia S, Kuperman G, Middleton B. Hospital information systems. In Wachter RM, Goldman L, Hollander H (eds). *Hospital Medicine. Second Edition.* Philadelphia, PA: Lippincott Williams & Wilkins (in press).

6 Barnett GO. History of the development of medical information systems at the Laboratory of Computer Science at Massachusetts General Hospital. *Proceedings of the ACM Conference on History of Medical Informatics.* New York: ACM Press; 1987.

7 Massachusetts General. EHR Web site: www.ehrweb.org/ehrweb/ehroverview/pages/massgen.htm (accessed April 7, 2005).

8 Gardner RM, Pryor TA, Warner HR. The HELP hospital information system: update 1998. *Int J Medication Inform.* June 1999; 64(3): 169-182.

9 Leavitt M. Electronic Medical Records. In Davidson PL (ed): *Healthcare Information Systems.* New York: Auerbach Publications; 2000.

10 Centers for Medicare and Medicaid Services, Office of the Actuary, National Health Statistics Group. www.cms.hhs.gov (accessed April 7, 2005).

11 Wennberg J, Gittlesohn A. Small area variations in health care delivery. *Science.* December 14, 1973; 182:1102-1108.

12 Tang PC, Hammond WE. A progress report on computer-based patient records in the United States. In Dick RS, Steen EB, Detmer DE (eds.). *The Computer-Based Patients Record: An Essential Technology for Health Care*, rev. ed. Washington, DC: Institute of Medicine, National Academies Press; 1997. www.nap.edu/readingroom (accessed April 7, 2005).

13 Dick RS, Steen EB (eds). *The Computer-Based Patient Record: An Essential Technology for Health Care.* Washington, DC: Institute of Medicine, National Academies Press; 1991.

14 Institute of Medicine. *To Err is Human: Building a Safer Health System.* Washington, DC: National Academies Press; 2000.

15 Institute of Medicine. *Crossing the Quality Chasm: A New Health System for the 21st Century.* Washington, DC: National Academies Press; 2001.

16 Department of Health & Human Services News Release. www.hhs.gov/news/press/2004pres/20040506.html (accessed April 8, 2005).

17 Ash JS, Bates DW. Factors and forces impacting EHR system adoption. *JAMIA.* www.jamia.org/preprints.html (accessed April 8, 2005).

18 Brailer DJ, Terasawa EL. *Use and Adoption of Computer-Based Patient Records.* Oakland, CA: California HealthCare Foundation; 2003.

19 HIMSS. *Ambulatory Technology Survey.* February 9, 2004. http://www.himss.org/content/files/ambulatory_tech_survey_0209.pdf (accessed April 8, 2005).

20 Center for Information Technology Leadership. *Patient Safety in the Physician's Office.* Oakland, CA: California HealthCare Foundation, April 2004.

21 Middleton B, Hammond WE, Brennan PF, Cooper GF. Accelerating U.S. EHR adoption: How to get there from here. *JAMIA.* www.jamia.org/preprints.shtml (accessed April 8, 2005).

22 Middleton B, Ghandi TK, Bates DW. The Role of Information Technology in Ambulatory Care Patient Safety. Prepared for the Ambulatory Care Patient Safety Workshop, convened by AHRQ and CMS, November 30, 2002. http://www.partners.org/cird/publications.asp (accessed April 8, 2005).

23 Wang SJ, Middleton B, Prosser LA, et al. A cost-benefit analysis of electronic medical records in primary care. *American Journal of Medicine.* April 1, 2003; 114:397-403.

24 Miller RH, Newman J. *Electronic Medical Records: Lessons from Small Physician Practices.* Oakland, CA: California Health Foundation; 2003.

25 Center for Information Technology Leadership. *The Value of Computerized Provider Order Entry in Ambulatory Settings: Executive Preview.* http://www.citl.org/research/ACPOE_Executive_Preview.pdf (accessed April 8, 2005).

26 Middleton B. In Demetriedes JE, Koldner RM, Christopherson GA (eds). *Person-Centered Health Records: Toward HealthePeople.* New York: Springer; 2005.

Section II

Principles for Transforming Practice

Chapter 4

Relationship

John H. Wasson, MD, and David Lansky, PhD

Relationship. We all think we know what it means. When it's right in the ambulatory healthcare world, relationship achieves improved patient outcomes, effective patient self-management and support, involved and empowered patients, families and friends, attention to comfort and privacy, high-quality organizational memory about the patient, and shared, collaborative decision making.

Relationship is not enhanced by simply teaching medical students communication skills. Like other system outcomes, relationship is enabled or disabled by the way a system is designed and the technological and other tools supporting the system. While many frequently assume that technology degrades relationship, when designed and used appropriately, technology can enhance relationship. Unfortunately, medical practice systems and the technology used to support the systems often fall short of delivering the best possible relationship.

This chapter traces the evolution of relationship in ambulatory practice, describes the attributes of effective patient-physician and care team interaction, and outlines a new vision of relationship that can deliver on the promise of individualized, efficient, and effective ambulatory healthcare. The organizing principle throughout is that interaction (relationship) is at the heart of most ambulatory care.

Printed by permission of
the Norman Rockwell Family Agency.

THE HISTORICAL VISION OF RELATIONSHIP

Norman Rockwell's paintings illustrate a traditional and idealized vision of the physician and patient-physician relationship. In one illustration, a grandfatherly-looking physician seated in an arm chair is using his stethoscope to listen to the "heartbeat" of a little girl's doll. The little girl, standing in front of him, presumably brought her doll baby to the doctor for a check up. In another illustration, a doctor sits on the side of a boy's bed reading a thermometer while the boy leans on the doctor's shoulders to get a closer view of just how sick the thermometer indicates he might be.

Rockwell's vision of the patient-doctor relationship involves trust. It is sensitive. It is important. As a paternalistic role-model, the doctor is both comforter and technical expert or diagnostician. The doctor's relationship with his patient matters for its own sake, independent of the disease the doctor may need to treat. The medical visits as illustrated by this artist are all about relationship. However, Rockwell portrays an era during which, in many ways, relationship was all or at the least the key offering healthcare could provide. Scientific/medical knowledge and diagnostic and therapeutic options and tools were much more limited.

"MODERN MEDICINE" AND THE PARADIGM OF THE 18-MINUTE VISIT

Contrariwise, if it was so, it might be;
And if it were so, it would be;
But as it isn't, it ain't.

Lewis Carroll, Alice in Wonderland

When Alice visited Wonderland, she learned that time was odd. She heard people saying very strange things. She saw that common sense was not very common at all.

What has happened in healthcare to change Rockwell's vision of relationship to one more closely resembling Alice's worldview or the White Rabbit's song: "No time to say hello—goodbye! I'm late, I'm late, I'm late." Obviously, most physicians no longer make house calls, and they certainly don't have time to "play doctor" with a child and her doll. With each passing decade, the amount of knowledge, the complexities of issues, and available options and tools that physicians must consider during an office visit have increased exponentially. However, the physician continues to have a primary duty to engage with the patient in a mutually respectful, high quality, trust-filled relationship.

Meanwhile, the 16 to 19-minute face-to-face visit is the norm[1,2,3] for what are now often called doctor-patient "encounters." This short encounter is in fact how primary medical practice is "designed." The design is locked-in by a payment system in which encounters are the basic "currency" for reimbursement. To meet financial targets, most primary care physicians must see between 18 and 25 patients per day. Twenty patients multiplied by 18 minutes per patient equals 360 minutes or 6 hours. The physician is required to spend additional hours beyond this for other important tasks, such as speaking with specialists, visiting hospitalized patients, accessing the medical literature to research challenging cases, reviewing laboratory and radiological results, returning phone calls, and more.

Physicians and other care providers work in a world that is normal to them. However, their world appears like Wonderland to most patients and families.[4] During the short visit, the doctor is focused on doing things, such as filling out forms and using diagnostic instruments. Some time may be spent talking, but much of the talk is *at* the patient and very little time is spent listening *to* the patient. In fact, data indicate that after asking patients what brought them in for the visit, physicians interrupt patients on average after hearing about 20 seconds of the patient's explanation. Some physicians may interrupt because they truly are not listening; others may need to clarify information such as the sequence of symptoms or occurrences. But whatever the reason for verbal interruptions, patient-physician encounters also are interrupted frequently by knocks on the door, beeper pages, or computer usage.[5] Equally discouraging, less than 10% of the visits include a question from the physician such as, "Do you understand what I've said?"

THE NEW VISION OF RELATIONSHIP

For quality care to occur, a meaningful connection must bridge the gap between physician and patient. That connection is still relationship. Relationship is not just the mechanism of care, it is caring and healing in and of itself. To achieve optimal outcomes, relationship must be built and sustained over time. In today's more complex healthcare world, relationship must be combined with other care-building blocks, such as knowledge, competence, and collaboration in order to produce the best possible health outcomes. Ambulatory practice in the 21st century will force relationship to assume new dimensions.

Modes of Care Delivery

The first dimension involves new modes of care delivery—*team-based care* and *self-managed care.* Ambulatory healthcare will increasingly be provided by a team of practitioners rather than a single physician. The patient's relationship with all team members must be considered and will be facilitated (or not) by elements of practice design and technology use, as described later in this chapter. Much of the care for individuals with chronic diseases will be self-managed care. This means that ambulatory practitioners will need to properly educate and equip patients and families to effectively manage their own health.

Technology and practice design play a critical role in this process. The current model of ambulatory care delivery focuses on acute illness and meeting short-term needs through short doctor visits. These visits typically require the patient, and often family members, to spend several hours of lost-work time to travel and wait for a brief and unsatisfying encounter. Apparent efficiencies for the doctor require huge inefficiencies for the patient, employer, and society. This must change to a model that involves patients, families, physicians, and a multidisciplinary care team working together collaboratively and efficiently to manage long-term conditions.

Balance and Trust

The second dimension involves a new view of the patient-doctor relationship with an equal sign (=) between the two parties. The paternalistic vision of the doctor as all knowing and all powerful in the relationship has been replaced by equally balanced and technology-empowered practitioners and patients. The doctor and his or her team are independent professionals with expertise and professional resources to offer. The patient and family bring their own expertise and resources to the table. The degree of intimacy in the relationship is the patient's choice. As one patient notes, "My physician is not the sole expert on my body. It is my body and I am the expert on it. We are partners in taking care of it."[6]

Two-way trust is present in the new vision of patient-doctor relationship. Trust occurs when the "truster" believes that the "trustee" will act in the truster's best interests.[7] Numerous studies indicate that problematic experiences in the ambulatory setting are strongly related to lower trust, and that patients who distrust the healthcare system do not seek the medical care they need and do not follow their physician's recommendations.[8, 9, 10, 11] And when doctors mistrust their patients, the healthcare system is plagued with repeat and unnecessary testing, excessive paperwork, and an anxious liability environment.

Two-way trust can enhance care quality and patient outcomes, but trust has a number of significant wrinkles. The patient's trust in the physician may be misplaced. This occurs when the physician is not providing care that reflects the best available science and knowledge. Wide variability in practice patterns indicates that many physicians do not in fact provide evidence-based care. Patients or physicians also may be too trusting. Patients need to ask questions to assure that they are receiving best-practice, evidence-based care. Physicians providing "the right care" need to assure that patients understand and are following their recommendations. In the case of both misplaced trust and too much trust, relationship is not an absolute good that represents the best course for the patient.

The Emergence of Technology

Technology has changed the nature of how people relate to *other* types of businesses, such as credit card companies, banks, stores, and even hospitals. Patients already have a great deal of experience with technology and want it to enhance communication and increase convenience; they do not want technology to interfere with a relationship. For example, patients would like to be able to e-mail their physician to ask questions, but do not want to call their physician's office and be told through an automated system that their call will be answered in four minutes because they are the eighth caller in line.

Most clinicians have had direct or vicarious experience with healthcare technology in the form of electronic health records (EHRs). Although they recognize that EHRs offer many benefits, they also know (or have heard) that the implementation of an EHR is usually expensive and disruptive and that as many as half of all EHR installations fail. Furthermore, some clinicians recognize that the functions of an EHR do not accommodate both population and patient management.

Table 4-1 highlights the differences between the old and new vision of relationship and medical practice. Although the evidence base supporting the importance of effective patient-provider interaction is well established, the challenge lies in making the new vision "happen."

Table 4-1: Relationship and Medical Practice: Then and Now

Old Vision	New Vision
Relationship as primary in quality medical care	Knowledge, competence, and collaboration join relationship in being key to quality medical care
Physician all knowing and all powerful	Equality of physician and patient
Care provided by single practitioner who makes all the decisions	Team-based care; decision making shared with patient and family
Visits to meet episodic, acute care needs	Visits, self-management and other communications channels to meet ongoing, chronic care needs

ATTRIBUTES OF EFFECTIVE PATIENT-PHYSICIAN INTERACTION

Key attributes of effective interaction or relationship include patient-centered communication, shared decision making, access to the needed information, and effective self-care management and support. A brief description of each follows.

Patient-Centered Communication

When physicians are effectively communicating with patients, they are providing information about things that really matter to the patient in a language the patient can understand and at an appropriate level. When physicians are effectively obtaining information from patients, they are listening well. Listening enables the physician and staff to determine why the patient has initiated the visit—what is of concern to him or her. Explaining the reason for the visit is often very difficult for the patient.

Consider a patient who has a chronic illness—perhaps several chronic illnesses—and is taking multiple medications. The patient is not feeling well, but has only 10 minutes with a physician every eight weeks to address all health concerns. The patient could provide a wealth of information that would be helpful to the physician, but all of this has to occur within the first minutes of the visit. Moreover, as mentioned earlier, most visits are interrupted within the first half a minute, thus exacerbating the patient's already difficult communication task. Now add language and cultural barriers to the mix. Even without these barriers, the short face-to-face visits, which have been the paradigm for medical care, clearly will not work.

Continuing with our patient with multiple chronic illnesses, after examining the patient, the provider must allow sufficient time to give clear explanations about the diagnosis, develop a treatment plan, and ensure that the patient and family understand the information provided. Evidence of performance here is discouraging. In one study of routine outpatient visits, assessment of patients' understanding occurred in only 1.5% of the discussions between patients and physicians.[12] Patients want to understand what their physicians tell them. In fact, patients rate a physician's ability to explain information as the most desired physician quality.[6] Competence and ability to listen follow.

Not surprisingly, poor provider listening behavior and dysfunctional information delivery are among the top reasons patients sue their physicians.[13] The typical malpractice report reads: "Doctor did not listen to me regarding a medical problem and insisted that it was something else. Problem could have been avoided if doctor had listened."[14]

Shared Decision Making

An era of educated health consumers has greatly changed the paternalistic doctor-centric approach to making treatment decisions. Data support the conclusion that most, but not all, patients generally want to be involved in the treatment decision-making process. For example, a study of women with breast cancer indicated that 22% wanted to select their own treatment, 44% wanted to collaborate with their physician in selecting the treatment, and 34% wanted to delegate this responsibility to their physician.[15] A more recent study with men diagnosed with prostate cancer showed 43% of patients wanting an active role and 47% wanting a collaborative role.[16]

To play a leading or shared role in decision making, patients and families need to have access to the information, tools and resources that will facilitate *informed* decision making. Even if the provision of such information by physicians or the research conducted by patients are perfect, patients at times will make decisions for treatments that are less effective or less cost effective than what their physician recommends.[17]

Although informed, shared decision making clearly is beneficial and preferable, healthcare is not achieving this ideal. Only 42% of the women surveyed in the study mentioned earlier believed they had achieved their preferred level of *control* in decision making.[15] Braddock's study of informed decision making in outpatient practices indicates that only 9% of treatment decisions, which ranged from lower-level decisions about laboratory tests to complex decisions about procedures, were made by patients who were equipped by their physician with complete information.[12] Only a dismal 0.5% of complex decisions were "completely informed."

As illustrated in the previous paragraph, the word *control* often appears in the literature on healthcare decision making. The word implies a confrontation whereby one party gains control and one loses control. The language of *shared* or *participatory* decision making is preferred.

Access to the Patient's Health Information

However, the word *control* is appropriate in another context. In an era of EHRs, *control* over access to healthcare information, specifically the patient's own healthcare data, is likely to become an increasingly contentious issue both ethically and clinically. Should a patient have the right to disallow his or her cardiologist from seeing his or her psychiatric records? On the technical front, some EHR vendors and developers hesitate to design systems that would allow patients such control over specific information fields. Although patients increasingly are indicating that this level of control is something they want, the acceptance of such systems by physicians is uncertain because physicians are trained to seek and expect *all* information about the patient before diagnosing and treating the patient.

In our opinion, the patient must have complete and unimpeded access to his or her clinical record. The data belong to him or her, although the provider currently is expected to maintain the record. We feel that access should be provided without barriers, hesitation, or restriction whatsoever. In a technology-enabled ambulatory environment, patients will be able to build their own personal health records (PHRs) that contain the personal health information the patients choose to include from various providers. These records will be able to interact with EHRs, receiving and sending data in a format called the continuity of care record (CCR).

Effective Self-care Management and Support

The productive and efficient exchange of information is at the heart of true patient-physician collaboration. The patient's access to information is critical to the individual's ability to make informed treatment decisions and manage his or her own care. The Web has revolutionized patients' ability to access healthcare information, but patients continue to want their physician to sort the information for them and to direct them to the research guidelines that demonstrate which treatments work best.[6] Patients who feel they successfully manage their health and chronic conditions report that their physicians explain best-practice evidence-based guidelines, and provide them with educational material and instructions about where to get additional information.[6]

PRACTICE DESIGN AND TECHNOLOGY TO ENABLE RELATIONSHIPS

These attributes of strong patient-physician relationships can be supported through appropriate use of information technology. Table 4-2 summarizes where several contemporary technologies can be deployed to help clinicians understand and support patients more actively. Of course, these particular technologies will change rapidly. What's important is the practice's commitment to applying the most effective available communications tools to the vital function of patient-physician collaboration.

Table 4-2: Applying Technology to Improve Relationships

Establishing the Relationship	Reaching a Diagnosis and Collaboratively Developing a Treatment Plan	Monitoring and Following Up Treatment Plan	Self Management Support
Customized communication based on patient's preference: face-to-face, e-mail, Web, phone, or mail	Web-based surveys administered before patient comes to the office	E-mail, telephone, or phone reminders	Web care, group visits
Registries identify relevant patient subgroups for proactive care and individual care planning	Evidence-based guidelines available to clinician and patient	E-mail, telephone, or phone progress reporting by patient	Telephone care and follow up
		Remote monitoring with results available to physician's office	Reminder systems, prescription renewal
			Educational programs available in community, on Web, video

Table 4-3 illustrates how this array of tools can be applied to a specific problem to improve care and, through the example, illustrates the type of knowledge needed to plan efficient services. Once the services and methods to deliver them are thought through, the practice is in a good position to use technology to support the planned services, attain the level of desired efficiency, and monitor effectiveness. In caring for patients with pain (or any chronic disease), physicians, nurses, and medical assistants generally do a much better job working together on management and support of patient self-management. Relationship-enhancing practices customize communication and services on an ongoing basis.

Table 4-3: Planning Services for Effective Relationships

Planned Services	Efficient Services	Technology
Who are our patients? What are the services to meet 80% of the needs? How do we best assess patient needs, inform them, activate them, and support them?	How do we most efficiently segment our patients so that we can plan services for them? How and by whom should these services be given?	What is needed to support practice function, payment, and internal communication? What is needed to support productive interaction among individual patients, groups of patients, the practice, and community resources? What is needed for assessment, management, and follow-up support of patients? What is needed to measure outcomes of care and prevent errors?
Example: We have 10,000 adult patients. Most of these patients have access to the Web. Of these, 2,500 have pain and about 1,000 have pain and psychosocial problems. We can easily identify patients with pain and psychosocial problems using the vital sign process. Once identified, we will provide them information and resources to support better self-care.	With all our patients, we will focus over the next two years on patients with pain. We will segment patients with pain into those having high and not high confidence with self-care. For those with high self-confidence, we will rely on the Internet. For the others, we will use phone management by LPNs and group visits, which are revenue neutral in combination. For those patients with pain and psychosocial problems who lack confidence with self-care, we will automatically reschedule two face-to-face visits within 3 months.	We will use available Internet programs for patient assessment that automatically place the patient information into a registry. We will also use the problem solving program that is available on the Internet. The LPNs will use the phone follow-up protocol and forms that have been tested in controlled trials. We will use the registry to master scheduled follow-up for patients and titrate enrollment so that no more than 10 low-confidence patients with pain and psychosocial problems are scheduled for visits each month. We will use a wall display to track patients with pain by number identified each week, number using the Web, number accepting phone follow-up, and group visits. We will randomly select 10% of patients for phone assessment each year to determine how well we are doing.

The first sidebar on page 43 lists tips for improving the interaction. The second sidebar describes the CARE Vital Signs Process, illustrating how the planning fits efficiently into everyday work.

Tips for Improving Interaction

- Recognizing that almost all patient "action" or self-care will occur after the visit, consider means to leverage the clinical team's influence over that time period. For example, promptly following the visit, send the patient e-mail follow-ups with reminders and information about helpful Web sites.
- Consider how to improve patient-physician interaction over time, not just during the visit, but before and after the visit. For example, offer appointment scheduling and patient access to his/her own health records on the practice's Web site.
- Remember that although no two patients are the same, groups of patients do share characteristics that can be addressed in standardized ways in order to maximize the impact of approaches. For example, patients with high/low self confidence and hence high/low self-management abilities can receive "customized" communications. Similarly, diabetic patients who are very good at self-care, for example, are likely to learn more by attending groups with other persons who have diabetes so that they can discuss relevant issues and different methods of self-care that have worked and not worked.

CARE Vital Signs Process

CARE (checking, activating, reinforcing, and engineering) Vital Signs process works as follows:

During visits, patients are routinely screened for issues that might benefit from a self-management program through use of the survey tool described earlier. Typically, about half of the patient population aged 19–69 is found to have an important care need. The medical assistant (MA) or nurse then obtains the patient's weight, blood pressure, and pulse and asks about three to five common chronic conditions, pain, health habits, feelings, medication problems, the patient's confidence with his or her self-management skills, and completion of appropriate preventive tests.

The MA or nurse informs the clinician about these issues and provides the patient with information about self-management resources. The clinician works with the patient to identify care goals and priorities and the MA or nurse asks the patient to register for brief self-management programs. The MA or nurse phones the patient following the program to check on understanding and completion of patient self-management goals. Telephone follow-ups are used regularly to reinforce goals over time and to adjust the goals to changing circumstances.

Personalized interactions require regular inquiries about each patient's preferences, and modern data systems to store and retrieve what is learned about patient communication and care preferences. The time constraints of a typical office visit make it exceedingly difficult for patients and their families to relate relevant health concerns to the physician. Health issues that are critical determinants of overall health, such as depression, and alcohol and drug use, must be identified and managed. If not identified and managed, they will continue to significantly impact health outcomes. However, these issues are often difficult to uncover.

User friendliness is the key with technology. If the technology is not easy for the patient, family, and staff to use, it will harm rather than help interaction and relationship. The technology itself may be extremely complicated (for example, consider electricity), but it must be usable with the equivalent of "a flip of the switch." Users do not need or want to be involved with more than switch flipping.

All users must be engaged in the design of practice systems and technology. This requires bringing patients and families and practice staff to the table to describe their needs. It also requires listening to ensure understanding, establishing and using an understandable vocabulary, and giving up any preconceptions about what patients need or want or what physicians and their staffs need or want.

One technique successfully used by a number of ambulatory practices is to ask a half a dozen patients to review the practice's critical processes every four months. In addition to formal mechanisms for input, informal mechanisms, such as patient suggestion boxes—common in the hospital environment—and regularly asking simple questions, such as "How can we improve the care and services we provide?" can also yield helpful information. The "Tips" sidebar includes other thoughts about including the patient in the interaction-improvement process.

Some technologies should undergird all modern practices. Patient access to providers is a major issue to be considered in practice redesign and technology use to enable relationship. The patient wants to know, Can I reach my doctor on Saturday night by phone or e-mail? Is the communication two-way or one-sided? A mechanism such as e-mail can help ensure that the patient's questions are asked and answered and that the patient and family are equipped with the information needed to improve health outcomes.

Case Study: *For examples of enabling relationships through technology, see "Enhancing Relationships through EHR Use at ThedaCare Clinics," page 156.*

Web- or computer-based interaction technology can improve communication of the needed information. Screening tools for depression, alcohol/drug abuse, and domestic abuse administered before the patient sees the physician can enable a relationship-enhancing discussion between the clinician and patient and referral to appropriate specialists, particularly when introduced within the context of an already-established and trust-filled patient-physician relationship.

One example of Web-based interaction technology is a simple "How's Your Health" survey designed, tested, and implemented in various communities.[18, 19] The survey, which patients can take in advance of their visit, consists of a simple series of multi-choice questions about overall health, symptoms, medications, diet, tests taken, emotional issues, and health behaviors such as smoking and drinking, and is completed by patients on the Web.[20] After the patient finishes, he or she obtains a one-page health summary, which includes a brief assessment of relevant clinical issues. The patient is encouraged to take this to his or her physician and is also provided links to Web sites specifically related to relevant health needs. If appropriate given the patient's profile, the patient also receives a Condition Management Form with suggested self-care steps, symptoms to be aware of related to his or her condition, and guidance in tracking health conditions, such as blood pressure, cholesterol, and so forth.

In the office setting, computer-based technology can accomplish similar objectives. For example, in specialty practices in New Hampshire, patients are greeted by a receptionist and given a touchpad computer and asked to answer questions about their health before seeing the physician.[21] It takes approximately 30 minutes for the patient to complete the form. The receptionist transfers the data to a desktop system that creates a one-page summary report that is placed on the front of the medical record for the physician's review. The physician and patient thus can start the visit with a richer information base. During subsequent visits, the patient again uses the touchpad device to update the survey.

Such interaction technology tools help patients, their families, and care providers obtain and provide a much greater level of detail about the individual's care needs and preferences. The scarce minutes with the physician need not focus on information gathering, but can be better used to focus on developing a collaborative treatment plan.

Placing an EHR or registry into a practice without planning efficient services usually leads to gross underuse of the power of the technology or a complete misalignment of the technology with the needs of a modern practice based on relationships.

Consider the hundreds of EHRs now available that do not have easy-to-use relational databases that allow clinicians, for example, to generate a list or registry of patients with diabetes. The reason for this failure is that designers may not have considered how information in the EHR could be used in new ways beyond traditional paper-based, encounter-oriented care. Even EHRs used by large managed care organizations and the government include screens with language that patients could rarely understand. The vocabulary and graphical elements of an effectively designed EHR should support the effective exchange of information between patient and doctor in order to enhance relationship.

Case Study: *For examples of Web-based interaction in practice, see "Enhancing Patient-Physician Interaction at PatientCare Family Clinic," page 178.*

CONCLUDING COMMENTS

Practice system design and technology can be used to improve relationship and to remove from ambulatory practice the tyranny of the 18-minute visit. However, practice design and technology must be centered on the needs of patients and must recognize the importance of relationship at all levels. Relationship is about caring, trust, and instilling confidence that the practice knows the patient and his or her needs and concerns.

If not properly designed and implemented, any technology can create a "digital divide," excluding individuals without access to the technology, enabling physicians who are so inclined to "bury themselves" in the data rather than talking with the patient. Poorly designed software can draw clinician attention away from the patient, while poorly placed computer monitors can come in between patients and their doctors.

A technology-enabled practice has computer screens on pivoting arms or rolling carts so that the doctor sits side-by-side with the patient and both look at the screen to review information or fill in the questionnaire collaboratively. Working as equal partners, they literally build their relationship around their common look at the information. Technology helps build and support their relationship.

References

1 National Ambulatory Medicare Care Survey. 1995–1996 Summary. National Center for Health Statistics, November 1999.

2 Hu P, Rueben DB. Effects of managed care on the length of time that elderly patients spend with physicians during ambulatory visits: National Ambulatory Medical Care Survey. *Medical Care.* July 2002; 49(7):606-613.

3 Blumenthal D, Causino N, Chang Y, et al. The duration of ambulatory visits to physicians. *J Fam Pract.* April 1999; 48(4):264-271.

4 Wasson J, Benjamin R. *How's Your Health? What We Can Do to Make Our Health Better.* www.howsyourhealth.org (accessed April 8, 2005).

5 Rhoades DR, McFarland KF, Finch WH, et al. Speaking and interruptions during primary care office visits. *Fam Med.* July/August 2001; 33(7):528-532.

6 Chronic Care in America: *Improving the Patient-Physician Interaction: Findings from a Comprehensive Survey in the U.S.*, June 2003. www.faact.org (accessed November 18, 2004).

7 Thom DH, Hall MA, Pawlson LG. Measuring patients' trust in physicians when assessing quality of care. *Health Affairs.* July/August 2004; 23(4): 124-132.

8 Keating NL, Green DC, Kao AC, et al. How are patients' specific ambulatory care experiences related to trust, satisfaction, and considering changing physicians? *J Gen Intern Med.* January 2002; 17(1): 79-81.

9 Moore PJ, Sickel AE, Malat J, et al. Psychosocial factors in medical and psychological treatment avoidance: the role of the doctor–patient relationship. *J Health Psychol.* May 2004; 9(3): 421-433.

10 Hall MA, Zheng B, Dugan E, et al. Measuring patients' trust in their primary care providers. *Med Care Rsch.* 2002; 59(3): 293-318.

11 Thom DH, et al. Validation of a measure of patients' trust in their physician: the trust in physician scale. *Medical Care.* 1999; 137(5): 510-517.

12 Braddock CH, Edwards KA, Hasenberg NM, et al. Informed decision making in outpatient practice: time to get back to basics. *JAMA.* December 22, 1999; 282(24): 2313-2320.

13 Levinson W, Roter DL, Mullooly JP, et al. Physician-patient communication: the relationship with malpractice claims among primary care physicians and surgeons. *JAMA.* February 19, 1997; 277(7):553-559.

14 Wasson JH. Why isn't it better (editorial). *Ann Fam Med.* July/August 2004; 2(4):292-293.

15 Degner LF, Kristjanson LF, Bowman D, et al. Information needs and decisional preferences in women with breast cancer. *JAMA.* May 14, 1997; 277(18): 1485-1492.

16 Davison BJ, Parker PA, Goldenberg SL. Patients' preferences for communicating a prostate cancer diagnosis and participating in medical decision-making. *BJU Int.* January 2004; 93(1): 47-52.

17 Kravitz RL. Engaging patients in medical decision making. BMJ. September 15, 2001; 323:584-585.

18 Institute for Healthcare Improvement. How's your health? Survey tool bringing patients and physicians onto the same page. http://www.ihi.org/IHI/Topics/ImprovementMethods/ImprovementStories/HowsYourHealthSurveryToolBringingPatientsandPhysiciansontotheSamePage.htm (accessed April 8, 2005).

19 Wasson JH, Stukel TA, Weiss JE, et al. A randomized trial of the use of patient self-assessment data to improve community practices. *Eff Clin Pract.* January/February 1999; 2(1):1-10.

20 Health survey tool can be accessed at www.howsyourhealth.org (accessed April 8, 2005).

21 Nelson EC, Batalden PB, Homa K, et al. Microsystems in health care: Part 2. Creating a rich information environment. *Jt Com J Qual & Safety.* January 2003; 29(1): 5-15.

Selected Bibliography

Bell RA, Kravitz RL, Thom D, et al. Unsaid but not forgotten: patients' unvoiced desires in office visits. *Arch Intern Med.* September 10, 2001; 161(16):1977-1984.

Bethell C. *Patient-centered Care Measures for the National Health Care Quality Report.* Foundation for Accountability. www.faact.org.

Bethell C, Reuland CH, Halfon N, et al. Measuring the quality of preventive and developmental services for young children: national estimates and patterns of clinicians' performance. *Pediatrics.* June 2004; 113(6 Suppl): 1973-1983.

Brown JB, Boles M, Mullooly J, et al. Effect of clinician communication skills training on patient satisfaction. *Ann Intern Med.* December 7, 1999; 131(11):822-829.

Cooper-Patrick L, Gallo JJ, Gonzales JJ, et al. Race, gender, and partnership in the patient-physician relationship. *JAMA.* August 11, 1999; 282(6):583-589.

Glasgow RE, Funnell MM, Bonomi AE, et al. Self-management aspects of the improving chronic illness care breakthrough series: implementation with diabetes and heart failure teams. *Ann Behav Med.* Spring 2002; 24(2):80-87.

Godfrey MM, Nelson EC, Wasson JH, et al. Microsystems in health care: Part 3. Planning patient-centered services. *Jt Comm J Quality & Safety.* April 2003; 29(4):159-170.

Gosfield AG. The doctor-patient relationship as the business case for quality: doing well by doing right. *J Health Law.* Spring 2004; 37(2):197-223.

Greenfield S, Kaplan SH, Ware JE Jr, et al. Patients' participation in medical care: effects on blood sugar control and quality of life in diabetes. *J Gen Intern Med.* September-October 1988; 3(5):448-457.

Heisler M, Vijan S, Anderson RM, et al. When do patients and their physicians agree on diabetes treatment goals and strategies, and what difference does it make? *J Gen Intern Med.* November 18, 2003; 18(11):893-902.

Hess AM, Nelson AC, Johnson DJ, et al. Building an idealized measurement system to improve clinical office practice performance. *Managed Care Q.* Summer 1999; 7(3):22-34.

Hibbard JH, Greenlick MR, Kunkel LE, et al. Mode of payment, practice characteristics, and physician support for patient self care. *Am J Prev Med.* February 2001; 20(2):118-123.

Kaplan SH, Gandek B, Greenfield S, et al. Patient and visit characteristics related to physicians' participatory decision-making style. Results from the Medical Outcomes Study. *Med Care.* 33(12): 1176-87, December 1995.

Kennedy I. Patients are experts in their own field. *BMJ.* June 14, 2003; 326:1276.

Kravitz RL, Bell RA, Azari R, et al. Direct observation of requests for clinical services in office practice: what do patients want and do they get it? *Arch Intern Med.* July 28, 2003; 163(14):1673-1681.

Krupat E, Bell RA, Kravitz RL, et al.: When physicians and patients think alike: patient-centered beliefs and their impact on satisfaction and trust. *J Fam Pract.* December 2001; 50(12):1057-1062.

Krupat E, Irish JT, Kasten LE, et al. Patient assertiveness and physician decision-making among older breast cancer patients. *Soc Sci Med.* August 1999; 49(4):449-457.

Krupat E, Rosenkranz SL, Yeager CM, et al. The practice orientations of physicians and patients: the effect of doctor-patient congruence on satisfaction. *Patient Educ Couns.* January 2000; 39(1):49-59.

Lanksy D. Consumers' use of performance information to promote quality health care. Presentation at Open Society Forum: Professional Responsibility for Competence and Quality, April 5-6, 2001.

Lorig KR, Sobel DS, Stewart AL, et al. Evidence suggesting that a chronic disease self-management program can improve health status while reducing hospitalization: a randomized trial. *Med Care.* January 1999; 37(1):5-14.

Magari ES, Hamel MB, Wasson JH. An easy way to measure quality of physician-patient interaction. *J Ambul Care Manage.* July 1998; 21(3):27-33.

Markle Foundation. *Connecting Americans to their Health: Final Report.* New York: Markle Foundation; July 2004.

May C, Allison G, Chapple A. Framing the doctor-patient relationship in chronic illness: a comparative study of general practitioners' accounts. *Sociol Health Illn.* March 2004; 26(2):135-158.

Murden RA, Way DP, Hudson A, et al. Professionalism deficiencies in a first-quarter doctor-patient relationship course predict poor clinical performance in medical school. *Acad Med.* October 2004; 79(10 Suppl):S46-48.

Nelson EC, Conger B, Douglass R, et al. Functional health status levels of primary care patients. *JAMA.* June 24, 1983; 249(24):3331-3338.

Nelson EC, Batalden PB, Homa K, et al: Microsystems in health care: Part 2. Creating a rich information environment. *Jt Com J Qual & Safety.* January 2003; 29(1): 5-15.

O'Connor AM, Rostom A, Fiset V, et al. Decision aids for patients facing health treatment or screening decisions. *BMJ.* September 18, 1999; 319 (7212): 731-734.

Renders CM, Valk GD, Griffin SJ. Interventions to improve the management of diabetes in primary care, outpatient, and community settings: a systematic review. *Diabetes Care.* October 2001; 24(10):1821-1833.

Saultz JW, Albedaiwi W. Interpersonal continuity of care and patient satisfaction: a critical review. *Ann Fam Med.* September-October 2004; 2(5):445-451.

Stewart M, Brown JB, Donner A, et al. The impact of patient-centered care on outcomes. *J Fam Pract.* September 2000; 49(9): 796-804.

Street RL Jr, Krupat E, Bell RA, et al. Beliefs about control in the physician-patient relationship: effect on communication in medical encounters. *Gen Intern Med.* August 2003; 18(8):609-616.

Thom DH, Kravitz RL, Bell RA, et al. Patient trust in the physician: relationship to patient requests. *Fam Pract.* October 2002; 19(5):476-483.

Thom DH, Hall MA, Pawlson LG. Measuring patients' trust in physicians when assessing quality of care. *Health Affairs.* July/August 2004; 23(4):124-132.

Wasson JH, Godfrey MM, Nelson EC, et al. Microsystems in health care: Part 4. Planning patient-centered care. *Jt Com J Qual & Safety.* May 2003; 29(5): 227-237.

Wasson JH, James C. Implementation of Web-based interaction technology to improve the quality of a city's health care. *J Ambul Care Manage.* July 2001; 24(3):1-9.

Wasson JH, Jette AM, Johnson DJ, et al. A replicable and customizable approach to improve ambulatory care and research. *J Ambul Care Manage.* 20(1):17-27, January 1997.

Wilson IB, Kaplan S. Physician-patient communication in HIV disease: the importance of patient, physician, and visit characteristics. *J Acquir Immune Defic Syndr.* December 15, 2000; 25(5):417-425.

CHAPTER 5

Service

Susan Edgman-Levitan, PA

Service. It's such a simple word, yet *Webster's Dictionary* defines the word as a noun in 26 different ways, ranging from those appropriate to healthcare, such as "an act of helpful activity," to those entirely beyond healthcare's domain, such as "a branch of the armed forces."

Most people have a clear concept of what the word means when used in conjunction with the word *customer* in realms other than healthcare, such as the hospitality and airline industries. Healthcare indeed has been slow in adopting a *customer service* orientation, notwithstanding the reality that dissatisfied patients, like dissatisfied airline customers, don't return.

THE NEW VISION OF SERVICE

Service quality in healthcare is more than valet parking, edible meals, fancy waiting rooms, and smiling receptionists. It is an understanding of basic customer service principles (see sidebar on page 50) and the ability to integrate these principles into clinical settings, whether ambulatory or inpatient.[1]

Service-oriented healthcare is patient- and relationship-centered healthcare. High quality patient-centered service optimizes the care experience for patients and their families. It is at the heart of the care experience and the clinical relationship described in Chapter 4. Service quality ensures that every time a patient has an encounter with a health provider, that encounter is a positive experience. Less-than-positive experiences are identified and quickly rectified by high quality service providers. Individual patient needs and preferences are also identified and patients and families are treated with respect and dignity. Communication is effective; care providers listen to patients and families and communicate in ways designed to meet the patient's specific needs and desires. Effective communication builds relationship and relationships are what make healthcare work. Equally critical in both inpatient and outpatient settings, are these service attributes really so revolutionary?

Service in ambulatory healthcare thus has four essential dimensions, which this chapter will describe:

- ***Access:*** Access involves getting needed care and getting that care quickly;
- ***Information and education:*** Targeted information for patients and their families directly impacts health outcomes and service quality;
- ***Emotional support:*** Support comes from care providers, family, and friends; and
- ***Coordination and continuity:*** Patient-centered care is based on continuous relationships that are empowered with needed information.

Basic Principles of Service Quality

- Providing services *for* and not *to* customers.
- Treating everyone fairly, equally, and with respect.
- Providing facts and making sure they are understood.
- Communicating effectively and honestly.
- Responding to comments and complaints positively.
- Meeting customer needs as unique individuals.
- Working as a team.

THE RESEARCH ON WHY SERVICE QUALITY IS IMPORTANT

Ambulatory practices and other healthcare providers need to worry about service quality for many reasons. Among these are the more obvious motivations, such as

- A satisfied patient returns for additional visits and generates positive word-of-mouth, and its flip side . . .
- A dissatisfied patient is unlikely to return and likely to share negative stories with friends and family.

Data from numerous research studies indicate four other reasons why service quality is important:

- Service quality is highly associated with care quality;
- Service quality is highly associated with care outcomes;
- Service quality and staff satisfaction go hand-in-hand; and
- Patients and families can provide information that improves healthcare processes and services for themselves as well as the clinicians.

Although much of the research to date has occurred in the hospital setting, other studies illustrate that conclusions are transferable to ambulatory and other healthcare settings.

First, service quality is highly associated with care quality. Medical groups and health plans that patients rate positively in such surveys as CAHPS, also receive high HEDIS scores on technical measures of quality of care. Ambulatory surveys conducted through the CAHPS program, which is funded by the Agency for Healthcare Research and Quality (AHRQ), focus on patients' experience in three service domains: access, interpersonal care, and administrative/customer service. HEDIS performance measures, sponsored and maintained by the National Committee for Quality Assurance (NCQA), focus on effectiveness of care and other indicators of quality. Health plans that have a high CAHPS score for a measure of access—"getting needed care"—and "health plan information and customer service" also have a high score with most of the HEDIS quality measures.[2] Reports of problems with care related to access, information, and education are highly associated with poorer ratings of care quality.[3]

Second, service quality is highly associated with care outcomes. A study of patients hospitalized for a heart attack in nearly two dozen New Hampshire hospitals showed that patients with positive reports about their care experiences in nontechnical aspects of care, such as patient education and discharge planning, had better health outcomes. A year after discharge, their overall health (physical health, mental health, and chest pain) was better than those of patients in hospitals with negative care-experience ratings.[4]

Similarly, a study on postdischarge acute myocardial infarction patients in the southeast indicated a strong association between meeting patients' information needs—one measure of service quality—and their general health status.[5] "The results suggest that providers of care should ensure that they meet the information needs of patients with specific conditions because patients' perceptions of both quality of care and quality of life are associated with the clinicians' ability to transfer key information to their patients," concluded the study's authors.[5] Should the correlation between the effective provision of information by clinicians to patients and how well those patients do really be surprising?

Third, service quality and staff satisfaction go hand-in-hand. Organizations that do a really great job with customer service also tend to provide their staff with a great place to work. It is almost impossible to find high employee satisfaction in organizations that have low patient satisfaction.[1] The reason is that employees and patients are often frustrated or angry about the same things, such as poor systems and processes and ineffective training. Leadership and culture play a key role. Research in industries beyond healthcare indicates that service-oriented organizations focus on the needs of those they serve and their employees. They share attributes, such as a participatory style of decision making, and supervisory methods that focus on listening, coaching or mentoring, and teaching.[6]

Research projects suggest that Magnet facilities—for example, those that have received recognition through the American Nurses Credentialing Center's Magnet Services Recognition Program—achieve positive outcomes for patients and nurses.[7] Patients experience lower mortality rates, shorter lengths of stay, and increased satisfaction. Nurses experience increased job satisfaction, resulting in better nurse retention and recruitment rates and lower rates of nurse burnout.

Another study in the physician world showed that general internists with a high level of professional satisfaction had patients with higher scores on overall satisfaction with the healthcare they received.[8]

Fourth, patients and their families can provide information that will help healthcare providers to improve care processes and services. As Paul Cleary notes,

> Patients are the best source of information about a (provider's) communication and education processes, and they are the *only* source of information about whether they were treated with dignity and respect. Their experiences often reveal how well a (provider) is operating and can stimulate important insights

into the kinds of changes that are needed to close the chasm between the care provided and the care that should be provided.[9]

Unlike choices such as what restaurant to patronize or which car to buy, healthcare consumers do not always have the choice of which medical practice, hospital, or doctor to use. An employer or health plan may be the decision maker. Some experts have suggested that this has allowed a portion of providers to be less concerned than they should be about service quality and performance improvement. Research does suggest that providers who focus on service quality achieve very significant benefits. For example, physicians who use patient satisfaction surveys to shape the care and services they provide report that the impact on the quality and efficiency of their practices has been positive.[10]

More research on the link between service quality and care quality, clinical outcomes, and patient/staff satisfaction is definitely needed in ambulatory settings. Much of the research to date has focused on the impact of patient-physician communication, which is only one component of service quality. A thorough review of the service-related research is beyond this chapter's scope, but additional studies are cited in the resource section at the end of the chapter.

THE SERVICE REDESIGN PROCESS

Four principles or strategies can enable ambulatory practices to achieve effective and efficient service redesign: consider the patient's perspective; focus first on the needs of the largest patient group; address emotional experiences frequently encountered by patients and their families; and center the patient-physician encounter on only those elements that can best be accomplished through face-to-face interaction. A brief description of each follows.

Strategies for Considering the Patient's Perspective

In order to redesign ambulatory practice to improve service quality, the individuals doing the design work must experience care through the patient's eyes. Understanding and promoting patient-centered care thus starts with collaboration between providers and patients and their families. Significant breakthroughs can be achieved in all service dimensions when patients are part of the design process. Conversely, the healthcare world is full of failed processes created by well-meaning clinicians and managers who neglected to consider the patient's perspective.

Walkthroughs are the simplest way for a practice of any size to give staff and clinicians the patient's perspective. System, flow, and service-oriented problems or rules and procedures that may have outlived their usefulness can be identified readily. During a walkthrough, one staff member or physician plays the role of the patient and another staff member or practitioner accompanies the "mock patient" as the "mock family member." They go through an office visit exactly as the patient and family do, taking notes to document what they see and how they feel during the process. Following the mock visit, they share their notes and improvement ideas with the organization's leadership.

Many ideas typically can be implemented easily and can result in significant benefits. For example, during walkthrough experiences, clinicians may learn that their conversations and those of their staff can be heard by patients and families sitting in the waiting room, thereby breaching confidentiality and trust. Increased awareness of voice levels and a white noise machine in the waiting room can rectify the situation. Another medical practice might discover that patients are asked to complete a form to obtain information that never is used by anyone. The form could be dispensed with immediately. Flow problems, such as asking patients to check in at two different places (this made sense 15 years ago, but no longer does), often can be identified.

A similar technique called *patient shadowing* can be equally instructive. A staff member requests permission to accompany a patient through the visit and takes notes on the patient's experience.

Formal or informal patient and family *surveys* can provide information on improvement opportunities. Surveys can be conducted by mail or by telephone following patient visits. The effort can be as extensive as desired. Simply equipping a staff member with one or two open-ended questions, such as "What was it like getting care at our practice?" and "What can we do to improve the care and service we provide?" can provide feedback that will make a significant difference. Informal telephone surveys following a visit can also be used to obtain feedback about a specific intervention being tested in the practice.

Focus groups provide another means of obtaining detailed service-related information from patients and families. Through a moderator-led discussion, ambulatory practices can collect information about a specific problem and new improvement ideas. It can be helpful to invite patients with a similar condition or with similar needs to participate in a focus group so that detailed, targeted questions can be asked of a major patient population. Consultants need not be hired; numerous resources are available to guide medical practices in conducting their own focus groups.[11]

Patient and family advisory councils provide one of the most effective strategies for involving families and patients in the design of care. Conceived by the Institute for Family-Centered Care (IFCC), such councils include individuals who represent the constituencies served by the medical practice. The Council meets regularly and serves as a "listening post" for the practice staff. The IFCC's book titled *Developing and Sustaining a Patient and Family Advisory Council* provides detailed guidance.[12]

Considering the patient's perspective provides benefits beyond the information obtained. It also teaches staff and clinicians to make "seeing things through the patient's eyes" a regular practice. For example, physicians often do not enter their offices through the same doors used by patients. The practice looks distinctly different when the patients' door is used. Similarly, many physicians and staff have not experienced their practice's telephone answering system from the patient's perspective. Messaging systems often confront patients—the customers—with a long list of options. Doctors and pharmacies can select one of the earlier options. Patients have to listen until the bitter end. Why not let patients press "1"?

Practices may wish to consider beginning staff and new clinician orientation by using one of the strategies outlined in this section. This can be both inspiring and energizing.

Case Study: *For examples of obtaining patients' perspective in practice, see "Putting the Patient in the Center of the Radar Screen at ThedaCare Clinics," page 157.*

Focusing on the Needs of the Largest Patient Group

Practices can start the service redesign process by focusing on meeting the needs of the practice's largest patient cohort. For example, a family practice in a rural area may see lots of mothers with young children. These should be the focus for service design. The information needs of mothers with young children are going to be very different than those experienced by elderly patients with chronic conditions, which may comprise the largest cohort seen by an internal medicine practice. Elderly patients typically have extensive access and continuity of care needs; young mothers typically have extensive emotional support needs. Customizing care for the largest patient population offers an efficient use of practice resources. This does not mean that the needs of smaller patient groups should be ignored, only that major energy should be devoted to the key customer group(s).

Addressing Patient and Family Emotional Support Needs

Patients and their families often experience considerable anxiety and fear surrounding an office visit. They wonder whether they will find a parking spot, arrive on time, wait for a long time before seeing the doctor, be asked questions that they cannot answer, have a test that hurts, or receive bad news, for example. Everything that practices do to redesign service must address patient and family emotional experiences. Many of the design strategies described later in the chapter focus on preparing the patient and family for the visit. Providing information in advance about where the practice is located, what the patient and accompanying family member can expect during the visit, and what they need to bring with them can address key concerns.

Centering the Patient-Physician Encounter

Face-to-face time for patients with practitioners is very limited. That time should be spent on only those elements that can best be accomplished face-to-face. Everything that can be removed from the office visit time and done in advance or following the visit should be designed to occur outside the office. Preparing patients for office visits and equipping them with the information needed to care for themselves after the visit will result in making more predictable what is now so random for practitioners and patients alike.

SYSTEM DESIGN AND TECHNOLOGY TO ENABLE SERVICE QUALITY

Numerous design and technology-enabled strategies that can enhance ambulatory service quality are described here. Information technology is often at the center of various efforts to improve the patient's care experience, particularly efforts focused on improved and customized communication, information exchange, and expedited care. However, as noted by clinical IT experts, technology can change everything, but it's about the patient, not the technology.[13] IT plays a supporting role, when possible. Since all patients are not technologically savvy, pencil and paper or other types of backups are needed to ensure the effectiveness of service redesign. For example, a practice that relies on e-mail for getting information out to patients in advance of visits needs to have an alternative way to relay information, such as by mail or by telephone.

Access Improvement Strategies

Access to services is a prerequisite for care. If individuals cannot *access* services, they certainly cannot *receive* care or services. As mentioned earlier, access involves getting needed care and getting that care quickly. Timing is an essential component of healthcare. *When* something happens is often as important as *what* happens. Ambulatory care is plagued by service delays. Patients often wait weeks for appointments with their primary care doctor and then perhaps months for appointments with specialists to whom they are referred. Diagnostic tests involve further delays and patients often wait what seems like an excruciatingly long time to receive test results.

Patients want and need access to service, not 9 to 5, not even 24/7, but 24/7/365. Access involves visits to the doctor's office, but it also involves nonvisit-based care and assistance with self-management. These might be provided via every possible route of delivery, including mail, voice, and electronic means. Optimal access uses available medical practice capacity to serve patients at the time, in the location, and in the manner most convenient to patients. It also ensures that the most appropriate provider meets the patient's needs.[14]

Open Access Scheduling

Open access scheduling—also known as *advanced access* and *same-day scheduling*—is a method of scheduling in which all patients can receive an appointment slot on the day they call, almost always with their personal physician. According to the experts who designed and implemented the model, Mark Murray and Catherine Tantau, it is effective in both managed care and fee-for-service environments. "It has one very simple yet challenging rule: Do today's work today," they note.[15] In practices that use open access scheduling, physicians start their day with approximately 70% to 75% of time slots open for patients who call for appointments that day. The remaining appointment slots are filled by patients requiring follow-up visits.

Open access scheduling does not differentiate between urgent and routine appointments. The goal is to meet the patient's service needs *today* rather than at some future time. Open access scheduling also does not try to control the daily patient demand for care, but rather to maximize the daily capacity to provide care to meet that demand. *Demand* for health services on any given day is directly related to the size of a practice's patient population. It is quite predictable. *Capacity* is the number of available or open appointments at the beginning of the day or the *supply* of clinicians' time. In essence, the open access model applies the principles of queuing theory and industrial engineering to match the demand for appointment visits with the supply.

To make this possible, the backlog of patients waiting for appointments must be "worked down" and kept to a minimum. Working down the backlog requires increasing the capacity of the practice temporarily by adding additional appointment slots for a finite period or hiring temporary help. The literature suggests that appointments can be worked down in two or three months, and that after that time no additional resources are required.

In addition to reducing backlog and balancing supply and demand, four other elements of the model are critical to its successful application:[16]

- Reducing the variety of appointment types;
- Developing contingency plans for unusual circumstances;
- Working to adjust demand profiles; and
- Increasing the availability of bottleneck resources.

A six-step method for making the transition from traditional scheduling to open-access scheduling is presented in *The CAHPS® Improvement Guide.*[1] Kilo and colleagues offer additional guidance for the transition process.[14] Through its Breakthrough Collaboratives, the Institute for Healthcare Improvement (IHI) has helped hundreds of medical practices to successfully implement open access scheduling. The organization currently also offers Web-based training and detailed resources in this area.[17] For example, scripts that staff can use when patients call to schedule appointments and when patients arrive late for appointments are available on the IHI's Web site (www.ihi.org).

Case Study: *For an example of open-access scheduling in practice, see "Open Access at ThedaCare Clinics," page 158.*

Streamlined Patient Flow

Dissatisfaction with service quality also stems from the all-too-common waits for diagnostic tests, test results, treatments, specialty services, and hospital admission. These waits often result from inefficiencies of administrative and clinical processes.

Analyzing the patient's "flow" through the visit and measuring "cycle times" can help a medical practice identify problem areas and ways to reduce waits by eliminating unnecessary steps or preparing the patient better for visits. An *office visit cycle time* is the amount of time that a patient spends at a medical office, as measured in minutes. It begins and ends when the patient walks through the office doors. Waits can occur during any step of the patient visit, such as waiting to check in, moving to an exam room, moving to check out, and checking out. Thus, to take steps to minimize delays, a practice must first determine where waits occur. A tool that can be used by patients and practices to measure specific elements of the cycle time is available on the IHI's Web site. At a minimum, practices should distinguish between the time the patient spends with the physician or other care team members and the time spent waiting. "The goal is not to reduce total cycle time, but to maximize the time the patient spends with the physician or other members of the care team," notes the IHI.[18] The goal cited by that organization is to decrease the office visit cycle time to 1.5 times the actual time spent with the clinician.

Methods of production planning and prediction are important. Practices need to be able to model capacity according to the predicted demand. Successful teams participating in the IHI's Idealized Design of Clinical Office Practices have used huddles, which involve brief meetings of care team members to discuss how to eliminate logjams, and other forms of immediate adjustment. These may be needed not just daily, but hourly in order to adjust the allocation of resources as new information arrives about practice needs.

Cycle time improvement strategies will vary widely based on the type of ambulatory practice, but strategies cited in the literature include:[19, 20]

- Shifting tasks previously handled by specialists to other professionals such as physician's assistants and nurse practitioners;
- Previewing medical records prior to visits in order to better anticipate what might be needed;
- Designing office work space so that people whose work is contiguous are in contiguous spaces;
- Pre-register patients through Web-based or telephone registration, whenever possible;
- Standardizing exam rooms by stocking them with supplies and equipment stored in a standard way; and
- Developing and using standardized order sheets and patient information and instruction sheets for common conditions and procedures.

Many practices take steps to achieve continuous flow, a system in which workflow is managed to avoid in-process waiting. Work is completed when it is generated, rather than batched in groups. Batching creates delay in workflow and patient flow.

Strategies to Improve Communication and Information Access

Customized communication, which is designed to meet the patient's specific needs and desires and is provided in the form and at the time desired by the patient, is a critical component of the vision for high quality service. So too is access to information by the patient and family when desired and in the preferred form.

Electronic health records (EHRs) and Internet connectivity greatly enhance access to both specific patient information and to general resources that are helpful in educating patients and families. Patients experience the benefits of rapid and accurate access to information during office visits, e-mail correspondence, and telephone conversations with the practice. When a patient calls the practice for a clinical or administrative reason, his or her record is available within seconds. This makes almost any process, such as scheduling an appointment, providing for medication refills, or answering a billing question quicker and easier.

Communication and information access/provision are inseparably and integrally related to service, relationship, and reliability. Material presented here thus is complementary to material appearing in Chapters 4 and 6. Information technology and practice design can have an enormous positive impact on a practice's ability to assure service quality. This section highlights specific initiatives that can make a significant difference to the services offered by many medical practices.

Helping Patients Prepare for the Visit and Communicate Their Care Needs

Patients often report that they leave office visits with their questions unasked, unanswered, or answered in ways they do not understand. They also report that they are ill-equipped to make informed decisions about treatment and prevention alternatives.

Strategies to address these communication and education problems range from no-tech or low-tech solutions to high-tech, inter- and intra-operational, Web-based ones.

A *patient question list*, also known as a "*doc talk card*," is one low-end strategy that requires few resources but is effective in generating communication and increasing patient satisfaction.

It works like this: The person scheduling the patient for the office visit encourages the patient to write down questions he or she wishes to ask the doctor and bring the list to the visit. Alternatively, a member of the office staff mails a card to the patient in advance of the visit, typically asking patients to generate two to five questions about their medical problems or their reason for the visit. The patient writes this information on the card, which is then attached to the patient's chart for the physician's review prior to the visit. Some practices give the cards to patients when they arrive for the visit to be completed in the waiting room, but this does not allow the patient to think about the visit fully or consult family members about issues.

An initiative conducted by Massachusetts General Hospital (MGH)-based John D. Stoeckle Center for Primary Care Innovation uses a pre-visit, paper-based packet to help prepare and better educate patients for office visits. Packets are customized by type of visit or condition and mailed to patients in advance of their visit. For example, educational materials for 50-year-old adults coming in for their annual physical exams include PSA testing, colonoscopy screening, and bone density information. A short form included in the packet requests the following information:

- Health topics the patient would like to discuss or would like more information about;
- Three health concerns the patient wants to address during the visit;
- An updated medication list which the patient reviews for accuracy and completeness;
- Recent changes in personal or family health history;
- Shared decision making videos on a variety of topics; and
- A health maintenance tracking tool.

Completed forms are given to physicians before the visit. In the future, MGH hopes to use a secure Web-based patient portal to distribute and collect this information.

The Center for Information Therapy (CIT) offers a Web-based system to launch patient-specific "information prescriptions" (Figure 5-1). "By using the system, medical practices can help patients come to the visit with a better description of their symptoms, a clearer understanding of what tests might be ordered, and perhaps even knowing what clothes to wear to minimize dressing delays in clinical examinations," notes Donald Kemper, CEO and Founder of Healthwise, Inc., CIT's parent organization.[21]

These strategies remove from the visit all activities that can be conducted in advance of the visit. This allows clinicians to focus on what can best be achieved through the visit—diagnosis, collaborative development of a treatment plan, and emotional support. The strategies also reduce patient and family anxiety about the visit.

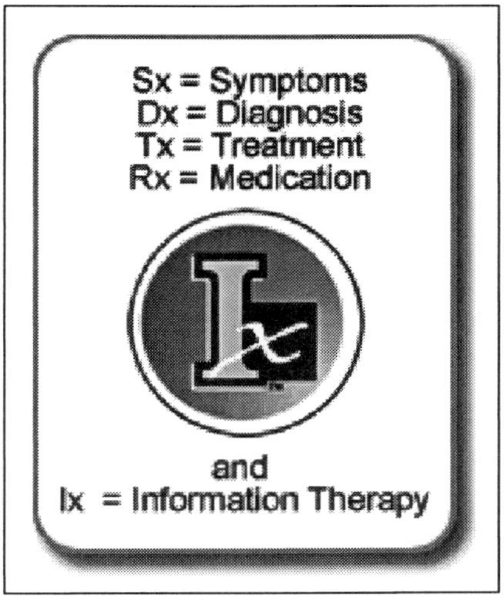

Figure 5-1: Information Therapy Prescription: IxTM. From Kemper DW. *The Business Case for Information Therapy.* Center for Information Technology. Used by permission.

Information therapy, a generic term, is the timely prescription and availability of evidence-based health information to meet individuals' specific needs and support sound decision making. Unlike free-floating health content on the Web, information therapy prescriptions are delivered to the patient as part of the process of care, with only the information relevant to his or her current moment in care.

Ix™, an acronym used to invoke other medical prescription-related terms (see graphic), is a trademark of Healthwise, a nonprofit organization based in Boise, Idaho. Healthwise offers comprehensive evidence-based, decision-support information for consumers and directs the Washington, D.C.-based CIT.

Physicians and other providers can use CIT's physician-generated, system-generated, and consumer-generated Ix™ prescriptions to promote health, manage chronic disease, prevent medical mistakes, achieve patient-centered care, improve healthcare efficiencies, and improve the overall quality and experience of care.

In Chapter 4, John Wasson and David Lansky described Web- or computer-based (touchpad) technology that helps patients and their families provide physicians with an increased level of detail about their care needs and preferences in advance of the visit. The basic idea is that, prior to a visit, each patient completes a questionnaire about the status of their functional health, clinical health, and health risk. The clinical team then uses that information to design and deliver a treatment plan appropriate to the individual. In effect, the patient provides the clinician with the information essential to service quality.

This kind of technology is being used in a few ambulatory clinics nationwide, such as the mammography center at MGH. Patients are instructed to arrive 15 minutes early and given a touchpad to complete a 140-item questionnaire, which they formerly had to complete using paper and pencil. The touchpad system enables even patients with severe disabilities to provide detailed information, such as family history, medications, and so forth. The receptionist transfers the data electronically to the physicians who thus are spared the job of collecting patient history. This system also enables the physician to give detailed recommendations to women about important risk factors, in effect providing genetic counseling at the visit, a process that previously required weeks to complete.

Patients and their families frequently complain that they have to provide the same information to multiple individuals during a visit. The one-time provision of information enabled by this kind of touchpad-based technology, among other technologies, improves a critical aspect of service quality.

Offering Patients Access to Their Own Health Records

Medical practices can offer patients access to their paper, electronic, or Web-based medical record in order to facilitate information sharing and communication about care needs. The patient and family should not be denied access to the patient's chart unless the patient requests it. Access to information in the medical record enables patients to better understand their condition and treatment plan, to feel more in control of their health, and to identify and correct inaccurate information. Web access to medical records allows patients to print out copies of test results, medication lists, and physician visit notes and instructions from any location at any time of day or night.

Not all patients are interested in accessing their medical record, of course, but research indicates that a significant portion (36%) is interested.[22] The most common reasons cited by patients for wanting to look at their record were to see what their physician said about them, to be more involved in their healthcare, and to understand their condition better. EHRs are making it easier to share information. Studies indicate that the sharing of medical records has a consistently positive impact on patient-physician communication, with the sole exception of communication with psychiatric patients.[23]

Targeted Clinical Advice and Information via the Web or E-mail

Research studies indicate that about half of adults in the U.S. have used the Internet to locate health information.[24] "The Net friendliness of clinicians and provider organizations—as rated by the e-patients they serve—is becoming an important new aspect of healthcare quality (and service)," note two experts.[25] They urge a major upgrade in designing a medical practice system in which patients who use the Internet are recognized as a valuable new type of resource for managing their own care, providing care for others, and helping professionals improve the quality of their services.

Research conducted at MGH related to e-savvy neurology patients, in fact, suggests that Internet-based support groups are creating an impressive variety of online health resources.[26] These researchers urge physicians to take a bottom-up approach to support groups by referring patients to the groups and participating in discussions.

Technology-enabled systems for providing customized information to patients are being used in many ambulatory practices nationwide. For example, Partners HealthCare provides its clinic-based physicians with an Intranet site called Primary Care Operations Improvement (PCOI). Clinicians can obtain documents and materials for their own education and to give patients on anything from the availability of flu vaccines to marriage license forms. Patients are provided similar access to information via a Web site. Customizing content enhances the patient's ability to care for him- or herself and satisfaction with service quality.

The sidebar on page 61 provides information on selected publicly available Web sites to which physicians can direct patients or use themselves for the provision to patients of customized information.

Selected Web Sites for Patient Education

American Academy of Family Physicians (AAFP)
http://familydoctor.org

All of the information on this Web site, which won the MD NetGuide's 2004 Nettie Award for Excellence on the Medical Internet for Best Patient-Friendly Site, has been written and reviewed by physicians and patient education professionals at the AAFP. Patients can search the site by conditions or topic area.

MedlinePlus
http://medlineplus.gov

Provided by the U.S. National Library of Medicine and the National Institutes of Health, this Web site has information on more than 650 health topics (conditions, diseases, and wellness), drugs (both prescription and over-the-counter medicines), a medical encyclopedia, a dictionary, health news, directories of doctors, dentists, and hospitals, and other resources. More than 165 interactive tutorials from the Patient Education Institute are also available.

Patient Education Institute
www.patient-education.com

The Patient Education Institute develops and distributes evidence-based patient education products and systems for healthcare organizations of all types. Products include

- XP Clinical: Used in clinics and physician offices to prescribe patient-specific information, verify comprehension, and document education and informed consent;
- X-Plain Tutorials, which combine physician-reviewed text, graphics, animations, narration, interactive questions and feedback; and
- X-Plain On-Demand, which allows clinics and hospitals to display, print, and e-mail the summaries, as it documents patient education.

Wired.MD™
www.wired.MD

wired.MD developed the streaMed™ Patient Education Solution, delivering videos (CCTV, DVD, VHS, streaming video formats) and text handouts for use at the point of care and beyond. It offers 310 patient and consumer health education videos and more than 1,300 education handouts.

Making medical information available to patients via electronic means is often critical to "activating" or involving patients in their care. Practices that send patients clinical updates or reminders via Web portals or e-mail systems are better able to achieve the goals of improved relationship (through reaching out and "touching" their patients), service (by letting patient know that the practice is thinking about patient health needs even when the patient is not present), and clinical reliability (patients know that the practice's system will not let them "fall through the cracks").

Group Health Cooperative in Seattle, which has a strong leadership commitment to keeping the patient at the center of planning and implementation of care, provides patients with a Web site, called MyGroupHealth. The site is designed to meet patient's needs outside the exam room. The organization's research indicates that 77% of the organization's patients want to ask questions where no visit is necessary, 71% want to schedule appointments, 71% want to refill prescriptions, and 70% wish to obtain results of medical tests.[27] Through MyGroupHealth, patients can do such things as review their test results, obtain information relevant to the results, and communicate about the results directly with their physician via secure messaging e-mail. The clinical information that a physician shows the patient in the exam room can be reviewed by the patient at home in his or her living room. "Condition centers," health tools, and discussion groups are available to patients.[28] Mark Handley, MD, Medical Director, notes that patients are respectful of clinicians' time and that e-mail capability accomplishes the following:

- Gives patients a channel for communicating that is not bound by clinic hours;
- Enables patients to avoid visits and enriches and empowers them with information; and
- Works as an extension of the relationship between the clinician and patient rather than a substitute.[27]

E-mail communication offers numerous service-enhancing benefits. It is convenient, fast, asynchronous (i.e., both people do not have to be available at the same time), unobtrusive (i.e., it does not interrupt the recipient on either end), and easy to track and manage, unlike telephone messages. Because it facilitates communication between patients and their doctors, e-mail can improve patient-centered care and service quality.

Coordination and Care Continuity Strategies

Patients and their families often identify lack of coordination and care continuity as a source of dissatisfaction about service quality. Patient dissatisfaction with primary care physicians frequently stems from difficulty getting needed referrals to specialists.[29] Care delays generate increased patient and family anxiety and contribute to a greater risk of adverse clinical outcomes.[30] Continuity of care, which matches the individual's ongoing needs with the appropriate level and type of care, treatment, or service across multiple providers, is critical to patient safety and service quality.

Information about the patient must be transmitted from healthcare provider to the next. All too frequently, patients who have been referred to a specialist by their primary care physician arrive at the specialist's office with no information in-hand or on-hand at the specialist's office. Thus, the specialist has no idea why the patient is there and must start the information gathering process from scratch. Then, after the specialist sees or treats the patient, the patient returns to the primary care doctor who has no idea what treatment the specialist provided or what follow-up care is recommended.

Technology such as EHRs, Webcast services, and audio and videoconferencing, can dramatically improve access to critical medical information and the transfer of such information between providers. X-rays and test results, medical records, and clinical recommendations can be discussed and shared among physicians, patients, and families alike.

Case Study: *For examples of coordination and care continuity strategies, see "Providing Consistent Non-Urgent Care at ThedaCare Clinics," page 159; and "Enhancing Care Coordination at PatientCare Family Clinic," page 180.*

CONCLUDING COMMENTS

Most patients and families want to be empowered with information about medical conditions and treatment strategies. Patient complaints related to service quality in ambulatory and other settings often occur when patients feel they are being denied needed information. The frustrations experienced when attempting to obtain test results or copies of laboratory reports or trying to ask a clinical question following an appointment are all too common. In a very fundamental yet global way, practice redesign and technology can improve service quality and patient safety because they are the building blocks for enhanced, compassionate human relationships.

References

1 Edgman-Levitan S, Shaller D, McInnes K. *The CAHPS® Improvement Guide: Practical Strategies for Improving the Patient Care Experience.* Cambridge, MA: Harvard Medical School Department of Health Care Policy; October 2003. Available at www.cahps-sun.org (accessed April 8, 2005).

2 Schneider EC, Zaslavsky AM, Landon BE, et al. National quality monitoring of Medicare health plans: the relationship between enrollee's reports and quality of clinical care. *MedCare.* December 2001; 39(12):1313-1325.

3 National Research Corporation-Picker Institute, unpublished data; 2001.

4 Fremont AM, Hargraves JL, Rowe RM, et al. Patient-centered processes of care and long-term outcomes of myocardial infarction. *J Gen Intern Med.* December 2001; 16(12):868-869.

5 Larson CO, Nelson EC, Gustafson D, et al. The relationship between meeting patients' information needs and their satisfaction with hospital care and general health status outcomes. *Int J Qual Health Care.* October 1996; 8(5):447-456.

6 Heskett JL, Jones TO, Loveman G, et al. Putting the service-profit chain to work. *Harv Bus Rev.* March-April 1993; 164-174.

7 Aiken LH. Superior outcomes for Magnet Hospitals: The evidence base. In McClure ML, Hinshaw AS (eds). *Magnet Hospitals Revisited: Attraction and Retention of Professional Nurses.* Washington, DC: American Nurses Publishing; 2002, 61-81.

8 Haas JS, Cook EF, Puopolo AL. Is the professional satisfaction of general internists associated with patient satisfaction? *J Gen Intern Med.* February 2000; 15(2):140-141.

9 Cleary PD. A hospitalization from hell: a patient's perspective on quality. *Ann Intern Med.* January 7, 2003; 138(1):33-39.

10 Reed MC, Devers K, Landon B. Physicians and care management: more acceptance than you think. Issue Brief #60 from Center for Studying Health System Change, January 2003. Available at www.hschange.org (accessed April 8, 2005).

11 Bader GE, Rossi CA. *Focus Groups: A Step-by-Step Guide* (3rd ed). San Diego, CA: The Bader Group; 2001; or MGMA: Size Matters: Focus on Satisfaction by Using Patient Focus Group, MGMA Web site: www.mgma.com (accessed April 8, 2005).

12 Webster PD, Johnson B. *Developing and Sustaining a Patient and Family Advisory Council.* Bethesda, MD: Institute for Family-Centered Care; 2000. Available at www.familycenteredcare.org (accessed April 8, 2005).

13 Handley M. In the trenches: integrating information therapy into the clinical workflow at Group Health Cooperative. Available at www.informationtherapy.org (accessed April 8, 2005).

14 Kilo CM, Triffletti P, Tantau C, Murray M. Improving access to clinical offices. *J Med Pract Mgmt.* November/December 2000; 16(3): 126-132.

15 Murray M, Tantau C. Same-day appointments: exploding the access paradigm. *Fam Pract Mgmt.* September 2000; 7(8):45-50.

16 Murray M, Berwick DM. Advanced access: reducing waiting and delays in primary care. *JAMA.* July 16, 2003; 290(3):332-333.

17 Institute for Healthcare Improvement's Web site: www.ihi.org.

18 Institute for Healthcare Improvement. Office visit cycle time. www.ihi.org/IHI/Topics/OfficePractices (accessed April 8, 2005).

19 Backer LA.Strategies for better patient flow and cycle time. *Fam Prac Mgmt.* June 2002. www.aafp.org/fpm (accessed April 8, 2005).

20 Edgman-Levitan S, Shaller D, McInnes K. *The CAHPS® Improvement Guide: Practical Strategies for Improving the Patient Care Experience.* Cambridge, MA: Harvard Medical School Department of Health Care Policy (under grant from Centers for Medicare & Medicaid Services); October 2003, p 69.

21 Kemper DW. *The Business Case for Information Therapy.* Center for Information Therapy. Available at www.informationtherapy.org/rs_white_papers.html.

22 Fowles JB, Kind AC, Craft C, et al. Patients' interest in reading their medical record: relation with clinical and sociodemographic characteristics and patients' approach to health care. *Arch Intern Med.* April 12, 2004; 164(7):793-800.

23 Ross SE, Lin CT. The effects of promoting patient access to medical records: a review. *JAMIA.* March/April 2003; 10(2):129-138.

24 Fox S, Fallows D. *Internet health resources: health searches and e-mail have become more commonplace, but there is room for improvement in searches and overall internet access.* Washington DC: Pew Internet and American Life Project, July 16, 2003. Available at www.pewinternet.org (accessed April 8, 2005).

25 Ferguson T, Frydman G. The first generation of e-patients (editorial). *BMJ.* May 15, 2004; 328(7449):1148-1149.

26 Lester J, Prady S, Finegan Y, Hoch D. Learning from e-patients at Massachusetts General Hospital. *BMJ.* May 15, 2004; 328(7449):1188-1190.

27 Handley M. In the trenches: integrating information therapy into the clinical workflow at Group Health Cooperative. Available at www.informationtherapy.org/conf_mat04/Handley_PPT.pdf (accessed April 8, 2005).

28 Hereford J. What information therapy means to patients and health care delivery systems. Available at www.informationtherapy.org/conf_mat03/Hereford_Ward.pdf (accessed April 8, 2005).

29 Grumbach K, Selby JV, Damberg C, et al. Resolving the gatekeeper conundrum: what patients value in primary care and referrals to specialists. *JAMA.* July 21, 1999; 282(3):261-266.

30 Murray M. Reducing waits and delays in the referral process. *Fam Pract Mgmt.* March 2002; 9(3): 39-42.

Selected Bibliography

Bauby J-D. *The Diving Bell and the Butterfly.* New York: Alfred Knopf; 1997.

Charles C, Gauld M, Chambers L, et al. How was your hospital stay? Patients' reports about their care in Canadian hospitals. *CMAJ.* June 1, 1994; 150(11):1813-1822.

Cleary PD, Edgman-Levitan S. Health care quality: incorporating consumer perspectives. *JAMA*. November 19, 1997; 278(19):1608-1612.

Cleary PD, Edgman-Levitan S, Walker JD, et al. Using patient reports to improve medical care: A preliminary report from 10 hospitals. *Qual Manag Health Care.* Fall 1993; 2(1):31-38.

Coulter A, Cleary PD. Patients' experiences with hospital care in five countries. *Health Aff* May-June 2001; 20(3):244-252.

Covinsky KE, Rosenthal GE, Chren MM, et al. The relation between health status changes and patient satisfaction in older hospitalized medical patients. *Gen Intern Med.* April 1998; 13(4):223-229.

Delbanco TL, Stokes DM, Cleary PD, et al. Medical patients' assessments of their care during hospitalization: insights for internists. *J Gen Intern Med.* December 1995; 10(12):679-685.

Edgman-Levitan S, Cleary PD. What information do consumers want and need? *Health Aff.* Winter 1996; 15(4):42-56.

Frampton S, Charmel P, Gilpin L. *Putting Patients First.* San Francisco, CA: Jossey-Bass Publishers; 2002.

Gerteis M, Edgman-Levitan S, Daley J, Delbanco T (eds). *Through the Patient's Eyes: Understanding and Promoting Patient-Centered Care.* San Francisco, CA: Jossey-Bass Publishers;1993.

Gibson R, Singh JP. *Wall of Silence.* Washington DC: Lifeline Press; 2003.

Gilmore JH, Pine BJ. The four faces of mass customization. *Harv Bus Rev.* January-February 1997; 75 (1): 91-101.

Goodman, John. Basic facts on customer complaint behavior and the impact of service on the bottom line. *Competitive Advantage: ASQ Newsletter.* June 1999; 8(1).

Greenfield S, Kaplan S, Ware JE Jr. Expanding patient involvement in care: effects on patient outcomes. *Ann Intern Med.* April 1985; 102(4):520-528.

Greenfield S, Kaplan SH, Ware JE Jr, et al. Patients' participation in medical care: effects on blood sugar control and quality of life in diabetes. *J Gen Intern Med.* September-October 1988; 3(5):448-457.

Institute of Medicine's Committee on Quality Healthcare in America: *Crossing the Quality Chasm A New Health System for the 21st Century.* Washington DC: National Academies Press; 2001.

Kaiser Family Foundation & Agency for Healthcare Quality and Research. *Americans as Health Care Consumers: An Update on the Role of Quality Information;* 2000.

Kaplan SH, Gandek B, Greenfield S, et al. Patient and visit characteristics related to physicians' participatory decision-making style: results from the Medical Outcomes Study. *Med Care.* December 1995; 33(12):1176-1187.

Kaplan SH, Greenfield S, Ware JE Jr. Assessing the effects of physician-patient interactions on the outcomes of chronic disease. *Med Care.* March 1989; 27(3 Suppl):S110-127.

Kruegar RA, Casey MA. *Focus Groups: A Practical Guide for Applied Research.* Thousand Oaks, CA: Sage Publications; 2000.

Krupat E, Fancey M, Cleary PD. Information and its impact on satisfaction among surgical patients. *Soc Sci Med.* December 2000; 51(12):1817-1825.

Leebov W, Afriat S, et al. *Service Savvy Healthcare: One Goal at a Time.* San Francisco, CA: Jossey-Bass/AHA Press; 1998.

Leebov, W. G. Scott, et al. *Achieving Impressive Customer Service: 7 Strategies for Healthcare Managers.* San Francisco, CA: Jossey-Bass; 1998.

Leebov W, Scott G, et al. *Service and Quality Improvement: The Customer Satisfaction Strategy for Health Care.* Chicago: American Hospital Publishing, Inc.; 1994.

Price R. *A Whole New Life.* New York: Plume Press; 1994.

Robinson A, Thomson R. Variability in patient preferences for participating in medical decision making: implication for the use of decision support tools. *Qual Health Care.* September 2001; 10 Suppl 1:i34-38.

Roth MS, Amoroso WP. Linking core competencies to customer needs: strategic marketing of health care services. *J Health Care Mark.* Summer 1993; 13(2): 49-54.

Seelos L, Adamson C. Redefining NHS complaint handling—the real challenge. *Int J Health Care Qual Assur.* 1994; 7(6):26-31.

Seybold PB. Get inside the lives of your customers. *Harv Bus Rev.* May 2001; 79(5):80-89,164.

Tait AR, Voepel-Lewis T, Munro HM, et al. Parents' preferences for participation in decisions made regarding their child's anesthetic care. *Paediatr Anaesth.* May 2001; 11(3):283-290.

Veroff DR, Gallagher PM, Wilson V, Uyeda M, et al. Effective reports for health care quality data: lessons from a CAHPS demonstration in Washington State. *Int J Qual Health Care.* December 1998; 10(6):555-560.

von Eigen KA, Walker JD, Edgman-Levitan S, et al. Care partner experiences with hospital care. *Medical Care.* January 1999; 37(1):33-38.

Wagner EH, Austin BT, Davis C, et al. Improving chronic illness care: translating evidence into action. *Health Aff.* November-December 2001; 20(6):64-78.

Wagner EH, Grothaus LC, Sandhu N, et al. Chronic care clinics for diabetes in primary care: a system-wide randomized trial. *Diabetes Care.* April 2001; 24(4):695-700.

Wasson JH, Godfrey MM, Nelson EC, et al. Microsystems in health care: Part 4. Planning patient-centered care. *Jt Com J Qual & Safety.* May 2003; 29(5):227-237.

Winawer S. *Healing Lessons.* Boston: Little Brown; 1998.

Chapter 6

Reliability

Charles M. Kilo, MD, MPH, and Joseph E. Scherger, MD, MPH

> *"Mistakes are at the very base of human thoughts, embedded there, feeding the structure like root nodules. If we were not provided with the knack of being wrong, we could never get anything useful done. We think our way along by choosing between right and wrong alternatives, and the wrong choices have to be made as frequently as the right ones. We get along in life this way. We are built to make mistakes, coded for error . . . The capacity to leap across mountains of information and land lightly on the wrong side represents the highest of human endowments."* [1]
>
> Lewis Thomas, MD

Reliability. The word conjures up different images for different people—a dependable worker, the morning newspaper by the front door, a dependable car, a cell phone that works. In the medical office practice, the meaning of reliability seems intuitive. Based on our experiences as healthcare professionals, as occasional patients ourselves, as parents of children, and as adult children of elderly parents who must interact with the health system, we know how far health delivery systems are from being truly reliable. The goal of high reliability is an aspiration, but an obviously worthy one.

Reliability and the concept of highly reliable organizations are just starting to gain traction in healthcare. This field promises to be extremely fascinating as we explore how to design our systems—both our work systems and our technology systems—to help us deliver on this aspired promise of highly reliable care. Of course, highly reliable medical practices, like high reliability organizations, don't just happen; they have to be intentionally and thoughtfully designed to achieve such performance.

Reliability is a familiar concept in the engineering and manufacturing worlds where it is defined as "the measurable capability of an object to perform its intended function in the required time under specified conditions."[2] The term reliability is also used extensively in the testing and measurement worlds, where it is defined as the ability of a measure to yield the same or compatible results in different clinical experiments or statistical trials.

A search for books on the topic of reliability yields such titles as *Practical Reliability Engineering*[3] and *Handbook of Reliability Engineering and Management*,[4] which imply that reliability is a discipline in engineering. In other words, when products or production processes are designed in those fields, the concept of reliability is an intentional part of the *design process*. Reliability doesn't happen by accident. Highly reliable production processes, products, and services are specifically designed to provide a consistent, dependable product. Engineers start with the end product characteristics in mind including product reliability, assuming that a wide variety of stressors will be placed on the product due to various user conditions.

A more formal definition of reliability in the world of medical practice draws from each of these definitions: *Reliability is the capability of a process, procedure, or health service to perform its intended function in the required time under existing conditions.*[5] But we prefer to state the concept in a more straightforward way that has meaning to clinicians: Reliability is *the ability to provide the right care at the right time, every time, for each patient without failure.*

THE INTERSECTION OF SAFETY AND RELIABILITY

While healthcare "safety" has received widespread attention over the past decade, the concept of reliability is a more robust concept that holds great applicability and potential in the ambulatory environment. Focusing on safety will not necessarily produce highly reliable systems, but focus on highly reliable systems must by necessity create highly safe systems at the same time. Safety is a subset of, a result of, or a component of reliability.

To understand this, it is helpful to examine the history of safety in healthcare. Research on the frequency of adverse occurrences started emerging as recently as the early to mid 1990s, primarily through studies in tertiary care hospitals conducted by Leape, Brennan, Bates, and others.[6,7,8] By the end of the 1990s, the incidence of medical errors was well-documented in the hospital setting, but remained totally undocumented in ambulatory settings.

Since publication in December 1999 of the Institute of Medicine's (IOM) report, *To Err is Human: Building a Safer Health System*,[9] healthcare safety has received considerable attention in the professional and policymaking communities and within the public at large. The report indicated that up to 98,000 Americans die each year as a result of medical errors—the equivalent of a jumbo jet crashing every 36 hours. Report findings included the critical observation that errors ("errors" representing the failure of a planned action to be completed as intended or the use of a wrong plan to achieve an aim) occur because of system failures and that error prevention is accomplished through designing safer systems of care.

The IOM's second report in 2001, *Crossing the Quality Chasm: A New Health System for the 21st Century*,[10] identified six key areas for healthcare quality improvement focus: safety, effectiveness, responsiveness (patient-centeredness), timeliness, efficiency, and equity. The report noted that safety will be achieved and errors reduced not by asking practitioners to work harder or even smarter, but by fundamentally changing the way care is organized and delivered.

Those at the forefront of efforts to reduce medical errors are now focusing efforts on the design and implementation of safe care systems. They view system problems or failures, rather than individual negligence of healthcare practitioners, as being at the root cause of why "bad things" happen in healthcare. Common in highly complex, high-risk engineering fields, such as the aviation and nuclear industries, this worldview starts with the premise that things can and will go wrong, and that therefore the challenge is to proactively design systems that make it difficult for humans to err.

In healthcare, this approach means that the people components of our systems (for example, nurses, physicians, and others), technological components (for example, computers), pharmacological components (for example, drugs and drug delivery systems), management components (for example, policies and procedures), and financial components (for example, the reimbursement system that affects care decisions), must be designed properly and integrated into a cohesive, functioning whole.[11] How these components function *together* determines the quality of the output of a system. That is the nature of a system.

Figure 6-1 illustrates the relationship between safety, error prevention, and system reliability.

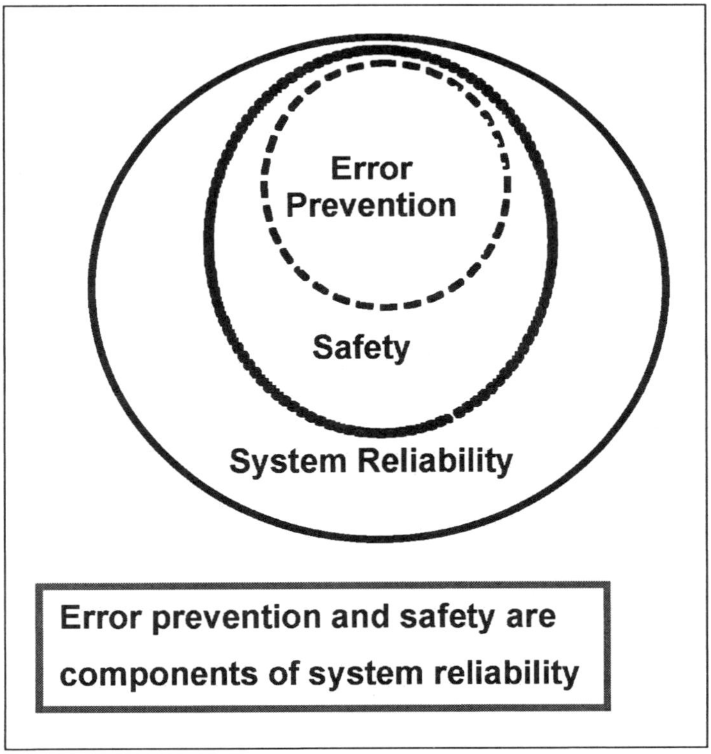

Figure 6-1: The Relationship between Error Prevention, Safety and System Reliability

By the early 2000s, safety had become an industry unto itself. However, attempts to translate safety efforts into the ambulatory world were largely absent or unsuccessful. Understanding the reasons for such lack of success is critical to the success of future ambulatory system improvement. While failures in the hospital setting are more frequently fatal due to the high-risk nature of procedures and high level of patient acuity, failures in the ambulatory setting are not as visible and tend to be much less severe. Patients leave the doctor's office and go home, where the effects of decisions are not as visible or easily monitored. Patients in physicians' offices are most often not as sick as those seeking care at hospitals. And lastly, the interventions used tend to carry a lower overall risk in the ambulatory environment. These dynamics have made it difficult for the safety industry to penetrate the ambulatory world to the extent achieved in hospitals.

Furthermore, practitioners in ambulatory settings often have simply not embraced safety initiatives because the "language" of safety provides a negative frame. The words *errors, failure,* and *patient safety* imply to many people some sort of practitioner deficit. The healthcare community historically has dealt with errors in a punitive manner, rooting out the "bad apple" practitioners by suspending their licenses and imposing fines or punitive court verdicts.

Language matters. "Decision makers respond differently to different but objectively equivalent descriptions of the same problem," note psychologist Irwin P. Levin and colleagues.[12] A significant issue in the ambulatory environment is to use language that fits with practitioner mindsets and needs. No sports team has as its primary goal "to make the fewest errors." While teams track errors, their primary metric of concern is who wins the game—i.e., who scores the most points. Likewise, errors and safety are critical to track in the ambulatory environment, but practitioners believe that they benefit from a primary focus on how they are doing at "winning the game." In other words, individual practitioners have a very hard time engaging the practice down the street in competing to produce the safest practice. Practitioners have a much easier time engaging fellow practitioners in thinking about practice reliability and beginning to see which practice can produce the most reliable results.

The word *reliability* provides a positive framing for practitioners; it also provides a clearer discipline around which they can wrap their arms. Reliability engages ambulatory providers much more strongly in efforts to enhance the quality of care.

THE NEED FOR RELIABILITY

The need for such engagement is pressing. As mentioned in Chapter 1 and many other publications such as the IOM's *Crossing the Quality Chasm,*[10] an abundance of research spanning the past decade provides some startling data on the absence of system reliability in ambulatory care—i.e., data on the poor clinical performance of medical practices. The outcomes currently achieved fall far short of providing *all* the effective care that can help the patient.

The presentation of performance data is not intended to place blame, but only to provide an imperative to think differently about medical practice. Data from a number of different sources provide differing insights into how practice systems fail and give clues as to the work needed to improve those systems. Data on clinical outcomes from health services researchers provides one look at health systems, whereas data on malpractice claims provide a different look. Data on service quality, such as the ease of access to practices, provides yet more information.

Consider, for example, ambulatory practice performance with patients with chronic conditions. The data demonstrate significant performance failures: One study indicates that only 23% of individuals with hypertension are taking medications that controlled their condition. This is found in all groups: uninsured, insured, poor, and average income.[13]

Patients interviewed for a recent study of medical errors and harms in primary care[14] provide another source of insight. They report that the most common incidents are related to

- Technical failures of misdiagnosis;
- Failure to disclose test results;
- Inadequate patient education;
- Relationship breakdowns;
- Disregard for patient concerns; and
- Access breakdowns created by long waits for appointments.

Medical malpractice data confirm the perceived importance in the patient's eyes of failure to diagnose. Diagnosis-related allegations—including failure to diagnose, delayed diagnosis, and misdiagnosis—represented nearly half of all allegations in medical malpractice cases tracked by the Risk Management Foundation of the Harvard Medical Institutions.[15]

The sidebar below outlines common preventable system failures that lead to patient harm in the ambulatory setting.

Common, Preventable Systems Failures That Lead to Patient Harm

- Failure or delay in ordering diagnostic tests
- Misinterpretation of test results
- Lack of systems to identify patients in high risk categories
- Poor rapport between patient and physician
- Poor communication among multiple providers
- Failure to coordinate care
- Lack of follow-up systems
  - Abnormal lab results
  - Imaging studies
- Medication errors
  - Drug/dose/route
  - Monitoring for side effects and toxicities
  - Incomplete medication history
- Lack of an updated medication allergy history
- No quality improvement process

Unfortunately, to discuss the need for greater reliability, the only real choice is to point to national outcomes studies such as these. Very few practices today measure their own performance in any level of detail, and this is a critical part of the problem. Even practices currently using electronic health records (EHR) frequently do not measure their performance; adoption of an EHR neither assures highly reliable care nor does it necessarily make performance measurement easy.

QUANTIFYING RELIABILITY

When measured with reliability scales prevalent in the manufacturing industry, ambulatory care does not perform at all well. Reliability is quantified in manufacturing as "the number of actions that achieve the intended result divided by the total number of actions taken." Thus, the defect rate is one minus reliability. For example, 10^{-2} means that the action fails to achieve its intended result 1 time in 100, a 1% defect rate.

Motorola, which invented the "Six Sigma" concept, General Electric, and others have applied that concept's reliability goals not only to manufacturing but to general operations and management. *Sigma* is a statistical term that measures how far a given process deviates from perfection. The central idea behind Six Sigma is that if you can measure how many defects you have in a process, you can systematically figure out how to eliminate them and get as close to zero defects as possible.[16] "Simply put, adopting the goal of Six Sigma quality means setting tolerance limits for defective products at such high levels that fewer than 3.4 defects occur per million units (or opportunities). These limits are set to include all observations within 6 standard deviations of the mean," explains Mark Chassin[17] (Table 6-1).

Table 6-1: Reliability and Defect Rates

Rate of Reliability	Defect Rate	"Sigma" (approximate)
90%	10%	1
99%	1%	2
99.9%	0.1%	3
99.99%	0.01%	4
99.999%	0.001%	5
99.9999%	0.0001%	6

The reliability of healthcare processes consistently falls far short of achieving Six Sigma quality goals (Table 6-2). In fact, most studies demonstrate that reliability of the application of clinical evidence or recommended care in the ambulatory world is significantly less than 90%.[18]

Table 6-2: Healthcare Outcomes Reliability

Reliability	Outcome
50-75%	Beta blockers and aspirin use following myocardial infarction Hemoglobin A1c every 6 months in diabetes Known preventive treatments
99%	Adverse events in hospital Deaths in high risk surgery
99.9%	Neonatal mortality General surgery deaths
99.99%	Deaths in routine anesthesia
99.999%	Blood Banking
99.9999%	?

WHY IS AMBULATORY CARE SO UNRELIABLE?

The question we must ask is why office practices lack high reliability. The answer to this has nothing to do with a poorly motivated workforce. Most physicians and medical practice staff are hard working, highly motivated, and well intended. The answer lies in the design of ambulatory systems—the design of medical practices.

In fact, the current design of medical practices is an unintentional design. It is a historical design continually brought forward into a future in which that design is clearly outdated. The current approach to ambulatory practice, with few exceptions, has been unchanged over the past several decades. For example, at the present time, most medical practices keep their records on paper, there is little advanced technology-enabled knowledge management, and care continues to be driven solely by the traditional one-on-one doctor-patient visit.

But the medical practice is a system—it is a collection of individuals and other parts that share the aim of high quality care. No one person alone can provide great care today; all practitioners are interdependent upon others and upon other parts both within and outside of practices. As with any system, the quality of the output of the system is dependent upon the design of the system. If practitioners desire a higher quality output from the system—from medical practices—then practitioners have to design smarter systems.

Organizations that require highly reliable, safe performance must intentionally design their processes to produce these results. In fact, as mentioned earlier, there is a body of literature on the design of high reliability organizations, and medical practices stand to benefit enormously from studying this literature.

HIGH RELIABILITY ORGANIZATIONS

A close look at the attributes of high reliability organizations that are intentionally designed for consistently high performance and accident prevention can shed light on desirable system design for ambulatory care.

The nuclear disasters at Three Mile Island and Chernobyl in 1979 and 1986 and the Challenger shuttle disaster in 1986 spawned significant sociological study of the organizational aspects of safety. Charles Perrow, originator of the Normal Accident Theory, explained the Three Mile Island accident, which involved the melt down of the core of a nuclear reactor that threatened to spill a massive quantity of radioactive contaminants, as follows:

> "The cause of the accident is to be found in the complexity of the system. That is, each of the failures—design, equipment, operators, procedures, or environment—was trivial by itself. Each one had a backup system, or redundant path to tread if the main one was blocked. The failures became serious when they interacted."[19]

Perrow describes some accidents as "normal" or inevitable due to interactive complexity and tight coupling of highly interdependent parts in a system. Changes in one part of the system can rapidly affect other parts of the system, with little opportunity for recovery. The results can be disastrous.

In the early 1990s, researchers, including Karlene Roberts, Todd La Porte, and others, studied complex systems, such as U.S. air traffic control, fire-fighting teams, and utility grid management to determine what made them work or not work. They defined *high reliability organizations* as the subset of high-risk, high-complexity organizations that experience a record of high safety over long periods of time.[20] Despite inherently risky environments, these organizations experience fewer than the normal number of accidents.[21]

In the healthcare arena, the study of accidents or mishaps in a particularly high-risk area—anesthesiology—commenced comparatively early, during the late 1970s and 1980s under the direction of Jeffrey Cooper, David Gaba, and their colleagues. They identified key characteristics of high reliability organizations that have a "climate of safety:"[22]

- Senior leadership articulates an institutional commitment to safety and conveys it uniformly throughout the organization.
- Following standard operating procedures and safety rules is a part of the behavioral norms.
- The organization proactively manages safety and carefully monitors ongoing safety processes and operating procedures.
- Resources and redundancy are provided to allow safe operations.
- Communication between workers and across organizational levels is frequent and candid.
- There is openness about errors and problems; they are reported when they occur.

In fact, highly reliable organizations focus on failure. They study and simulate how failure could happen and design systems and the link between system components to be as mistake-proof as possible. Decision making is both centralized and decentralized, allowing an unimpeded flow of communication. Leadership is committed to a culture of safety, and staff ideas are always welcome. Adoption of best practices and organizational transformation are top priorities. The sidebar at the top of page 75 summarizes attributes of high reliability organizations. The sidebar below it outlines the IOM's five principles for the design of safety systems in healthcare organizations.

Attributes of High Reliability Organizations

- Focus on failure rather than success; don't like it when they have the wrong outcome.
- Failures are generalized rather than localized.
- Cognitive infrastructure is well-developed.
- Focus on reliability rather than efficiency.
- People take their time, pay attention to details, and concentrate on the work at hand.
- Flexible structures and processes reduce the chance of multiple failures that result in catastrophic organizational accidents.
- Education, hands-on learning, and problem solving are welcomed.
- Information is actively sought and shared.
- Failures are actively received as learning, and new ideas are encouraged.
- Doing the same activity in the face of changing events is avoided.
- Communication is valued; divergent views are encouraged.

Principles for the Design of Safety Systems in Healthcare Organizations[23]

Principle 1. Provide Leadership
- Make patient safety a priority corporate objective and everyone's responsibility.
- Make clear assignments for and expectation of safety oversight.
- Provide human and financial resources for error analysis and systems redesign.
- Develop effective mechanisms for identifying and dealing with unsafe practitioners.

Principle 2. Respect Human Limits in Process Design
- Design jobs for safety.
- Avoid reliance on memory and on vigilance.
- Use constraints and forcing functions.
- Simplify key processes.
- Standardize work processes.

Principle 3. Promote Effective Team Functioning
- Train in teams those who are expected to work in teams.
- Include the patient in safety design and the process of care.

Continued.

Principle 4. Anticipate the Unexpected
- Adopt a proactive approach: examine processes of care for threats to safety and redesign them before accidents occur.
- Design for recovery.
- Improve access to accurate, timely information.

Principle 5. Create a Learning Environment
- Use simulations whenever possible.
- Encourage reporting of errors and hazardous conditions.
- Ensure no reprisals for reporting of errors.
- Develop a working culture in which communication flows freely regardless of authority gradient.
- Implement mechanisms of feedback and learning from error.

DESIGN PRINCIPLES FOR HIGHLY RELIABLE AMBULATORY CARE

"They always say time changes things, but you actually have to change them yourself."
Andy Warhol [24]

"The ultimate judge of the quality of our work is the patient, end of story."
Don Berwick[26]

The vision for reliable ambulatory care is care that provides what the patient wants and needs when the patient wants and needs it. Don Berwick, President of the Institute for Healthcare Improvement (IHI), described this from the patient's perspective: "To have health care with no needless deaths, no needless pain or suffering, no unwanted waiting, no helplessness, and no waste."[26]

As discussed in Chapter 4, the patient's experience with healthcare quality or reliability in many cases has more to do with his or her relationship with the physician and less to do with actual clinical care, unless something very dramatic happens in terms of a poor outcome. Patients' ability to judge the true reliability of the care they are receiving is most often limited at best. However, this clearly does not relieve us of our responsibility to provide highly reliable care—and to document it to ourselves, our patients, and others.

The challenge we face is to design our system so that we move from significantly less than a 90% reliability rate to a rate closer to 99%. The reality is that this will require very intensive changes in ambulatory system design.

A three-level design for safe and reliable care, focused on prevention, identification, and mitigation, was proposed more than five years ago by Michael Cohen and Charles Kilo:[27]
- ***Prevent:*** Design the system to prevent failure.
- ***Identify:*** Design procedures and relationships to make failures visible when they do occur so that they may be intercepted before causing harm.
- ***Mitigate:*** Design procedures and build capabilities for mitigating the harm caused by failures when they are not detected and intercepted.

What does this mean, in practical terms? Designing for failure prevention, identification, and mitigation can best be accomplished through standardizing and simplifying practice systems. Standardization reduces an individual's need to rely on memory. Standardization strategies include using standing orders and evidence-based guidelines that are embedded into daily practice.

Simplification in healthcare generally involves reducing the number of handoffs required for a process to be completed.[28] For example, consider the steps involved when a physician gives an order in the traditional way. The order must be provided, transcribed, and then entered into a computer, perhaps in a number of different locations. Simplification strategies include taking extra steps out of processes, delegating the step to someone else who may be better suited to handle the step, and making information available where and when it is needed. The sidebar below provides examples of practices that enhance reliability.

Two ambulatory models—the Chronic Care Model (now commonly called the Planned Care Model) from the Improving Chronic Illness Care Program, and the Idealized Design of Clinical Office Practices from the IHI—have succeeded in enhancing care reliability. John Wasson and Edward Wagner describe these models fully in Chapter 2.

Examples of Reliability-Enhancing Practices

- Standardized forms for data collection
- Tickler systems
- Referral tracking processes
- Automated drug-drug interaction checking
- Chronic disease data registries and proactive management
- Automated reminders for preventive services
- Specialist/diagnostic appointment scheduled before patient leaves office
- Follow-up of no shows and cancellations

KNOWLEDGE MANAGEMENT AND CLINICAL DECISION SUPPORT SYSTEMS

In past eras, individuals who could memorize enough of the information presented in medical school were reasonably well assured of being reasonably good doctors when they finished their formal education. That era is over, as described earlier. Knowledge management tools are now essential to having the right knowledge available at the right time—during the patient visit.

Knowledge management can be defined as systems or tools that continually link to and update information about the best available scientific and practice knowledge and deliver that knowledge directly into the care process. As outlined in the IHI's Idealized Design of Clinical Office Practices, knowledge management assures a match between new science and best practice: "The knowledge is not just scientific, but also includes knowledge of the patient's unique history, desires, social, and cultural background."[29]

Reliability requires having all the necessary information at hand each time a patient interacts with the practice.[31]

EHRs help ensure that the patient's information is readily accessible in one place; clinical decision support system (CDSS) tools ensure that evidence-based knowledge is available to the practitioner at the point of care. Investing in EHRs may be the most expensive part of the conversion to IT in ambulatory healthcare, but EHRs are now an imperative for high-reliability, quality ambulatory care. Without question, the first decade of the 21st century will see patient information becoming digitally based. As in banking, this could occur across a healthcare delivery system and into rural areas, just as a matter of doing business. The home base of the patient's record could be in the ambulatory practitioner's office.

CDSSs integrate information on individual patient characteristics with a computerized knowledge base to generate patient-specific assessments or recommendations designed to aid clinicians and/or patients in making clinical decisions.[31] CDSSs can also be used to help clinicians with preventive and monitoring tasks, prescribing of medications, and diagnostic and treatment decision support.[31]

At times, the knowledge-based or evidence-based element of reliability may come into conflict with the theme of individualized relationship. This occurs, for example, when a patient wants care that is scientifically of no value, or even harmful. Practitioners need to accept this challenge willingly, without criticism of either the patient or the science. Their task involves maintaining processes of education, interaction, and encouragement that seek always to reconcile this conflict. This involves helping patients to understand existing knowledge, and helping interpret the science through the appropriate lens to match the individual's needs. The IOM's second report notes that, "The best care results from the conscientious, explicit, and judicious use of current best evidence *and* (emphasis added) knowledge of patient values by well-trained, experienced clinicians."[32]

High-quality knowledge management and decision support tools are becoming widely available. The most common are medication interaction programs loaded on hand-held computers, called personal digital assistants (PDAs). Tablet-sized computers which can be carried into the exam room and have a wireless connection to the Internet are also widely available. The expectation now is that knowledge management and decision support software should be able to answer almost any clinical question in less than a minute at the point of service.

Case Study: *For examples of obtaining patients' perspective in practice, see "Putting the Patient in the Center of the Radar Screen at ThedaCare Clinics, page 157.*

Population Management and Disease Registries for Chronic Conditions

The words population management and disease registries (Figure 6-2) seem at odds with the vision of individualized care that meets individual patient needs. This is not the case. As outlined by the IHI in *Idealized Design of Clinical Office Practices*, proactive population management provides the failsafe systems for tracking and anticipating individual patient needs. Systems coordinate care across boundaries of people, place, time, and organizations.[29] Individual care is enhanced by a practitioner's deep knowledge of his or her population of patients. Population knowledge informs individual care.

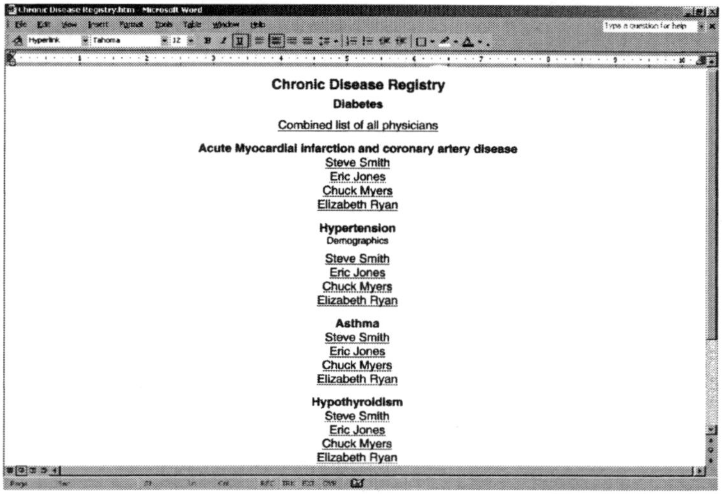

Figure 6-2: Sample Page of Chronic Disease Registry in a Small Ambulatory Practice

The effective management of chronic conditions, the central application of population management, requires the patient's intimate and continuous involvement in the care process. Self-management must be recognized as central to high quality, reliable patient care. "Self-management programs must be flexible enough to allow for tailoring to individual patient preferences, as well as culturally, linguistically, age, gender, and lifestyle appropriate," notes the 2004 IOM report.[33]

Chronic care delivery models, appropriate to most ambulatory care settings, provide a planned, systematic approach to care, attention to the information and self-management needs of patients, use multidisciplinary care teams, and ensure unfettered and timely access to clinical information. Table 6-3 illustrates reliability gains that might be achieved through systematically designed and improved diabetes management programs, for example.

Table 6-3: Reliability in Diabetes Management

Reliability	System Design	Improvement Methods
50-75%	Historical	Lecture-based CME Try harder
75-90%	Registries intermittently used Early care teams Some clinical standards	Targeted improvement initiatives
90-95%	Planned care Fully developed care team Integrated IT into smart workflow Detailed measurement systems Clear clinical standards with exception reporting Intensive self-management support Automated Web-based disease management and follow-up Redundant systems	System improvement integrated into work Team meetings focused on quality Strategic planning Failure mode and effects analysis (FMEA)
>95%	?	?

Case Study: *For examples of population management and disease registries in practice, see "Improved Reliability and Quality of Care at SETMA," page 168.*

SAFETY SYSTEMS

Healthcare safety is enhanced by systems designed to identify and mitigate opportunities for error. Electronic prescribing systems with capabilities for drug-drug interaction checking provide one example (Figure 6-3). Proactive fail-safe reminder systems that bring patients into practitioners' offices when they otherwise might have forgotten the visit are another example. Such systems anticipate needs and help the patient to remember what he or she should be asking the practitioner. The systems ensure follow-up when it is needed, and, equally important, *only* when it is needed.

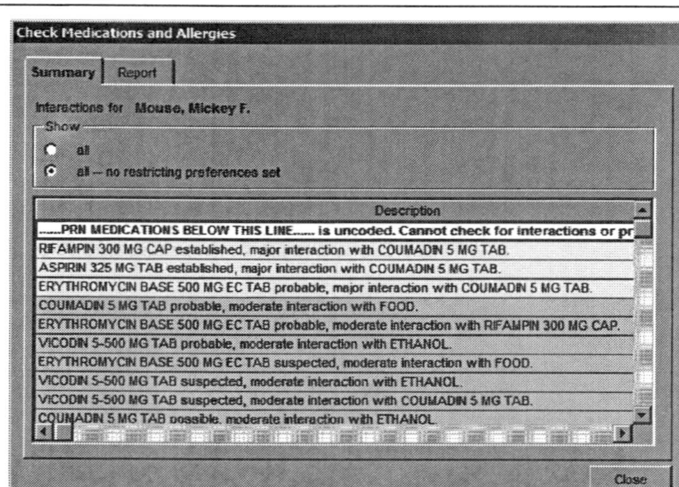

Figure 6-3: Medication Interaction-Checking System

CONCLUDING COMMENTS

High reliability in ambulatory care—in our specific practices—is possible, but such care requires that we intentionally design our care systems. The knowledge and technological capabilities to design such systems is available today. The specific application into our practices will require insight; knowledge of system design; accurate measurement of practice performance; knowledge and skills around system improvement; focused, intent leadership; and the appropriate use of technology.

There are many barriers to our progress. While many information technology tools are available today, they frequently do not provide the full functionality that we need to create highly reliable medical practices. In addition, the technology's effectiveness is fully determined by how well a practice incorporates those tools into its overall care systems. As stated previously, most practices using an EHR today use only 10-25% of the capabilities of those systems. Most of these practices still do not and cannot measure their own performance.

High reliability ambulatory practice requires a merger of leadership, workflow design, and technology application all focused on the common goal of providing the right care at the right time, every time, for each patient without failure.

References

1 Thomas L. *The Medusa and the Snail: More Notes of a Biology Writer.* New York, NY: Viking Press; 1974, 37–39.

2 Ushakov IA (ed). *Handbook of Reliability Engineering.* Updated American edition. New York: Wiley-Interscience; 1999.

3 O'Connor PDT. *Practical Reliability Engineering.* New York: John Wiley & Sons; 2002.

4 Ireson WG, Coombs CF, Moss RY (eds). *Handbook of Reliability Engineering and Management,* Second Edition. New York: McGraw-Hill; 1996.

5 Personal communication with Don Berwick and Tom Nolan, Institute for Healthcare Improvement, 2004.

6 Brennan TA, Leape LL, Laird NM, et al. Incidence of adverse events and negligence in hospitalized patients. *New Engl J Med.* February 7, 1991; 324 (6): 370-376.

7 Leape LL, et al. Preventing medical injury. *Quality Rev Bull.* 1993; 19:144-149.

8 Bates DW, Cullen DJ, Laird N, et al. Incidence of adverse drug events and potential adverse drug events. *JAMA.* July 5, 1995; 274 (1): 29-34.

9 Institute of Medicine. *To Err is Human: Building a Safer Health System.* Washington, DC: National Academies Press; 2000.

10 Institute of Medicine. *Crossing the Quality Chasm: A New Health System for the 21st Century.* Washington, DC: National Academies Press; 2001.

11 Moray N. Error reduction as a system problem. In Bogner MS (ed). *Human Error in Medicine.* Hillsdale, NJ: Lawrence Erlbaum Associates; 1994, 71.

12 Levin IP, Schneider SL, Gaeth GJ. All frames are not created equal: A typology and critical analysis of framing effects. *Organizational Behavior and Human Decision Processes.* November 1998; 76(2):149-188.

13 Hyman DJ, Pavlik VN. Characteristics of patients with uncontrolled hypertension in the United States. *N Engl J Med.* August 16, 2001; 346(7):544.

14 Kuzel AJ, Woolf SH, Gilchrist VJ, et al. Patient reports of preventable problems and harms in primary health care. *Ann Fam Med.* July/August 2004; 2(4): 330-340.

15 Personal communication with Frank Federico, Harvard Risk Management Foundation, 2002.

16 What is Six Sigma? The Road to Customer Impact. www.ge.com/sixsigma (accessed April 11, 2005).

17 Chassin MR. Is health care ready for Six Sigma Quality? *Milbank Quarterly.* 1998; 76(4): 1-14.

18 Personal communication with Roger Resar, Institute for Healthcare Improvement, 2004.

19 Perrow C. *Normal Accidents: Living with High-Risk Technologies.* New York: Basic Books; 1984, 7.

20 Roberts KH. Managing high reliability organizations. *Calif Mgmt Rev.* 1990; 32(4): 101-114.

21 Pexton C. Ideas for achieving higher reliability in healthcare. Six Sigma Healthcare Web site: http://healthcare.isixsigma.com (accessed April 11, 2005).

22 Gaba DM, Singer SJ, Sinaiko AD, et al. Differences in safety climate between hospital personnel and naval aviators. *Human Factors.* Summer 2003; 45(2):173-185.

23 Source: Institute of Medicine: *To Err is Human: Building a Safer Health System.* Washington, DC: National Academies Press; 2000, 165-182.

24 Andy Warhol quote as appeared in Quote DB. www.quotedb.com/categories/time (accessed April 11, 2005).

25 Berwick DM. Keynote address to the First Annual Crossing the Quality Chasm Summit. As quoted in Institute of Medicine: *Report of a Summit: The First Annual Crossing the Quality Chasm Summit: A Focus on Communities.* Washington, DC: National Academies Press, 2004, 6.

26 Berwick DM. *Crossing the Quality Chasm: Health Care for the 21st Century.* Powerpoint Presentation, 2004.

27 Cohen MR, Kilo CM. High-alert medications: Safeguarding against errors. In Cohen MR (ed). *Medication Errors.* Washington, DC: American Pharmaceutical Association; 1999.

28 Institute of Medicine. *To Err is Human: Building a Safer Health System.* Washington, DC: National Academies Press; 2000, 172.

29 Institute for Healthcare Improvement. *Idealized Design of Clinical Office Practices.* www.ihi.org (accessed April 11, 2005).

30 Kilo CM.Guest Editorial: The practice of tomorrow. *Hippocrates.* May 2000; 14(5).

31 Institute of Medicine. *Crossing the Quality Chasm: A New Health System for the 21st Century.* Washington, DC: National Academies Press, 2001; 152.

32 Institute of Medicine. *Crossing the Quality Chasm: A New Health System for the 21st Century.* Washington, DC: National Academies Press; 2001, 76.

33 Institute of Medicine. *Report of a Summit: The First Annual Crossing the Quality Chasm Summit: A Focus on Communities.* Washington, DC: National Academies Press, 2004, 9.

SECTION III

ACHIEVING THE VISION

CHAPTER 7

Leadership and Management Systems: The Foundation for Transformation

Charles M. Kilo, MD, MPH, Bruce Bagley, MD, Jill K. Arena, FACMPE, and Jeffrey L. Kegarise, OD

"If you don't know where you are going, any road will get you there."

"All systems are perfectly designed to achieve the results they achieve. If you want a different result, you have to change the system."

Many clinicians will find the title of this chapter puzzling. Leadership and management systems...they aren't something we learned about in medical school, we received virtually no training on business management in residency, no one asks us about management on our board examinations, and it isn't a part of accreditation or credentialing.

Yet leadership and management systems are obviously central to the success of any organization, large or small, including medical practices. It is imperative that medical groups interested in transforming themselves have physicians who understand that their role goes beyond the exam room, and leaders who help to focus everyone's attention on system design, management, and system improvement.

This chapter will begin by discussing the prevailing culture of medical group leadership as background information. This prevailing culture affects almost all medical groups today in one way or another. It frequently affects the group's ability to effectively implement critical changes such as bringing information technology into the practice. We will then discuss the roles of leadership necessary for high performing practices, the medical practice as a "system," system improvement, and the role of information technology in leadership and management.

THE PREVAILING CULTURE OF LEADERSHIP

In discussing the prevailing culture of leadership, we do so with no intent to criticize, but rather to help elucidate the current situation so that we can discuss the leadership necessary to advance the performance of the medical group. These cultural norms are abundantly obvious in most ambulatory practices, even those with more mature management structures. While the reader's organizations may have addressed many of these issues, remnants of this culture remain pervasive in healthcare today and will probably be easily recognized by most.

Physicians obviously have a primary role in the management of most medical groups. They often view their management responsibilities as secondary to providing care, however, and they tend to hope that they have hired a practice manager who can handle the troubles that arise so they can focus on patient care. The physician's job, after all, is to care for patients—most of us didn't go into medicine to become business managers.

The problem is that physicians frequently hire or appoint "managers" not to truly lead, but instead to put out fires, to manage the administrative work that no one else wants to deal with, and to protect the group from the turbulent healthcare environment.[1, 2] Because physicians are so focused on clinical care—one physician with one patient at a time imparting the empathy and knowledge that creates care—our general handshake agreement in the practice is "I won't tell you what to do and you don't tell me what to do."

The medical practice, large or small, tends to consist of independent agents (i.e., physicians) who happen to work together for a variety of reasons such as the sharing overhead and a sense of camaraderie. It is for these reasons that the traditional medical practice—the predominant practice of today—can be aptly called a condominium practice. They share things, but they really work quite independently and separately. Stated differently, in the traditional practice, "We practice together separately." This is called autonomy, and physicians do a lot to preserve it.

We understand that this is not per se intentional on the part of most physicians—rather, it is a cultural norm adopted from decades past, but it is a very strong culture that bears calling out so that it can be addressed, when necessary. There are many things about our prevailing culture that serve the system well. Autonomy can be very helpful in a physician's determination to care for patients. Autonomy can also be a major barrier to making effective group decisions and can paralyze progress. In many medical groups, it is perfectly acceptable for any one physician to approach a group decision by stating "that may be okay for the rest of you, but I'm not going to do that." This aspect of autonomy, if allowed to persist, thwarts progress, as any one decision is amenable to veto by any one physician. This may play out overtly, or it may play out very subtly by behavior that simply demonstrates that "you can't tell me what to do."

Autonomy is exacerbated when physicians relegate leadership to others because they do not appreciate management as "real work." When physicians choose leaders, they frequently work to undermine the leader's authority to lead. They do so, again in both overt and subtle ways, because they do not want their independence—or autonomy—threatened.

There are obvious problems with this approach, however. The lack of leadership and management is the single most common cause of the inability to achieve and sustain meaningful change. Medical practices are business organizations and "systems." Organizations and systems neither manage themselves nor do they tend to spontaneously improve themselves. System improvement toward higher performance requires focused, intent leadership and managerial processes. Real leadership has to make hard choices that may not be comfortable for everyone, and that each individual will not necessarily agree on. Leadership and managerial processes enable improvement and higher performance—they are prerequisites. They are the foundations upon which all great organizations are formed.

So how should a healthcare organization proceed? Given the current societal and regulatory pressures to improved performance and lower costs, many medical groups and physician leaders now find themselves with the will to improve but a lack of certainty about how to proceed.

THE PRACTICE AS A SYSTEM

To improve an organization, leaders must understand that organizations are systems, and improving the performance of the organizational system requires a deep knowledge of system improvement and measurement.[3,4,5]

The old adage "all systems are perfectly designed to achieve the results they achieve" provides vital guidance for leaders. The implication is clear: If you want to change the performance of a system, then you have to change the design of the system. Organizational improvement—system improvement—does not occur by simply encouraging people to try harder or even training individuals to work smarter. This is the traditional and current approach in healthcare as evidenced by the fact that we use traditional continuing medical education (CME), or subject matter lectures, as our primary method of trying to improve care. Abundant literature demonstrates that such traditional lecture-based, medical content-oriented CME are ineffective at driving performance improvement.[6,7,8]

What is a system, and what does an understanding of systems tell us about driving performance improvement? A system is a set of interdependent parts sharing a common purpose. Interdependence of parts and a common purpose—these are fundamental characteristics of any system. When the parts act in ways discordant with interdependence or when a common purpose is absent, a system stumbles. Its performance fails to achieve the highest possible levels.

The "interdependent parts" in healthcare include not just physicians, nurses, and others but the individual patient, our computer systems, the medical record system, the machinery we use to monitor patients, the devices we use to diagnose and treat patients, and more. To achieve optimal outcomes, these parts must work together to achieve the common purpose—they have to be designed to work together.

In most medical practices today, the "interdependent parts" often lack a common purpose and/or the desire to act interdependently. Developing a common purpose requires that medical groups go beyond the generic purpose of providing unmeasured "high quality care" to providing a measured quality of care and then intentionally seek to improve that performance.

What does true interdependence mean? It means that the components of the system *must* work in a coordinated fashion in order to produce optimal outcomes; they must understand their dependency on each other. The physician is dependent upon the medical assistant to collect accurate clinical information and to manage the medical record; the medical assistant is dependent upon the phone system and the schedule system to provide great service; the nurse is dependent on the medical record management system to enhance relationships; a pharmacist is dependent upon the physician to prescribe appropriately.

In a system, it is not the individual but rather the entire system that produces results. The structure of the system—its parts, its design, and the interactions between its parts—determines its performance. Individual parts are important to performance, but more important is how these parts work together.

Traditional CME fails to improve measurable outcomes of care because it is designed around individual learning, not around changing systems of care. Smart people in poorly designed systems do not achieve optimal performance. Ambulatory practices should strive to specifically and intentionally design relationship, service, and clinical reliability into their care systems through system engineering, leadership, and cultural change. The requirement of leaders, or of anyone who intends to drive the improvement of care, is to become a "systems thinker"—to understand the "systemness" of the care we provide. While leaders themselves may not be system experts, they need to ensure that the practice either has within it or is closely associated with individuals who do have such expertise. They are crucial—large medical group or small—to the improvement of outcomes.

To survive, systems must have a capacity to adapt to an ever-changing environment. Darwin described this process as biological evolution—a static system within a changing environment produces deteriorating performance over time. Unchanging systems are doomed to extinction. Healthcare systems continually interact with their environment—new technologies and treatments, evolving payment structures, emerging diseases, shifting epidemiology, and evolving patient, family and societal expectations. The current environment of healthcare epitomizes change, so medical practices must continuously adapt.

Change and adaptation must be a property of the system itself, and it is the leader's job to organize this—to ensure the appropriate management systems are in place to understand and manage performance in the dynamic environment; to drive meaningful, intentional, and necessary changes in performance to meet the environmental challenges; and to help others in the organizations see the necessity of those changes.

THE ROLES OF LEADERS IN EFFECTIVELY MANAGED PRACTICES

With a firm understanding of systems, the next job of leaders in the new world of high performing medical practices is to understand the roles of leadership. Innumerable books and articles have been written about leadership, some of the best being by such great business thinkers and writers as Peter Drucker, Warren Bennis, Edgar Schein, Michael Hammer, Charles Handy, Michael Porter, Stephen Covey, John Kotter, Frances Hasselbein, Marshall Goldsmith, and Richard Beckhard.

The sidebar on page 89 provides a list of the roles of effective leadership. Readers will note that many of these roles are foreign to many medical practices. This is changing as healthcare professionals increasingly immerse themselves in studying the leadership necessary to drive effective performance improvement. Yet many leadership roles are sufficiently soft and ethereal that they turn off physicians. Implemented ineffectively or half-heartedly, the roles and function of leaders do indeed become fluff. It is the leader's role to ensure that this does not occur.

These roles are both specifically operational, such as assessing staff skills and providing staff training, and at the same time very strategic, such as making sure that the practice has clear goals and that it is working toward them.

Most medical practices want to provide high quality care. However, neither the specific goals nor the group's vision statement are generally more specific than that, and rarely does the practice have measures of quality—they have an assumption of the quality with little demonstrable data to substantiate such claims. There is a pervasive belief in the medical profession that if we are well trained, well intentioned, and work hard, then quality care will result. Unfortunately, when rigorous measures are used, we often fall short.[9]

If leaders seek to improve the performance of their practice, then the goals have to be very specifically and clearly stated. Physicians and staff should understand them, and should be held accountable to them. Specificity of goals lets people know what direction they are supposed to be moving in.

Case Study: *For examples of identifying the objectives for IT, see "Defining Business and Clinical Objectives" page 169, and "Defining the EHR's Clinical and Financial Objectives at Thedacare," page 162.*

The Roles of Leaders in High-Performing Medical Practices

Leaders in high-performing practices do (and have) the following:

1. ***Mission, Vision, and Values:*** Leaders help the organization develop meaningful mission and vision statements and a set of organizational values. For example, the leaders should ensure clear answers to critical questions such as: What is important to the practice, what defines the group as a group, what is acceptable behavior, what does the practice seek to become.
2. ***Performance Goals:*** Leaders help the organization establish measurable goals and they monitor progress towards those goals.
3. ***Communication:*** Leaders continually communicate a clear, consistent set of messages that express the goals and values of the organization. They use effective communication to reiterate performance expectations of clinicians and staff.
4. ***Management Structure:*** Leaders shape the management structure and management systems as necessary, to ensure that the practice is run effectively. They continually ask if the organization has the right people in the right positions doing the right work to provide effective management.
5. ***Improvement Structure:*** Leaders also shape the improvement structure such that it is clear to everyone in the organization how improvement happens. They continually ask if the organization has the right people with the right knowledge about improvement in the right positions doing the right work

Continued.

to help drive performance improvement. Staff skills should be periodically assessed and training should be provided to keep staff updated on new skills.

6. ***Manage Resources:*** Leaders monitor and manage organizational resources. They provide resources such as time and money for critical initiatives.
7. ***Hold Accountable:*** Leaders hold everyone in the organization accountable for their individual behavior, their team behavior, and their performance.
8. ***Learn:*** Leaders should be voracious learners, inquisitive about new knowledge both within their industry and in other industries. Leaders cannot afford to be insular in their thinking. They should routinely get out of their organization and out of their industry in order to garner critical improvement ideas.
9. ***Coach:*** Leaders help everyone in the organization be better than they are. They coach team members as needed to be good managers and to be effective clinicians for example.
10. ***Celebrate:*** Leaders help the organization celebrate success therein keeping a positive environment in the organization for people to thrive.

It may or may not seem obvious that leaders need to shape and refine their "managerial systems" as well. This includes managing the governance structure of the organization, such as designing the managerial positions; assessing individual performance of those positions; reviewing how decisions are made, how often meetings occur, who sits on the board of directors and why, how the board and other decision makers are kept abreast of changes in the industry; and much more. The smaller a medical group is, the easier it is for group members to believe that these structures do not apply to them. This is a major mistake because such beliefs tend to foster weak leadership and leadership structures in those groups.

Case Study: *For examples of building consensus and change management in practice, see "Laying the Groundwork for EHR Consensus, Managing Change, and Aligning Incentives at ThedaCare," page 164, and "Laying the Groundwork for EHR Consensus at SETMA," page 169.*

A list of managerial systems for the medical practice along with the necessary information technology components to help accomplish those functions is noted in Table 7-1.

Table 7-1: Medical Practice Management Systems

Management System	Purpose	IT Components
Financial and strategic planning	• Easy-to-access financial information provides detailed accounting of costs and revenues • Accounts receivable and accounts payable are easily tracked and understood • Budgets are updated regularly • Budgets are understandable to all staff and financial accountability is established and monitored; staff at all levels participate in the budget process • Business planning is effective and used to guide resource allocation	• Spreadsheet • General ledger • Practice management software
Human resources	• Supports hiring and retaining high-quality staff • HR policies are written, updated regularly, and accessible—a shared set of policies and manuals stored where everyone can access them • Performance reviews conducted on a regular basis • Hiring and firing procedures are in place	• Internal Web site (intranet) • Designated network directory
Information system	• Strategic decisions about what IT components are necessary • Effective selection, implement, and maintenance of IT systems • Network security, anti-viral, and anti-spam management • Production of performance metrics • Provides training and support to staff	• All IT systems
Improvement and performance management	• Continuous access to useful performance metrics • Selected metrics posted on "data wall" for staff to see • Data collection methods for customer surveys • Methods for "innovation" and testing changes in practice	• Electronic health record (EHR) • Practice management system (PMS) • Population-based reports from EHR and PMS • Spreadsheets

THE IMPLICATIONS FOR INFORMATION TECHNOLOGY

Information technology such as electronic health records (EHR), practice management systems (PMS), secure messaging software, a practice's Intranet resources, and electronic access to knowledge resources are all obviously vital parts of the medical practice of the future. A transformed practice's IT is in fact made up of much more than an EHR—it is a sophisticated set of electronic components that cross a number of operating platforms. Those platforms include server-based products linked with Internet-based products, palm-based applications, and diagnostic devices.

Information technology is the specific subject of Chapter 8. We address it in this chapter as well because a practice's IT system, including the EHR, is such a significant part of the redesigned system. A practice should not contemplate building an IT system without contemplating a redesign of the practice overall. IT and the EHR are essential enablers of the transformation—they are a platform for redesign. Medical groups should use the opportunity that IT adoption presents to directly address many other organizational issues such as

- Rationalize management structure and processes;
- Create specific, measurable goals that include improving relationship, service and clinical reliability;
- Plan for data collection and understand how the IT system needs to be designed to allow the group to do so;
- Planning for investment and tracking of return on investment;
- Implement new work flows; and
- Redefine tasks and train staff for new tasks.

Table 7-2 demonstrates the IT system components of GreenField Health, a four-physician internal medicine practice in Portland, Oregon. A simple perusal of this list demonstrates the necessity of smart work flow design with the technology in mind. The number of components, even for this small practice, is impressive and speaks to the need for IT integration. Both people and technology touch every part of the practice, so every part must be designed with considering both people and IT.

Table 7-2: IT System Components at GreenField Health, Portland, OR

Component	Purpose and Function
Electronic health record	Electronic record keeping and enhanced knowledge management via such tools as integrated guidelines, drug-drug interaction checking, automated risk assessment, and much more
Practice management system	Timely billing and management of accounts receivable
Specialized encounter forms	Enhance data management within the EHR
Disease registry	Obtain population-based data for the practice and for specific providers
Scanning	Place outside paper documents into the system for electronic storage, viewing, and retrieval
Secure messaging (secure e-mail)	Electronic communication with patients and other health professionals in a secure, HIPAA-compliant manner. Improve work flow including the transferring of medical records and sending consult notes to other practices
Network faxing	Where secure messaging is not available, network faxing helps improve work flow including the transmission of medical records and sending prescriptions or refill requests directly to pharmacies
Interface with lab, radiology, hospital documents	Efficiently import labs from outside sources directly into the EHR's database so that information is not just electronically visible, but available for measurement
Electronic ECG	Paperless electrocardiogram integrated into the EHR
Electronic spirometer	Paperless spirometry integrated into the EHR
Practice decision support	Decision support and knowledge management tools to enhance the EHR
Patient decision support	Decision making tools specifically designed to assist patients in making effective decisions based on deeper knowledge and their individual values
Medical group intranet	Shared network location for general organization and community information
Patient e-newsletter	Regular electronic mass communications with the practice's customers
Online clinical information	Make high quality information available to patients
Remote connectivity (e.g., from home or other offices)	Allow IT system access from remote locations such that physicians and staff can work from home and can have access to patient records during weekend call, for example
Internet connectivity	Connect the practice's network to the internet
Security (i.e., antivirus, antispam, back-up systems)	Guard against unwanted intrusion and provide a high degree of system security and stability
Spreadsheet	Allow financial modeling
General ledger	Manage financial statements including balance sheet, cash flow, and income statements
Word processing	Letter writing and other general word processing
Voice recognition	Increase speed of note generation

Most organizations will develop their IT system in a stepwise fashion. Leaders should create an overall road map for the IT system that they are planning to build—a roadmap that is built around a specific set of needs and strategic goals of the practice. If a product doesn't integrate well with other components of the IT system and with the practice's workflow, then be careful about purchasing it. Integration is key for overall system efficiency. Stand-alone, non-integrated products frequently serve as a barrier to improvement and may limit efficiency.

Like other components of the overall practice system, IT needs to be intentionally built into the overall practice system design. What does this mean? It means a practice benefits the most if it puts in a lot of work in preparation for the IT system and the EHR well before implementing them. Systems are redesigned by taking time to carefully analyze the work that is being done, who is doing it, and how it is being done. Do not assume that the way things currently work are the way things should work.

Practices should examine their office systems to seek opportunities for improved efficiency. For example, some critical yet time-consuming work flows include message handling, prescription refills, patient triage, documentation, and billing. To intentionally *not* design these and other tasks implies that it is acceptable for everyone to do their own thing. Everyone doing their own thing, even relatively so, is a recipe for inefficiency, mistakes, and errors, and overall performance problems.

When leaders begin to examine their work process, one of the first things they recognize is the widely disparate methods of doing common tasks. From clinical care to administrative functions, variation in how we do things is abundant in the medical practice. This leads to significant variation in performance. Performance is nearly always improved when work can be standardized.

Leaders can help the team develop rational, standardized, reliable methods for work such as managing refills, managing visits, managing the work within visits, lab ordering, lab tracking, clinical review and patient notification. Each of these tasks, and many more, benefit from the use of IT, but they can benefit more or less depending on how skilled the leadership is at organizing the daily work in accordance with the IT capabilities.

The goal of any EHR implementation should be to install a system that will not only support the core business of the practice, but also provide opportunities improvements in efficiency and quality. With the increasing need to measure and report performance improvement data, make sure your vendor understands the issues surrounding such measurement and can eventually build in the clinical quality improvement support you want and need. Clinical measurement has been largely accomplished in the paper world by retrospective chart audits, which can be extremely time consuming and costly. EHRs provide the opportunity to collect clinical data for improvement and reporting as a byproduct of the process of care, but both the processes and the way data are entered are crucial to accomplishing this goal.

The use of standard measure sets endorsed by the National Quality Forum and National Committee on Quality Assurance will allow vendors to more easily design systems to capture and report the necessary data.[10, 11] A significant portion of the practice income in the future may be determined by the ability to collect and report quality improvement data. Such "pay for performance" will initially focus on providing incentives for improved systems within the office and later change to incentives for actual clinical outcomes.

Case Study: *For examples of improving workforce efficiences, see "Achieving Increased Workflow Efficiences at SETMA," page 170, and "Improving Work Flow at PatientCare Family Clinic," page 180.*

CONCLUDING COMMENTS

Interdependency, true teamwork, a defined purpose, measurable performance, and intentionally designed systems are central to high performing practices. It is the role of leaders to understand these items and to manage them in the medical group, irrespective of its size. The new world of electronic medical practices with tools such as the EHR and performance management requires tenacious leadership and smart planning. Dealing effectively with objections, barriers and a few reluctant souls will be major challenges that leaders face.

Modern improvement science does not primarily concern itself with putting out fires or solving sporadic problems. Instead, it aims for demonstrable long term performance improvement, which requires a focus on basic system design. This is the domain of leadership. It requires a strategic change in how we frame our work and what sights we set our eyes on for the future. It is where effective leadership and continual improvement necessarily merge into one.

References

1 Silverson J, Kornacki MJ. *Leading Physicians though Change: How to Achieve and Sustain Results.* Tampa, Florida: American College of Physician Executives; 2000.

2 Reinertsen JL. Zen and the art of physician autonomy maintenance. *Ann Int Med.* June 17, 2003; 138(12)992-995.

3 Berwick DM. Developing and testing changes in delivery of care. *Ann Intern Med.* April 15, 1998; 128(8):651-656.

4 Berwick DM. A user's manual for the IOM's 'Quality Chasm' report. *Health Aff* (Millwood). May-June 2002; 21(3):80-90.

5 Berwick DM, James B, Coye MJ. Connections between quality measurement and improvement. *Med Care.* January 2003; 41(1 Suppl):I30-38.

6 Davis D, O'Brien MA, Freemantle N, et al. Impact of formal continuing medical education: do conferences, workshops, rounds, and other traditional continuing education activities change physician behavior or healthcare outcomes? *JAMA.* September 1, 1999; 282(9):867-874.

7 Davis DA, Thomson MA, Oxman AD, et al. Changing physician performance. A systematic review of the effect of continuing medical education strategies. *JAMA.* September 6, 1995; 274(9):700-705.

8 Tu K, Davis D. Can we alter physician behavior by educational methods? Lessons learned from studies of the management and follow-up of hypertension. *J Contin Educ Health Prof.* 2002 Winter; 22(1):11-22.

9 McGlynn EA, Asch SM, Adams J, et al. The quality of health care delivered to adults in the United States. *New Engl J Med.* June 26, 2003; 348(26): 2635-2645.

10 http://www.qualityforum.org (accessed April 11, 2005).

11 http://www.ncqa.org/PhysicianQualityReports.htm (accessed April 11, 2005).

CHAPTER 8

Selecting and Implementing EHRs for the Physician Practice

Jane B. Metzger and Keith MacDonald

Achieving the new vision for medical practice outlined in previous chapters—characterized by enhanced relationship, service, and reliability—is difficult at best and is probably not possible without an electronic health record (EHR). Up until the current decade, use of information technology for functions beyond finance or administration in the ambulatory setting was limited to the largest healthcare systems, hospitals, and medical groups. That situation is changing. Web-based technology, mobile computing, reconfigured products and pricing models, and modular products provide new opportunities for physician practices of all sizes to leverage an EHR in their work to achieve this new vision.

This chapter provides practical information about effectively incorporating the necessary IT into the practice. It covers how a practice of any size—from the small, solo-physician practice to the large, multi-site and multi-physician practice—can obtain and implement an EHR. This process involves laying the necessary groundwork in setting objectives and planning; selecting a particular vendor's application; actually implementing the system; and managing the technology to achieve defined business and clinical objectives. The goal is to offer a balanced view of what can be achieved by physician practices.

The clinical piece—the EHR—is the focus of this chapter, with the understanding that the IT to support tasks such as scheduling and billing must work in concert with the flow of EHR data and combine to support the workflows of clinicians and other staff. In short, decisions about the EHR involve decisions about the other applications because the potential end-point has to support functional integration, independent of how that is achieved by technology in the background (e.g., through a single, integrated system or through applications linked using interfaces). Realistically, EHR implementation and adoption represent an incremental process, not a one-time project that is undertaken to achieve an "ideal state."

Because this chapter's mission is such a large one (by itself worthy of an entire book),[1] the focus here is on basic principles that can be applied in *most* situations to sort out options and make decisions. Whenever appropriate, specific recommendations are made for small practices and references provided to additional information resources either in the sidebars, endnotes, or the bibliography at the end of the chapter.

LAYING THE GROUNDWORK

Before selecting a vendor, physician groups and practices need to lay out what they are trying to accomplish and be sure that all physicians agree on the need to invest in IT to meet those goals (as discussed in Chapter 7). In larger practices, this will be a more formalized process. What is critical in any setting is that decisions are made regarding what is to be accomplished, what application(s) are to be replaced and purchased, and what resources the organization is realistically willing to commit.

Deciding What Is Important to Accomplish

EHRs are available with a range of functions and design approaches for accomplishing documentation and managing orders for prescriptions and other services. Available products also range in cost, related roughly to the complexity of the product's features, functions, and flexibility. A critical first step in any practice—especially for the physicians—is to agree on the problem or problems they believe are important enough to solve and therefore merit the investment of both money and energy. The EHR that can serve as a tool to achieve the vision described in this book is on the higher end of the range of products in terms of functional richness and flexibility, and is likely not the least expensive option in the marketplace. Reaching agreement about the need, the goals, and the commitment of resources is a critical first step.

Developing the "Business Case" for the EHR

The traditional approach for evaluating whether or not to proceed with a major business investment—a return on investment (ROI) analysis—is problematic for the EHR because some of the most important benefits are difficult to quantify in dollars. Many physicians who have led the way with EHRs made the investment with the conviction that paper-based medical records cannot support the care their patients deserve. Generally they have not conducted a traditional ROI analysis as part of their decision making.[2]

Most small practices, however, do identify the process improvement benefits and cost savings they expect to achieve. Certainly opportunities *do* exist for financial gains to offset the costs. In fact, depending upon the EHR chosen, how it is implemented, and the commitment of the practice to undertaking process changes, sizable financial gains are certainly available. Many of the areas in which physician practices have achieved benefits using an EHR, including some representing significant financial savings, are listed in the sidebar on page 99. These form the basis of the formal or informal "business case" that can convince a practice to purchase and install an EHR.

Opportunities for Achieving Tangible Benefits through Implementation of an EHR

The following areas of benefit for ambulatory EHRs reflect a wide range of demonstrated results:

- Reduced medical records costs through a reduction or elimination of paper charts, forms, and related supplies; a reduction in the associated expenses for copying, printing, storing and delivering paper charts, and a reduction or reassignment of medical records staff;
- Decreased transcription expenses;
- Improved workflow and intra-office communication for office visits, prescription refills, processing of test results, and telephone calls;
- Decreased telephone call volume related to prescription questions and test results (when e-prescribing and other electronic communication tools are implemented as part of the EHR);
- Improved chronic disease management and compliance with care protocols (in a growing number of cases, this now translates to an increase in payments for physicians under pay-for-performance bonus programs);
- Improved analysis and reporting for regulatory compliance, public health reporting and accreditation;
- Increased accuracy of visit charges, including a decrease in lost charges, an increase in relative value units or charges per visit, a decrease in claims denials and an improved billing cycle time (when used in conjunction with electronic billing); and
- Reduced malpractice insurance premiums.

Regardless of how a business case is framed, key decision makers (including at a minimum the physicians in the practice) must agree on what the desired benefits are and commit to achieving them. Achieving benefits almost always requires changes in the practice's processes. For example, reducing reliance on paper medical records can translate into decreased staffing in areas such as medical records. One large medical group studied by the authors operated a number of different physical locations and devoted significant staff resources to pre-visit chart completion reviews and delivery of patient medical records to clinics where they were needed. Eliminating these activities was expected to substantially offset the investment in an EHR. Actually achieving this type of savings, however, requires that *all* physicians document care online and, after sufficient information is electronic, agree to policy changes such as criteria for pulling paper medical records in advance of a visit less frequently (or rarely). It is important that the implications of each benefit in the business case be understood in this way.

Resources do exist for practices that wish to perform a traditional ROI analysis. For example, an Excel-based ROI benefits calculator is available from AC Group, Inc., *ACG 2003 Annual Report on Computer Systems in Physicians' Offices: Electronic Medical Records—Return on Investment,* May 2003 (available at www.acgroup.org).

One financial gain that can be factored into the business case for an EMR is fairly recent: the opportunity to qualify for additional reimbursement when certain levels of performance in delivering quality care can be demonstrated. "Pay for performance" programs have been established by health plans and employer groups in different parts of the country. California has a statewide initiative involving a number of the largest health plans.[3] Over the next few years, this model will grow, especially if, following current demonstration projects,[4] Medicare reimbursement incorporates pay for performance criteria. This change, combined with public reporting of performance information, increases the impetus for using the EHR as a tool to aid in delivering recommended disease and wellness management interventions (e.g., immunizations, screening, monitoring) more consistently. The California pay-for-performance program even includes rewards for the practice's use of an EHR.

Case Study: *For examples of developing a business case for the EHR in practice, see "The Business Case for IT at SETMA," page 171.*

Maintaining a Realistic Expectation about Costs

Typical prices for EHR software, hardware, training, and support range from $15,000 to $50,000 per physician.[5] Anticipated costs must also factor in ongoing software maintenance. One solo pediatric practice cited earlier spent $20,000 in 1995 for an EHR system and $40,000 in system upgrades and maintenance over the next seven years.[6] Beyond the investment in technology is the investment in transforming processes to incorporate the EHR and to achieve the desired model that enhances the patient relationship, service, and reliability.

In order to achieve consensus about the business case for IT, practice leaders must determine their "cost tolerance" upfront—how much money the practice is willing and able to spend. The capital needed for an EHR investment can be obtained through practice income or may need to be borrowed. Purchasing models now include the ability to spread start-up costs over a number of years. For some practices, hospitals or health systems in the market may offer EHR and related implementation services at an attractive cost of ownership, sometimes even including financing. Nonetheless, an EHR represents a big investment.

Although detailed EHR costs are typically not available at this point in the exploration process, practice leaders must still wrestle with and determine their comfort with investing capital and other resources. It is critical for physicians in particular to agree upfront about their ability to absorb the estimated dollar and human resource investments of an EHR. Without this understanding, the practice may start looking at technology it simply cannot afford or will not be able to implement. Very robust products (which require a large investment in set-up, training, and process change) may be entirely appropriate when the practice leadership and physicians are highly motivated to transform the practice; simpler tools are likely to be more appropriate for practices in which the physicians are not prepared to (or simply can't afford to) make such a big investment in change.

Creating a Roadmap

Practices are well-served at this point to create a roadmap for the steps and timeframe involved in selecting and implementing IT. The roadmap forces the practice to set appropriate and realistic expectations and to ensure that everyone is "on the same page" regarding how long the project might take and the level of commitment that will be involved. Roadmap guideposts might include the following:

- ***Establishing an EHR team:*** The size of the team, which will vary based on the practice's size, might include someone who will manage system selection and integration, someone who will oversee the clinical elements of process redesign, someone responsible for the financial aspects, and a technical expert.[7] Heavy involvement of physicians as both leaders and participants in every aspect is critical! So, too, is ensuring that the perspective of nurses and front- and back-office staff is always included.
- ***Evaluating the practice's current workflow:*** What are the problems with current processes? What do we hope to achieve through process improvement? It is important that a new model for workflow is in place to help in selecting the right vendor.
- ***Identifying possible vendors:*** How will this occur? Who will lead the effort?
- ***Identifying how potential products will be evaluated:*** What criteria will be used?
- ***Implementation planning:*** How will a realistic implementation plan be developed?

A roadmap organizes the effort and enables the practice to monitor its performance toward accomplishing technology-enabled business and clinical objectives, as described in Chapter 7.

FINDING AND SELECTING THE "RIGHT" EHR

With increased use of the Internet, development of wireless technology, and advances in end-user computing devices, the number of products and vendors is daunting. Companies that sell EHRs, practice management systems, document imaging systems, hand-held devices, Web-based applications, and so forth, number in the hundreds if not thousands.

For the physician practice or clinic, IT can be provided either by a collection of products and technologies or by one integrated application (see the sidebar on page 102). In order to solve an immediate problem, some practices opt to start with a single functional component of an EHR such as electronic prescribing or a disease management registry.[8] If these practices anticipate needing additional functionality in the near future, they are best served to consider modular EHRs with more comprehensive capabilities that they can "grow into."

Finding and selecting the "right EHR" involves looking at vendors with the practice's objectives in mind and matching the cost and complexity of implementation with the practice's resources and capacity for change. Basic principles for conducting the necessary homework in each of these areas follow.

Examples of the IT Components That Can Be Part of or Integrated with an EHR

- Billing/scheduling software
- Specialized encounter forms and data capture methods
- Scanning and document imaging software
- Dictation/transcription systems
- Disease registry
- Network faxing
- VPN (virtual private network) for secure use from home
- Internet connectivity
- Online clinical research and reference information
- Internal practice Intranet
- Secure messaging with other clinicians and external partners
- Interface with laboratory, radiology, or hospital information systems
- Interface with medical devices such as EKG, spirometry or PFT machines
- Patient e-newsletter, or electronic patient-physician communication
- External practice Web site for patients
- Security—antivirus, anti-spam, back-up

The Right Features and Functionality

The functionality of a comprehensive system for the physician practice or clinic can be separated into three partially overlapping domains, consistent with the clinical, business and patient care functions (Figure 8-1):

- *Business or financial tools* focus on more traditional practice management and billing functions, such as charge capture and coding assistance. However, new options have emerged for charge capture and online payer-based transactions using hand-held devices and Web-hosted solutions, and several EHR vendors offer tightly-integrated practice management system products.
- *Clinical tool*s focus on point-of-care functions such as prescription writing, order management, decision support, and visit documentation.
- *Patient tools* support communication functions such as telephone triage, patient reminders, appointment scheduling, and prescription refills.

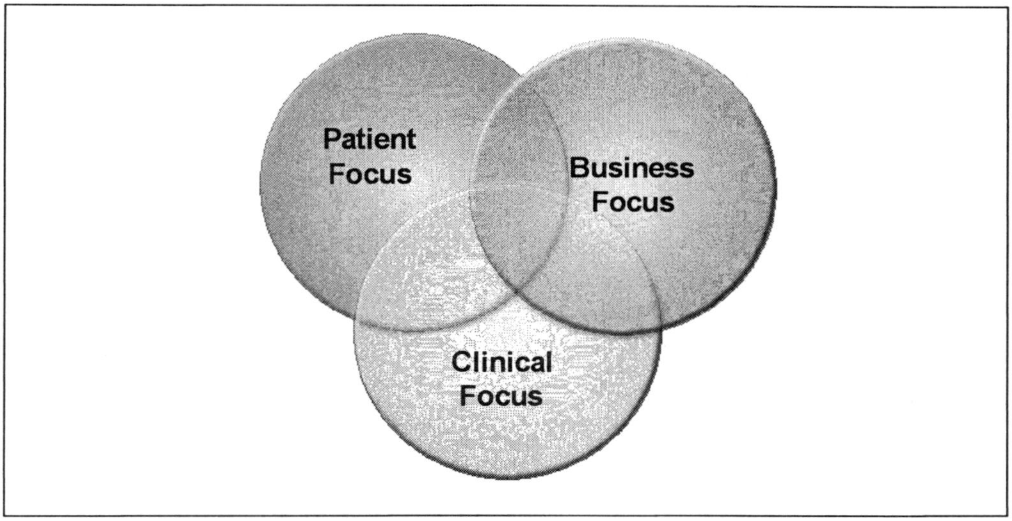

Figure 8-1: Three Functional Domains of Ambulatory Practice Systems

Key functions reside within each of the three domains, while some functions are shared between domains (Figure 8-2). A number of the shared functional components for an effective ambulatory-based system may be satisfied through one integrated vendor solution, or may require interfaces between different EHR, practice management and other vendor products.

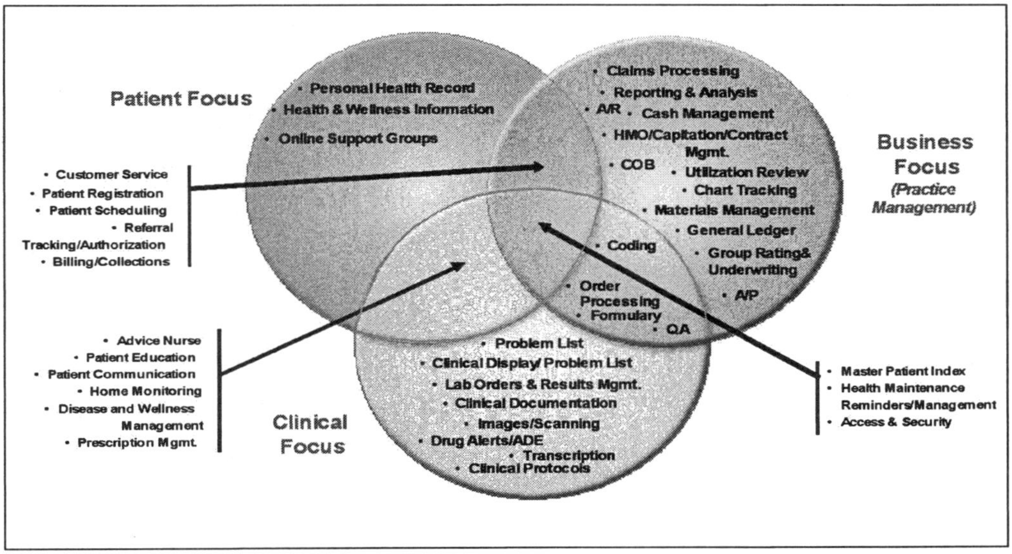

Figure 8-2: Functions of Comprehensive IT for the Physician Practice or Clinic

The key question in defining and evaluating EHR functionality is, "How much is enough?" The answer in each case is, "what we need to accomplish what we set out to do tempered by what we can afford." Reviewing what other organizations recommend regarding minimum and ideal functionality may help in answering these questions.

For example, the Institute of Medicine (IOM) has defined eight core functions as key capabilities of an EHR system:[9]

1. ***Health information and data:*** Immediate access to key information such as patients' diagnoses, allergies, and laboratory test results.
2. ***Results management:*** Quick access to new and past test results.
3. **Order management:** Computerized entry and storage of data on all medications, tests, and other services.
4. ***Decision support:*** Electronic alerts and reminders to improve compliance with best practices, ensure regular screenings and other preventive practices, identify possible drug interactions, and facilitate diagnoses and treatments.
5. ***Electronic communication and connectivity:*** Secure and readily accessible communication among clinicians and patients.
6. ***Patient support:*** Tools offering patients access to their medical records, interactive education, and the ability to do home monitoring and self-testing.
7. ***Administrative processes:*** Tools (including scheduling systems) to improve administrative efficiencies and patient service.
8. ***Reporting:*** Electronic data storage that uses uniform data standards to enable physician offices and healthcare organizations to comply with federal, state, and private reporting requirements in a timely manner.

The IOM defined these capabilities in an attempt to develop consensus on a standard definition of an EHR—one which the industry is currently lacking.

Another organization's analysis defined EHR functionality as 15 key capabilities the software could offer physicians, including how quickly and effectively the physician can view critical information in the record, document the patient visit, write prescriptions and order tests, manage the patient's chronic diseases and conditions, and other functions.[10]

Health Level Seven (HL7) is currently developing an Electronic Health Record Functional Model, and one of its special interest groups is seeking consensus on EHR system functionality.[11] HL7 develops IT-related healthcare standards with wide support from the Department of Health and Human Services (HHS), the Department of Veterans Affairs (VA), the Healthcare Information and Management Systems Society (HIMSS), and a grant from The Robert Wood Johnson Foundation, and through active participation of healthcare stakeholder representatives on its work groups. HL7's *Essential Now for Ambulatory EHR* list can be accessed on HL7's Web site (www.HL7.org).

Certification of EHRs for the physician practice promises to level the playing field and help medical practices make more rational choices in the crowded EHR market place. The Certification Commission for Healthcare Information Technology (CCHIT)[12] will create testing methods to certify that EHR products meet standards for functionality, interoperability, security and reliability. Formed in the fall of 2004, the commission will be developing not only minimum requirements for certification in the first year of the program, but also a roadmap for subsequent years. It is hoped that voluntary, private-sector certification of EHRs will help physicians and other healthcare professionals select and implement these products with greater speed and confidence.[13]

The challenge for every EHR purchaser is to figure out what is *essential*. Greater functionality is not necessarily better since it often brings greater complexity to change management. In the end, that determination must be based on what the organization needs to realize its goals. Table 8-1 arrays broad functional requirements with the likely categories of improvement that may be on the organization's list of goals. Note that EHR purchasers who strive for the vision described in this book have a long list of requirements!

Table 8-1: **EHR Requirements to Support a Practice's Improvement Goals**

Potential Organizational Improvement	Associated EHR Requirements
1. Improved clinical quality and disease management	• Patient registry for population management • Prescription management (including Rx checking) • Point-of-care decision support tools (wellness and disease management) • Outreach reports • Practice/process analysis reporting tools
2. Increased cost efficiency of operations	• Replacement of transcription (voice objects, voice recognition, easy notes writer tools) • Prescription refill processing • Team messaging
3. Increased revenue generation and reimbursement	• Clinical coding integrated with encounter notes • E&M coding advisor • Referral management • Quality tools to aid in performance improvement and reporting for pay for performance reimbursement
4. Improved access to data (reduce medical records costs)	• Basic charting capabilities (meds, problems, notes) • Interface to laboratory system(s) • Flexible display, graphing and query capabilities
5. Support of paperless environment	• Improved access to data (see above) • Document scanning and imaging
6. Patient interaction and empowerment	• Clinical e-mail (MD-patient communication) • Access to knowledge/tools for collaborative decision-making during encounters • Patient direct access to knowledge/tools for self-management • Patient direct access to medical
7. Support of all the relationship, service, and reliability process improvements described in this book	• Workflow/message management • Test result management • Quality tools (see above) • Improved access to data (see above) • Patient interaction and empowerment (see above)

Case Study: *For examples of finding and selecting the 'right IT' in practice, see* *"Determining EHR Core Functionality at SETMA," page 171, and "Selecting the Right IT Product at SETMA," page 173.*

Beyond EHR Functionality

Given that a large amount of the information necessary to treat a patient in the ambulatory practice setting originates from other sources, the ability to integrate information from external laboratories, hospitals, and other physician practices can be critical to both efficiency and quality goals for the practice. Standards for formats and content of this clinical information, which the industry has been slow to develop and adopt, are needed to achieve interoperability among disparate systems. The EHR standards being established by the CCHIT described earlier will include communication and data standards. EHR products that are not aligning with these emerging national standards will not represent a good investment for the practice in the long run.

While standards to protect patient privacy and ensure the security of electronic patient information have now been finalized under the Health Insurance Portability and Accountability Act (HIPAA), the approaches that EHR vendors employ to support these requirements can vary widely. Efforts to certify that vendors meet these national security standards are also just emerging.

Cost/Price Issues

In addition to thinking about possible EHR vendors based on product characteristics, it is important to evaluate them according to what they cost and the purchasing model(s) they offer. Practices will need to gather comprehensive estimates of the full cost of implementing an EHR system up front in order to fully prepare for the initiative. These costs include not only the purchase of the software and associated hardware, but also the costs associated with implementing the application and supporting it going forward (see sidebar below).

Components of EHR Vendor Costs

- One-time, usually upfront, fees for
  - Hardware (both server(s) and desktops);
  - Software (for the EHR as well as for related but separately-licensed software);
  - Network; and
  - Implementation and training.
- Ongoing licensing fees for
  - Maintenance;
  - Support; and
  - Upgrades.

There are two ways that some vendors structure the business proposition to fit the customer's agenda and resources:[14]

- ***Financing flexibility:*** This is the company's willingness to offer both monthly leases (subscription terms or application service provider—ASP—plans) and long-term license purchase agreements; and
- ***Modular implementation and pricing:*** This gives users the flexibility to implement systems in a flexible, modular way, as needed and as budgets allow.

Many practices find the concept of modular products appealing. Unlike one-stage products, these enable practices to enhance their operations on an incremental rather than one-stage basis. Practices need to ensure, however, that the product a vendor offers is truly modular and that the practice is not paying for more than the components physicians want and need. Vendors may indicate that functions can be "turned on" when the practice wants them, but the practice may in fact be purchasing and installing a more robust system than envisioned or required.

New EHR options are also becoming available to practices as community, regional, and metropolitan networks, hospitals, health systems, and other entities seek ways of hosting applications to ensure data sharing and interoperability with ambulatory practices in the community. Application-hosting alternatives include local hosting of an EHR at a local health system, hospital or large group practice, or remote hosting by the vendor using an ASP-based model with access via the Internet.

Practices should consider the issues of data control and access associated with remotely-hosted applications. Not all practices appreciate having their patient data reside on a vendor's system or hosted by another delivery system in the community, with access in either case dependent on the reliability of a high-speed Internet connection. The adequacy of provisions for security and patient privacy, in addition to other requirements for HIPAA, are important concerns. Some practices feel it is important to retain all patient data in a database they control. Other practices feel comfortable that their data will be protected and view remote hosting as a better way to leverage skills and resources they otherwise wouldn't have.[15]

Other cost or pricing practices that can make a difference include:

- ***Discounts offered by vendors:*** Most vendors offer discounts, so practices should not expect to pay full list price.
- ***Percentage price increases for maintenance costs quoted by vendors:*** Increases are normally negotiable and tied to the consumer price index (CPI) in some way.
- ***Licensing type:*** Perpetual licenses allow practices to buy the software and use it forever. Subscription licenses, which are becoming more common, allow the practice to use the software for a fee for a specified number of years, at the end of which the practice must purchase the license again.
- ***Timing of prices quoted by vendors:*** Salespeople eager to make quarterly or year-end goals might offer a specific price that is honored only up to a specific date.

When it comes to actually purchasing the technology, financing methods will need to be considered. Options used by small medical practices include:[16]

- A lease buy-back program with the vendor (typically of three years' duration);
- A bank loan with the practice as collateral (also typically over three years); and
- Tapping into the practice's revolving line of credit at the bank.

In each case, practices incorporate the regular lease or loan payments into their monthly operating expenses.

Case Study: *For examples of how practices deal with cost/price issues, see "EHR Costs and Financial Benefits for SETMA," page 172.*

Implementation Issues

A number of implementation issues require careful consideration by medical practices prior to and as a factor in selecting a vendor product. Issues include process re-engineering and workflow redesign, the training process, and productivity loss.

Workflow and Process Design

To achieve major relationship, service, and reliability transformation as described earlier in this book, leaders in medical practices will need to think extensively about workflow and process redesign. What workflow problems exist and what problems does the practice hope to solve through the use of IT?

If the envisioned change is a major one, the practice will need to ask and answer questions such as:

- How will the practice manage incoming telephone calls?
- Will the practice interact with patients on the Web?
- How will the practice manage laboratory results and prescription refills?
- How will the practice's care team be configured to support the flow of patient visits?
- How will documentation and electronic prompting be employed to advance new care models for disease and wellness management?

Even if the scope of the envisioned change is not dramatic, the workflow issues associated with each of these processes should be considered.

Training

Medical practices should thoroughly explore the vendor's approach, tools, and services for training end users. The quality of the vendor's remote training is particularly important for smaller practices because such training is typically all that is offered when purchasing a product. Because training takes time away from the practice's patient care activities, vendor-supplied tools and services are an important part of decision making about the right product solution.[17]

Practices can ask about and learn from the experiences of similar practices that have completed the training process. As medical practices increasingly adopt IT, it is expected that more vendors will offer easy ways for practitioners and staff to learn to use these new products, including Web-based and CD-ROM-based training. Vendors' user groups can provide additional support to practices beyond their initial training.

Case Study: *For examples of staff training in practice, see "Staff Training at SETMA," page 175.*

Productivity Loss

In selecting vendor products, practices should consider the impact of the new product on the practice's productivity. Medical practices inevitably experience a range of temporary productivity loss when implementing EHRs. Factors impacting the level of loss include the extent of required workflow and process change, the availability of templates and tools that effectively support the practice's workflow, the learning curve for end users (especially physicians), and the quality of the training provided in advance.

One study of implementation costs for EHRs indicated that an initial, first-month productivity loss of 20% could be expected, with a 10% loss in the second month, a 5% loss in the third month, and return to baseline productivity levels in the fourth month.[18] Talking with other practices that have implemented the products under consideration and understanding the level of transformation the practice undertook can be helpful in gauging the expected level of productivity loss.

Case Study: *For examples of implementation planning in practice, see "Implementation Planning at SETMA," page 174, and "System Implementation at SETMA," page 174.*

Evaluating Vendors as Long-Term Business Partners

The preparation stage should also consider the long-term viability of potential vendors and their ability to sustain an enduring relationship with the practice. No medical practice wants to invest capital in an IT product from a company that is at risk of folding or that may discontinue its support of the product in the future.

In evaluating vendors' long-term viability, practices can consider the following issues:

- *Longevity of the company,* including its history in the ambulatory marketplace;
- The company's *financing model:* Vendors supported by venture capital or that lack a net positive cash flow from revenue over successive quarters may be at greater risk of folding;
- The history of the *company's financial performance,* including consistent earnings and a track record of growth as indicated by increasing revenue, and employee growth;
- The size of the *customer market:* Number of licenses sold or the actual installed base of users specifically for the product being considered and in practices of similar size and specialty;
- The track record of *successful implementations:* Good customer reference checks can help;
- The frequency of *product updates:* Vendors that provide upgrades on an infrequent or irregular basis tend to have fewer resources and may have less staying power compared with companies offering updates on a regular cycle, such as twice a year;
- The company's understanding of *clinical workflow:* Does the sales and support staff understand clinical practice?; and
- The company's own *business partners:* The extent to which the company partners with other well-established vendors and leading standards-setting organizations provides a measure of its ability to see the big picture and collaborate to improve its product(s).

Evaluating these factors to identify a vendor that does not push the physician practice beyond the level of risk with which it is comfortable is difficult but important. One consultant annually rates healthcare EHR vendors using a point value system that takes into account factors such as company size, company financial viability, total annual revenues, cash flow, percentage of revenue related to EHR, EHR annual development costs, end-user satisfaction, number of employees, number of clients, cost per physician, and the company's ability to meet national, regional, and local standards.[19] Marketplace consolidation and emerging certification requirements may also facilitate the process of conducting vendor due diligence, and a sound vendor contract can minimize the potential viability-related risks down the line.

Where to Get Information to Help Develop a Vendor Short List

Compiling a short list of potential vendors from among the dozens that exist can be a daunting challenge. The Web sites and resources offered by national societies and associations including the American Academy of Family Physicians' Center for Health Information Technology (www.centerforhit.org), the Medical Group Management Association (www.mgma.com), the American College of Physicians (www.acponline.org), and the American Medical Informatics Association (www.amia.org) can help practices identify the universe of possible vendors and generate an appropriate short list. Other resources for narrowing the list include:

- Peer practices in the community.
- Proceedings and presentations from the HIMSS Davies Primary Care Award. The award recognizes primary care practices that have successfully implemented an EHR; winners tend to be very improvement-oriented and results-focused and their essays include information about vendor products they have used (www.himss.org).
- Vendor exhibitions such as those associated with the Medical Records Institute's annual meeting titled TEPR—Toward an Electronic Patient Record (www.medrecinst.com), the HIMSS annual meeting (www.himss.org), and the annual meetings of other associations mentioned above.
- Vendor ratings by organizations such as the AC Group (www.acgroup.org), KLAS (www.healthcomputing.com), HIMSS (www.himss.org), Gartner (www4.gartner/com), and others.

Table 8-2 provides a list of possible resources for EHR vendor identification and selection.

Table 8-2: Resources for EHR Vendor Identification and Selection

Resource	Offered By	Description
Ambulatory EHR Selector	HIMSS http://www.ehrselector.com/emrtoolkit/ASP/Default.asp	This online tool includes comparative information on products from 30 vendors. The tool allows physicians to select the features they want in an EHR, matches them with a product and allows product comparisons.
AC Group EHR Survey	AC Group Inc. www.acgroup.org	This annual survey ranks top EHR applications by functionality and provides basic cost information.
EHR Product Reviews	American Academy of Family Practice's Center for Health Information Technology www.centerforhit.org	These reviews are written by Academy members who currently use an EHR in their office. Reviewers are asked to rate products using a five-point scale on quality, price, support, ease of use, and impact on productivity. The reviews do not evaluate each product's features and functions, and are available only to AAFP members.
MGMA Buyer's Guide	Medical Group Management Association www.mgma.org/marketplace/	Information systems and services vendors are listed, but no evaluations are provided.
Electronic Medical Records: A Buyer's Guide for Small Physician Practices	California HealthCare Foundation www.chcf.org	This 20-page publication provides guidelines for evaluating EHRs, with a particular focus on practices of nine or fewer physicians.
HMT Online Resource Guide	Health Management Technology www.healthmgttech.com	This online tool allows users to search for products and services from more than 1,000 healthcare IT vendors, by typing in company or category/subjects, or alphabetically.
Healthcare Informatics Resource Guide	Healthcare Informatics Online www.healthcare-informatics.com	Annual print publication of more than 700 IT companies.
Physicians EHR	www.physiciansehr.com	Lists information about more than 200 vendors and includes a forum for discussing the pros and cons of different solutions.
Developing services to help physicians select EMRs	Physicians Electronic Health Record Coalition (PEHRC)	Formed in 2004 by 14 medical organizations (i.e., AAFP, AAP, ACP, AMA, etc.) to assist physicians, particularly those in small- and medium-sized practices.

Kicking the Tires

While it might be common for larger medical groups to narrow down the list of vendors and obtain more specific information about the vendors' products by issuing a formal request-for-information (RFI) or a request-for-proposal (RFP) to a short list of potential vendors, smaller physician practices are unlikely to have the resources to do so. It is more likely that the process of obtaining specific vendor information will be an informal one, and that the resources listed above will effectively serve to narrow down the practice's list of options.

Two aspects are particularly important in determining which product offers the best fit: ability to support the transformed process; and product usability.

Ability to Support the Transformed Process
In order to evaluate how well the EHR will support the redesigned workflow, practices should develop realistic patient care scenarios addressing key practice processes such as conducting a patient visit, documenting a telephone call, managing a diabetic patient, and refilling a prescription.

Product Usability
How easily physicians and staff can use a product often makes or breaks an EHR implementation. Dimensions of EHR usability, as defined in one report,[14] include how easily physicians and staff can:

- *Input* information using a variety of methods;
- *Customize* the sequence of activities, tasks, and screens to suit personal workflow preferences;
- *Understand* the meaning of menu categories, graphics, icons, and symbols;
- *Integrate* with practice management systems and claims processing services;
- *Access* the system remotely plus use a mobile device to dictate, view histories, document visits, and capture charges; and
- *Process*, exchange, and store graphics and images.

One of the best ways to judge a product's fit with the target workflow and usability is for physicians to visit another practice using the same EHR product, and/or to arrange for the vendor to conduct a product demonstration at the purchasing practice's offices. Reference sites should have demographics (i.e., practice size and specialties offered) and objectives that are similar to those of the purchasing practice. It is important to ensure that the product version demonstrated by the vendor is actually available for sale, not simply in development, and that it can be easily configured by the client for different scenarios (and has not been custom-configured by the vendor specifically for the demonstration).

Selecting the Best-Fit Vendor
In summary, successful selection of the final, best-fit vendor requires making tradeoffs among competing requirements—each of which will carry a different weight depending on its relative importance to the practice. In addition to cost, these tradeoffs include whether the vendor:

- Meets minimum functional requirements for achieving the practice's objectives;
- Meets—or is planning to meet—emerging EHR and interoperability certification requirements;
- Is configured and supported as needed for the practice (including remote-hosting and Web-accessibility considerations if desired);
- Is modular, flexible and usable;
- Reflects a sizable installed base of customers similar to the practice's—and is highly recommended by those customers; and
- Is supported by a vendor that represents long-term stability and viability.

Agreeing on the relative importance ranking for each factor (reflected as the percentage out of a total value of 100), rating the potential vendors for each factor, and summarizing the resulting scores across all practice physicians and other decision makers can point to a "winning" vendor.

Negotiating the Contract

Contract terms and their negotiations can be extensive. Understandably, practitioners are disadvantaged when negotiating with IT vendors who have vastly more experience and their own (not the practice's) interests in mind. Use of a lawyer experienced in IT contract-related issues is helpful.[20]

The sidebar below outlines contract issues, which may or may not be relevant or appropriate depending upon the size and scope of the IT investment.

Possible Contract Issues

- Product definition (how components are defined)
- Scope of the license (for example, nontransferable or the definition of authorized users)
- Pricing (total costs and ongoing costs)
- Implementation work plan (the steps and their timing)
- Personnel (for implementation and training)
- Payment terms
- Performance warranties
- Remedies and liability
- Change in vendor control
- Product obsolescence
- Exit strategies

Practices should remember to include provisions in the contract that address the practice's recourse should the vendor close or the product be discontinued. To reduce its risk, a practice should incorporate several elements into its vendor contracts:

- The technical approach and financial ramifications of exporting clinical data from the EHR to another application or database; and
- Data ownership and access—including the reversion of data to the practice in a usable form and format in the case of a vendor merger, acquisition, or closure.

IMPLEMENTATION PLANNING

Once the vendor product has been selected and the contract is signed (or even sooner as part of the contract negotiation process), practices will need to develop an implementation plan. A well-balanced implementation team is critical to developing new practice workflows and managing change. The team should include a designated project lead; representatives of physicians, nurses, and front-and back-office staff; and

IT support as appropriate to the practice. In small practices, this team may simply consist of a physician and the practice manager.

Vendors will often provide an initial implementation plan, but practices will need to confirm the necessary tasks, responsibilities, and time frames. The plan should spell out appropriate and realistic expectations for the practice, and should reflect the level of implementation support available from both the vendor and from practice-based staff.

Key components of an implementation plan include:

- Determining whether the product will be implemented in phases or will be rolled out all at once;
- Installing and testing the required technical infrastructure;
- Redesigning the practice's clinical and administrative processes;
- Configuring and testing the application and preloading patient data;
- Training clinicians and staff; and
- Monitoring the implementation's success against the practice's objectives.

A brief description of each follows.

Phased Implementation or All at Once?

The implementation plan needs to reflect whether the practice wishes to implement the EHR in a staged, modular manner, or all at once as a comprehensive system. This decision is often based on the initial objectives of the practice—reflecting what the practice set out to achieve—and its appetite or tolerance for change. The resulting decision dictates how the application will be configured, the technology tools deployed, and the training conducted. Some practices choose to roll out the application or any of its individual modules to one or more physicians as a short-term "pilot" to test the effectiveness of the product in achieving the practice's objectives. The more functionally complex the product, the more important is a dry run to learn what should be changed or enhanced before full roll-out. Piloting is also much more important in a large physician practice or medical group.

Technical Infrastructure

The technical infrastructure must be in place and any problems addressed before the new application goes live. Most vendors recommend the minimum level of computer hardware and software that will be required to support their applications, but they neither provide the equipment nor manage the actual implementation of these components. Practices that lack the IT savvy themselves often turn to local resources in the community (including computer retailers, resellers and independent contractors) to install the necessary infrastructure including:

- Network capabilities (including Internet access and wiring of exam rooms and offices); and
- Desktop and related hardware (including desktop and laptop computers, scanners, hand-held devices and printers).[16]

Some of the EHR products require high-speed Internet access, which can be obtained through a local Internet service provider or a local telephone or cable operator. Where technically and financially feasible, practices should also consider options for redundancy in case any critical portion of the technical infrastructure should fail. Keeping an extra computer or mobile device on hand and installing a failover dial-up line can prevent panic should key components fail on a busy clinical day. It is crucial for practices that maintain the EHR database within their own physical facilities to make regular, frequent back-up copies of the database, and store the back-ups securely —preferably at an off-site location.

If integration between the EHR and other IT applications (such as a practice management or billing system) is required, interfaces also need to be developed, tested, and operational before users go live on the system.[21] The vendors of both the EHR product and the other interfaced application will probably each need to be involved in this endeavor.

Finally, the location of computers, printers, and other hardware must support the practice's expected workflow and planned patient interactions. For example, practices using desktop devices in exam rooms configure them so that patients can view their own record and any Web-based information alongside the practitioner. An increasing number of practices use mobile user devices with wireless connectivity because of the flexibility this provides over hardwired devices.

Redesigning Processes

As stated previously, any clinical and administrative process redesign must fully reflect the organization's strategic objectives and must *precede* system set-up and implementation. Practices should identify processes that are ineffective or that do not support the future vision so that they can configure the EHR to effectively support the desired-state workflow. This step can entail significant effort if the practice elects to implement uniform care standards across the practice (an effort that is easily supported by an EHR).

Configuring the Application and Preloading Patient Data

Preparing the EHR application for use by the practice requires loading clinical reference data sets; building the core tools and templates that physicians will use for documentation and related workflow support; and loading essential patient data into the application.

Loading clinical reference data such as diagnosis codes, therapy codes and codes necessary for billing is typically provided for by the vendor. Practices may have multiple options among which to choose, and they will likely need to adapt or configure the available code sets for their own use.

Most vendors provide instructions and tools for building templates to document a visit and support other related workflow processes, though a smaller number provide the actual templates and forms *themselves* that the practice can use outright. For the EHR products in which clinical decision support tools are available, the actual rules that trigger alerts and inform physicians are rarely provided by the vendor. Practices can sometimes turn to other customers of the vendor to obtain examples of their forms, templates and decision support rules. Vendor user groups are a good forum for exchanging practical examples of these. The EHR's forms and templates and the rules on which they rely are not only critical components of the EHR's functionality, but they dictate the clinical workflow of the patient visit and all of the other critical processes in the practice. As such, the development of these templates and rules is one of the most critical parts of building the application and preparing for an effective implementation.

Because clinical data are the building blocks for many of the technology-enhanced practice changes, practices must determine which critical data are going to be included in an EHR, and how historical data are going to be transferred from the practice's paper records and other sources. By preloading historical patient data in advance of go-live, which is advised whenever possible, the practice can significantly increase the value of the electronic record for providers at the outset. Having physicians build electronic records from scratch is extremely time-consuming, reduces productivity significantly for a period of time, is almost guaranteed to reduce physician enthusiasm and acceptance, and increases the time period to achieve a steady state (when physicians can rely on the EHR for most of their patients most of the time). Involving physicians in considering these tradeoffs is important.

Transitioning from paper-based records to an EHR typically involves identifying a minimal data set (such as current medications, active problems, and recent test results) for a subset of the practice's patient population (defined, for example, as those patients who have been seen in the last 18 months, those who have upcoming appointments, or those with certain chronic illnesses). These historical data can be entered into the EHR in advance by local medical records staff or nurses or by a contracted physician or nurse; can be summarized by the physician and entered in advance by clinical support staff, or can be input into the EHR as patients are seen for the first time once the practice is "live" on the EHR. Electronic scanning of previous medical records is not usually recommended as a conversion approach because it is time-consuming and costly, and because scanning does not provide for the structured data necessary for automated decision support or population analysis.

In some cases, patients' paper charts may still be needed during the initial months (or years) while the practice is migrating to the EHR. As availability of online patient information increases, so too does the efficiency, reliability, and relationship-related benefits that can be achieved.

Training Clinicians and Staff

The implementation plan must consider training for physicians, other clinicians, and staff—not just on the application but for basic computer skills that might be needed. Some vendors offer a number of training options, including remote, Web-based training and computer-based training on CD-ROM. In most cases, vendors will train a selected staff member at the vendor's office, and then expect that staff member to train other members of the practice. Regardless of the training mode, the provision of training to physicians as close to go-live as possible allows for better retention of the new system functionality.

Practices sometimes use family members and friends as simulated patients in mock patient visits one morning or evening before the go-live date to help physicians become more comfortable with the new application and workflow and reduce their anxiety about what can go wrong. It is also critical to train staff with the actual screens and screen flows they will be using. Role-based training both shortens training session time and brings end users up the learning curve faster than generalized training. Staff lacking computer skills altogether can benefit from a basic course to become familiar with computer navigation before being trained to use the EHR.

Monitoring and Maintaining Implementation Goals and Technology

As a final step of implementation, the team should revisit the practice's objectives and goals and ensure they are making adequate progress toward meeting those. Regular communication is essential for ongoing performance improvement. Lessons learned need to be shared throughout the practice so that all staff benefit from their colleagues' experience.

The systems and technology require maintenance and ongoing support themselves. The level of required maintenance will depend on the structure of the application and the hosting arrangement. For example, a practice using a remotely-hosted application through an ASP or hospital will have fewer maintenance responsibilities than the practice that is running its own application.

Practices using remote-hosted applications will want to ensure that the vendor or host entity provides adequate assurances and information about the expected level of system up time; down-time procedures; the escalation process for addressing system problems; and how and when system upgrades will occur.

Practices running their own system applications will want to secure information from the vendor about:

- Maintaining an ideal system configuration and how to effectively support the application going forward;
- Accomplishing system backups; and
- When software upgrades will occur, how these will affect the practice, and how to best prepare for them.

Astute vendors provide practices as much preventive maintenance information as possible to increase the practice's ability to minimize unexpected problems and ensure the application is running optimally.

CONCLUDING COMMENTS

The EHR is critical to achieving the new vision for medical practice described in this book, one characterized by enhanced patient-physician relationships, high quality care with increased reliability, and better service. An increasing number of medical practices, both large and small, are integrating IT tools that range from simple, single-function products to comprehensive, multi-function EHR applications.

Many factors are changing the landscape to help make this possible: Vendors are offering a better mix of integrated and stand-alone products; computers and other technology are playing a bigger role in physicians' lives; and financial incentives are making it increasingly desirable and possible to bring EHRs into the ambulatory setting.

The key to success requires that everyone in the practice buys in, rolls up their sleeves, and approaches the task with the end result in mind. It is not easy work, but an increasing number of practices have done it and done it well. Success stories abound.

Practitioners need only read about the primary care[22] or organizational[23] Davies Award winners, listen to presentations at professional meetings, read the medical literature, or talk with peers in their community. All such stories attest to this fact: Physician practices and clinics can be successful in using the EHR to help them achieve major benefits for their patients, improvements in their own work environment, and increased satisfaction in delivering good care and service.

References

1 Miller J (ed). *Implementing the Electronic Health Record: Case Studies and Lessons for Success.* Chicago: HIMSS; 2005.

2 MacDonald K, Metzger J. *Achieving Tangible IT Benefits in Small Physician Practices.* Prepared for California HealthCare Foundation; September 2002.

3 Integrated Healthcare Association, www.IHA.org.

4 Doctors' Office Quality Information Technology (DOQ-IT), www.DOQIT.org.

5 Anderson MR. AC Group Releases 2004 EHR Survey. July 15, 2004. Available at www.acgroup.org (accessed Apr 11, 2005).

6 Cooper JD. Organization, management, implementation and value of EHR implementation in a solo pediatric practice. *J Healthcare Info Mgmt.* Summer 2003; 18(3):51-55.

7 American Academy of Family Physicians Center for Health Information Technology. Establish the EHR Team. www.aafp.org/x3873.xml (accessed April 11, 2005).

8 MacDonald K, Metzger J: *Achieving Tangible IT Benefits in Small Physician Practices.* Prepared for California HealthCare Foundation; September 2002, p 16. Available at www.chcf.org.

9 Institute of Medicine. *Key Capabilities of an Electronic Health Record System.* Washington, DC: National Academies Press; July 2003.

10 Barrett MJ, Holmes BJ, McAulay SE. *Electronic Medical Records: A Buyer's Guide for Small Physician Practices.* Prepared for California HealthCare Foundation by Forrester Research; October 2003.

11 Health Level Seven. HL7 Partners with Private and Public Healthcare Leaders to Develop Electronic Health Record (EHR) System Functional Model and Standard. [Press release] July 18, 2003. Available at: www.hl7.org/press/20030718.asp (accessed April 11, 2005).

12 www.cchit.org.

13 HIMSS. Industry Leaders Launch Health Information Technology Product Certification Initiative. [Press release] July 21, 2004. Available at: www.himss.org/pressroom (accessed April 11, 2005).

14 Barrett MJ, Holmes BJ, McAulay SE. *Electronic Medical Records: A Buyer's Guide for Small Physician Practices.* Prepared for California HealthCare Foundation by Forrester Research; October 2003, pp 9-10.

15 Metzger J. *Using Computerized Registries in Chronic Disease Care.* Prepared for California HealthCare Foundation by First Consulting Group; February 2004.

16 MacDonald K, Metzger J. *Achieving Tangible IT Benefits in Small Physician Practices.* Prepared for California HealthCare Foundation; September 2002, p 27. Available at www.chcf.org.

17 Metzger J, Turisco F. *Computerized Physician Order Entry: A Look at the Vendor Marketplace and Getting Started.* First Consulting Group; December 2001.

18 Wang SJ, Middleton B, Prosser LA, et al. A cost-benefit analysis of electronic medical records in primary care. *Am J Med.* April 1, 2003; 114:397-403.

19 Anderson MR. AC Group Releases 2004 EHR Survey; July 15, 2004, p 8. Available at www.acgroup.org (accessed Apr 11, 2005).

20 Dotting the I's and crossing the T's: Ensuring the best IT contracts. *Healthcare Finan. Mgmt.* February 2004; 58(2): IT2-31.

21 Leavitt M. Electronic Medical Records, Chapter 17 in Davidson PL (ed): *Healthcare Information Systems.* New York: Auerbach Publications; 2000.

22 http://www.himss.org/ASP/davies_primarycare.asp.

23 http://www.himss.org/ASP/davies_organizational.asp.

Selected Bibliography

AC Group, Inc. *ACG 2003 Annual Report on Computer Systems in Physicians' Offices: Electronic Medical Records—Return on Investmen;* May 2003.

Medical Records Institute. Sixth Annual Survey of Electronic Health Record Trends and Usage for 2004, July 2004.

Metzger J, MacDonald K. *Clinical Decision Support for the Independent Physician Practice.* I-Health Report Series, Prepared for California HealthCare Foundation by First Consulting Group; October 2002.

Metzger J, McCaskey J, Schlusberg C, et al. *The Importance of Clinical Data Standards.* First Consulting Group; February 2004.

Miller RH, Sim I, Newman J. *Electronic Medical Records: Lessons from Small Physician Practices.* Prepared for California HealthCare Foundation by University of California, San Francisco; October 2003.

Terry K. Doctors and EHRs. *Medical Economics.* 28:2, 72-84.

Section IV

The Changing Environment

CHAPTER 9

The Federal Government's Impact on Medical Practice and Information Technology Adoption

David W. Roberts, MPA, FHIMSS, and Thomas M. Leary, MALA

HISTORICAL PERSPECTIVE: EVOLUTION OF THE GOVERNMENT'S ROLE IN HEALTHCARE

Regulation of Pharmaceuticals and Medical Devices

Prior to the nineteenth century, medical practice was basically a private profession in which patients paid for services rendered and hospitals were largely charitable institutions. States exercised the principal control over domestically produced and distributed drugs and controls were markedly inconsistent from state to state.

Commercial abuses, as well as unsafe drugs and products, led to a public call for regulation. This regulation was the beginning of the formation of the U.S. Food and Drug Administration (FDA). The FDA is a scientific, regulatory, and public health agency that now oversees items accounting for 25 cents of every dollar spent by consumers. Its jurisdiction encompasses human and animal drugs, therapeutic agents of biological origin, medical devices, and radiation-emitting products for consumer, medical, and occupational use. The FDA has grown from a single chemist in the U.S. Department of Agriculture in 1862 to a staff of approximately 9,100 employees and a budget of $1.4 billion in 2005.

The FDA remained under the Department of Agriculture until June 1940, when the agency was moved to the new Federal Security Agency. In April 1953, the agency was transferred again, this time to the Department of Health, Education, and Welfare (HEW). Fifteen years later the FDA became part of the Public Health Service within HEW, and in May 1980 the education function was removed from HEW to create the Department of Health and Human Services (HHS), the FDA's current home.

With the election of President Franklin Roosevelt in 1930, the FDA had a receptive ear for needed changes in the law that mandated quality and identity standards for drugs and prohibited false therapeutic claims for drugs. Change was also influenced by a new generation of journalists and consumer protection organizations. Legislation was finally passed in 1937 following a therapeutic disaster in which a Tennessee drug company marketed a form of the new sulfa drug that contained an untested and highly toxic chemical that killed over 100 people, many of whom were children. The public outcry not only reshaped the drug provisions of the new law to prevent such an event from happening again, but propelled the bill itself rapidly through Congress.

The new law extended regulation to cosmetics and medical devices, and required that drugs be labeled with adequate directions for safe use. It created a pre-market approval process for all new drugs, requiring manufacturers to submit evidence of safety and effectiveness to the FDA. It strictly prohibited false therapeutic claims for drugs, although a separate law granted the Federal Trade Commission jurisdiction over drug advertising.

The Government's Role in Public Health

The development of the Public Health Service (PHS) also began in the nineteenth century. The origins of the PHS can be traced to the passage of an act in 1798 that provided for the care and relief of sick and injured merchant seamen. The earliest marine hospitals created to care for the seamen were located along the East Coast and loosely networked in an organization called the Marine Hospital Service. The scope of activities of the Marine Hospital Service began to expand beyond the care of merchant seamen in the closing decades of the nineteenth century, beginning with the control of infectious diseases. Responsibility for quarantine was originally a function of the states rather than the federal government, but the National Quarantine Act of 1878 conferred quarantine authority on the Marine Hospital Service. Over the course of the next half century, the Marine Hospital Service increasingly took over quarantine functions from state authorities.

As immigration increased dramatically in the late nineteenth century, the federal government also took over from the states the processing of immigrants, beginning in 1891. The Marine Hospital Service was assigned responsibility for medical examination of immigrants arriving at sites such as New York's Ellis Island, with commissioned officers playing a major role.

The Service continued to expand its public health activities as the nation entered the twentieth century. As the century progressed, PHS commissioned officers served their country by controlling the spread of contagious diseases such as smallpox and yellow fever, conducting important biomedical research, providing healthcare to underserved groups, supplying medical assistance in the aftermath of disasters, and in numerous other ways. Today, the PHS is the largest public health program in the world, and like the FDA, is part of HHS.

The Government's Role in Financing Healthcare

During the twentieth century, "Great Society" programs such as Medicare and Medicaid, financed by taxes, extended health benefits to the elderly and the poor. This evolution continued the federal government's deeper involvement in healthcare. During the latter half of the twentieth century, healthcare technology became more tied to health quality, and more sophisticated and expensive financing mechanisms were needed. The rise of employer-sponsored health insurance provided financing mechanism to cover working families. Today, with government as the largest purchaser of healthcare, and healthcare one of the most highly government-regulated industry, the two are inextricably intertwined.

The Government's Role Today as the Largest Purchaser of Healthcare

The U.S. spent $1.679 trillion on healthcare in 2003, according to new statistics from the Centers for Medicare and Medicaid Services (CMS), up 7.7% from 2002. Healthcare now consumes 15.3% of the country's gross domestic product, the world's largest outlay. Healthcare spending is about 4.3 times the amount spent on national defense. The amount spent per person from all sources increased 69% from 1993 to 2003.

Of the $1.679 trillion spent on personal healthcare in this country in 2003, Medicare accounts for almost 19% or $259 billion. Spending by all public programs, including Medicare, Medicaid, SCHIP (State Children's Health Insurance Program), and other programs, accounts for 44% of healthcare spending. Medicare is the largest single purchaser of healthcare in the U.S. Thirty-six percent of spending is from private health insurance payers and 16% is consumer out-of-pocket spending.[1]

The Medicare and Medicaid reimbursement methodologies have exerted a powerful impact on the delivery of healthcare. In 1983, the hospital payment system was reformed with the introduction of Diagnostic Related Groupings (DRGs). This new methodology introduced case-specific payments to hospitals based on diagnosis, age, gender, and complications. Thus, payment was transformed from *retrospective*—reimbursing for actual services rendered—to *prospective*, paying for the expected needs of the patient.

Physician reimbursement methodologies, and their influence on provider behavior, are further discussed in Chapter 10. Although government is the largest single payer for physician services, the reform of payment methodologies has not progressed at the same rate as it has for hospitals. While prospective payment using *capitation*—a fixed monthly fee for "managing" a patient—was introduced by managed care organizations in the 1980s, the vast majority of government payments to physicians remain on a fee-for-service basis. In the face of growing national concern about total healthcare spending, the government's setting of physician fee schedules has become a politically contentious process.

It is generally acknowledged that the present fee-for-service system locks in current behavior patterns. This current system produces systematic bias in pricing, in which new procedures get the most recently updated rates, and traditional services are tied to former rates subject to annual limits on increases. This system creates a major gap in value, driving disproportionate resource allocation into specialist practice and high-tech procedures. Above all, the current lack of reimbursement for use of appropriate information technology has severely limited the diffusion of these tools to improve care.

LEGAL AND REGULATORY BARRIERS TO INFORMATION TECHNOLOGY

While the reimbursement system described above exerts a major influence on the medical practice, certain laws and regulation have been considered additional barriers to the adoption of information technology. A 2004 GAO report[1] highlighted the impact of these laws.

While a benefit of information technology is its ability to seamlessly *connect* the physician practice to other entities in the healthcare system—hospitals, laboratories, and other practices—two federal laws closely regulate the relationships between a physician and those other entities. The first is the Stark physician self-referral law and the second is the Medicare and Medicaid anti-kickback law. Both have related statutes for implementation, and extremely strong penalties for noncompliance.

The Stark Law

The physician self-referral law, also known as the Stark law, prohibits a physician from making a referral to an entity with which the physician or any member of the physician's immediate family has a financial relationship, if the referral is for furnishing of a designated health service, and prohibits the entity from submitting the claim to Medicare or Medicaid for the service, unless an appropriate exception applies.

Common areas of risk under the Stark law include all relationships with hospitals, including medical director contracts, recruiting arrangements, personal service contracts, equipment leases, office leases, and the provision of free or below-market services by physicians to hospitals, or by hospitals to physicians.

The original Stark law ("Stark I"), enacted in 1989, prohibited only self-interested referrals for clinical laboratory services. In 1993, Congress broadened the Stark law ("Stark II") to include referrals of a broad array of "designated health services." In 1995, HHS published final regulations to implement Stark I. HHS then proposed regulations in January 1998 that addressed Stark II.

The final Stark II regulations are substantively different in a number of respects and provide physicians and other contracting parties more flexibility than originally anticipated under the proposed regulations. In fact, due to significant changes from the proposed regulations, HHS announced that it would issue the Stark II Regulations in phases. Regulations for Phase I were issued on January 4, 2001, and restate or modify definitions used throughout the Stark law; they also confirm or amend the description of arrangements that are exempt from the law. Phase II regulations will be issued in 2005; they will address the remainder of Stark II including additional exceptions to the law and will clarify the Stark law's application to the Medicaid Program.

The Anti-Kickback Law

The anti-kickback law provides both criminal and civil penalties for individuals and entities that knowingly offer, pay, solicit or receive bribes or kickbacks or other remuneration in order to induce business reimbursable by Medicare, Medicaid, or other governmental programs. The anti-kickback law may be distinguished from the Stark law in a number of important ways:

- The anti-kickback law applies to all services covered under the governmental programs, not merely the list of designated health services set forth above.
- The anti-kickback law provides civil as well as criminal penalties, while the Stark law provides only civil penalties.
- The anti-kickback law covers all individuals or entities guilty of prohibited conduct, while the Stark law covers only physicians.
- The anti-kickback law requires a showing of intent to violate the law.
- The safe harbors under the anti-kickback law are optional, unlike the Stark exceptions, which are mandatory.

GAO ESTIMATES POTENTIAL HEALTHCARE SAVINGS FROM IT ADOPTION

On October 31, 2003, the Government Accountability Office (GAO), the investigative arm of Congress, issued a 125-page report[2] at the request of Senator Edward Kennedy (D-MA) on the value of information technology (IT) to improve healthcare. The purpose of the study was to identify cost savings and other benefits reported by healthcare organizations that have implemented IT both in providing clinical healthcare and in administrative functions associated with healthcare delivery.

The GAO analyzed information from ten private and public healthcare delivery organizations, three healthcare insurers, and one community data network. The GAO found that the rapidly rising costs of healthcare, along with an increasing concern for the quality of care and the safety of patients, are driving healthcare organizations to use IT to automate clinical care operations and their associated administrative functions. The GAO found that IT is now being used for electronic medical records, order management and results reporting, patient care management, and Internet access for patient and provider communications, as well as automated billing and financial management. Those facilities analyzed in this study reported cost savings resulting from the use of IT, including reduction of costs associated with medication errors, communication and documentation of clinical care and test results, staffing and paper storage, and processing of information. Benefits included improved quality of care, more accurate and complete medical documentation, more accurate capture of codes and charges, and improved communications among providers that enabled them to respond more quickly to patients' needs. A 2005 GAO update on the topic[3] provided further support to the potential benefits of IT adoption.

LEGISLATION WITH SIGNIFICANT IMPACTS ON MEDICAL PRACTICE AND INFORMATION TECHNOLOGY

Medicare Modernization Act (MMA) of 2003

The Medicare Prescription Drug, Improvement, and Modernization Act of 2003 has been called the biggest expansion of the government-run health system for the elderly since its creation 38 years ago, adding prescription drug coverage and greater private competition to Medicare. Numerous provisions in this legislation will have an impact on medical practice and the role of information technology.

- Section 101 (Electronic Prescribing Provisions). Under this section, not later than September 1, 2005, the Secretary of HHS must establish initial standards for e-prescribing based on input from the National Committee on Vital and Health Statistics. From January 1 through December 31, 2006, the legislation mandates a voluntary pilot demonstration project be carried out to test the selected initial standards. From January 1 through March 31, 2007, the HHS Secretary must evaluate the results of the demonstration project and issue a report to Congress on this evaluation not later than April 1, 2007. On April 1, 2008, the Secretary of HHS will issue final electronic prescribing standards. This section also specifies that each CMS-endorsed discount drug card program would implement a system to reduce the likelihood of medication errors and adverse drug interactions and to improve medication use.
- Section 108 provides for grants to physicians to implement electronic prescription drug programs. It requires 50% matching funds from non-federal sources; $50 million is authorized for FY07 and additional funds as needed are authorized for FY08 and FY09.
- Section 238 provides for the Institute of Medicine (IOM) to study performance measures within 18 months. The goal is to align performance to payment for service. The report will identify key data and information technology requirements.
- Section 417 provides for extension of telemedicine demonstrations for up to eight years and doubles the available authorized funding to $60 million. This conference position was consistent with Sec. 415 (House bill) and Sec. 441 (Senate bill) that provided for Medicare healthcare demonstration programs.
- Section 649 proposes a three-year CMS pay-for-performance demonstration program using healthcare information technology at four separate sites.
- Section 942 establishes a new Council for Technology and Innovation within CMS.
- Section 1012 proposed the creation of a new 11-member commission to focus on standards development acceleration and adoption. The commission is directed to finalize a report of recommendations for Congress no later than October 31, 2005.
- Section 1014 calls for a national debate led by a 15-member commission to conduct community meetings around the nation on how to improve healthcare. Politicians and association advocates are specifically prohibited from serving on the commission. This proposal resulted from a Senate bill provision (Sec. 620) that provided for the establishment of a Citizens' Healthcare Working Group, through the Agency for Healthcare Research and Quality (AHRQ), to engage the American public in the national debate over choices about the services they want covered, what healthcare coverage they want, and how they are willing to pay for coverage.
- Section 1016 includes $200 million in grant funding over 54 months for loans to providers to implement technology. This provision resulted from the Senate bill (Sec. 608 and 609) that provided for improvements in the healthcare infrastructure and for the establishment of a Capital Infrastructure Revolving Loan Program.

Other Recent Healthcare IT Legislative Initiatives

The 109th Congress took office in January 2005 and immediately continued the debate over how to improve the quality of healthcare utilizing technology. A few bills that did not pass into law in the 108th Congress are being considered again during the 109th Congress.

H.R. 663 and S. 720 (Patient Safety and Quality Improvement Act)
These are companion bills submitted into the House and Senate that contain a number of provisions to improve patient safety. They include establishing a Medical Information Technology Advisory Board to make recommendations to the HHS Secretary regarding medical information technology, including: (1) the best current practices in medical information technology; and (2) methods of implementing records security.

H.R. 2915 (National Health Information Infrastructure Act of 2003)
This is a piece of legislation directing the HHS Secretary to appoint a National Health Information Officer for HHS to maintain national leadership in the planning, development, and adoption of a national health information infrastructure. It also directs the Secretary to develop or adopt (and periodically update) voluntary, national data and communications standards that promote the interoperability of health information technology (HIT) systems across all public and private health care settings.

H.R. 3035 (Medication Errors Reduction Act of 2003)
This bill proposed to establish an informatics grant program for hospitals and skilled nursing facilities in order to encourage healthcare providers to make major information technology advances for systems that use common data standards.

S. 2570 (The Health Care Assurance Act)
This bill is being offered as a vehicle to address concerns with the U.S. healthcare system, particularly to improve Americans' health and reduce healthcare costs by reorienting the nation's healthcare system towards prevention, wellness, and self care. While the primary purpose of this legislation is to provide healthcare coverage for all Americans who are currently uninsured, the legislation's $540 billion price tag over the next 10 years would be offset by improving program integrity and efficiency, reducing medical errors, increasing the use of medical technology, and increasing preventive health measures, including improving healthcare quality and consumer education.

The legislation includes a provision that would provide for demonstration programs to test best practices for reducing errors, testing the use of appropriate technologies to reduce medical errors (e.g., hand-held electronic medication systems), and research in geographically diverse locations to determine the causes of medical errors. To assist in the private sector's development of needed technology standards, this legislation would provide for ways to examine the use of information technology and coordinate actions by the federal government to ensure that this investment will further the national health information and infrastructure. This section of the legislation is projected to save $150 billion over the next ten years.

THE GOVERNMENT AS A DIRECT HEALTHCARE PROVIDER: THE DEPARTMENTS OF DEFENSE AND VETERANS AFFAIRS

As seen above, the federal government has become progressively more involved in financing healthcare for large sectors of the country's population. Concurrently, the executive branch and its agencies have become a substantial direct provider of healthcare, as the Departments of Defense (DoD) and Veterans Affairs (VA) fulfill their mission to provide healthcare for America's former and current military members and their eligible dependents.

Department of Defense

For the DoD, providing healthcare to military personnel dates back to the colonial era. Over time, Congress expanded the requirement to include family members, retirees, and other eligible beneficiaries. The passage of the Civilian Health and Medical Program of the Uniformed Services (CHAMPUS) in 1966 began the modern era requirements for care that have had a significant impact on the business processes of care delivery.

By the 1980s, the search for ways to improve access to quality medical care, while keeping costs under control, led to several CHAMPUS "demonstration" projects in various parts of the United States. After several years of working through the demonstration process, the CHAMPUS Reform Initiative program was expanded to a uniform, multi-tiered program known today as the TRICARE program. As the clinical care delivery model was being changed, the Military Health System (MHS) leadership began developing electronic solutions to aid clinicians in care delivery. Most notably, the Composite Health Care System (CHCS) expanded military medicine's ability to provide quality care, reduce errors, and increase efficiency. The CHCS system allowed laboratory, radiology, scheduling, and eligibility information to be gathered and managed electronically, and gave providers capabilities that, along with computerized provider order entry (CPOE), were designed to improve the quality of care delivery within the MHS. CHCS is deployed around the world to gather clinical data on over 50 million outpatient appointments and 70 million prescription transactions annually.

As technology has improved, CHCS has been augmented by over 40 clinical data systems, which has required the MHS to develop a fully functioning electronic health record (EHR). As electronic capabilities have evolved, so have the MHS's requirements. The system is now in the process of deploying the Composite Health Care System II (CHCS II) program. When completely deployed, CHCS II will fully integrate the MHS's 75 hospitals and 435 clinics around the world under one EHR that allows data to be accessible anywhere in the world.

Veterans Affairs

Throughout their history, similar challenges faced the VA. As medical procedures have advanced, military personnel have returned from the battlefield with wounds they would not have survived in previous wars. This has placed enormous budgetary demands on the clinical care provided at VA facilities. The VA has expanded its healthcare delivery to meet the needs of these returning heroes and has had to develop business processes to keep pace with changing clinical environments.

Recognizing the need to integrate HIT solutions into the business processes, in 1985 the VA developed the Decentralized Hospital Computer Program (DHCP). The DHCP was transformed into the Veterans Health Information Systems and Technology Architecture (VistA) in the 1990s. The evolution of the VA to a cabinet-level agency occurred in 1989, just prior to the Gulf War. With the change came increased responsibility and visibility of the programs the VA initiated. Throughout the 1990s, the VA sought to improve the quality and efficiency of care. Like the MHS, a multi-tiered care model was adopted that required more clinical data to improve clinical decision support. The evolution of the health IT systems incorporated the Computerized Patient Record System (CPRS). Released in 1997, the CPRS system created a single interface for clinicians to access and review patient information using real-time order entry and clinical alerts.

The philosophy has continued with the VA's latest move to the HealtheVet-VistA program, which is expected to enhance the flexibility of care delivery through advances in technology that connect the clinicians to the veterans and families.

In unfavorable federal budget environments, a great deal of emphasis is placed on government efficiency. Given that reality, the MHS and VA have taken steps to streamline the delivery of care between the two systems. The agencies have nearly completed a seven-year process to incorporate common vocabulary and data elements in their data systems. The program, formerly known as the Government Computerized Patient Record, evolved into a Federal Health Information Exchange, in which critical data was downloaded from the CHCS I system to the VistA system. As the government focus has increasingly emphasized interoperable systems, the MHS and VA have nearly completed information flow between the two systems on a bi-directional basis through the Joint Electronic Medical Record Interoperability Program. Although the impact of the Bi-Directional Health Information Exchange and the resulting collaborative effort on the Clincal and Health Data Repository has not yet been realized, it will demonstrate to the industry that interoperable data sharing in real time between disparate systems is possible.

Consolidated Health Informatics (CHI) Initiative

HHS, DoD, and VA have joined together in a partnership with a total of 23 federal agencies/departments who use health data for agreements to build adopted standards into their health IT architecture. The goal of this initiative is to set uniform data and messaging standards in 24 target domains for the electronic exchange of clinical health information to be adopted across the federal government. These standards are part of the foundation of the National Health Information Infrastructure (NHII) that will serve consumers, patients, health care providers and public health professionals. Standardized information exchange, with privacy and security protections, makes it easier for healthcare providers to share relevant patient information and for public health professionals to identify emerging public health threats. Standardized information exchange also makes portable electronic medical records more likely and easily achievable.

GOVERNMENT INFLUENCE THROUGH RESEARCH FUNDING

The government plays yet another highly significant role in its funding of healthcare research and development. Over the last 10 years, grant research funding from the National Institutes of Health (NIH) has increased from $10.6 billion in fiscal year 1994 to $28 billion in fiscal year 2004. Not surprisingly, the 27 institutes and centers have experienced an increase in grant proposal requests from 24,000 in fiscal year

1994 to 36,000 in fiscal year 2003. Federal funding has expanded to HIT initiatives, too. According to a 2005 congressional presentation, congressional program requests for HIT funding has increased dramatically over the past several years, as members of Congress began to learn the value of HIT from their constituents.

Within HHS, research into the application and benefits of HIT has been directed by AHRQ. With quality improvement and cost containment as key drivers for Medicare policy, CMS has turned to AHRQ for usable tools to measure quality outcomes. The Physician Focused Quality Initiative builds upon ongoing CMS strategies and engages the HIT community in programs designed to:

- Assess the quality of care for key conditions affecting many Medicare beneficiaries;
- Support clinicians in providing appropriate treatment of the conditions identified;
- Prevent health problems that are avoidable; and
- Investigate the concept of payment for performance.

Within the Physician Focused Quality Initiative, three projects have received national attention:

The Doctor's Office Quality (DOQ) Project: An integrated approach to measuring quality of care for chronic disease and preventive services in clinician offices, DOQ is being developed by Medicare Quality Improvement Organizations (QIOs) in Iowa, California, and New York.

The Doctor's Office Quality Information Technology (DOQ-IT) Project: Designed to promote the adoption and implementation of EHRs in small clinician offices to improve quality and outcomes, the DOQ-IT project calls upon QIOs to assist in implementation of IT in those settings. Piloted in four states, the program is entering a national roll-out phase.

In funding these projects, CMS sees HIT improvements as a way to improve quality and control costs to the Medicare and Medicaid programs. The first step is to achieve accurate data collection. When the data is sufficiently accurate, CMS will initiate pay for performance programs to reward top performers in a particular care setting. The impact of the program is expected to further the implementation of EHRs as well as quality improvement.

In October, 2004, AHRQ awarded $139 million in contracts and grants under its **Transforming Healthcare Quality through IT (THQ-IT) program,** with the following goals:

- Improve patient safety by reducing medical errors;
- Increase health information sharing between providers, labs, pharmacies, and patients;
- Help patients transition between healthcare settings;
- Reduce duplicative and unnecessary testing; and
- Increase knowledge and understanding of the clinical, safety, quality, financial, and organizational value and benefits of HIT.

Concurrently, AHRQ established the National Resource Center for Health IT to serve as a repository for lessons learned by the funded programs. The projects have received a second year of funding from Congress and will continue to expand.

THE GOVERNMENT'S ROLE IN THE PAY-FOR-PERFORMANCE AND PATIENT SAFETY MOVEMENTS

The government has taken a leadership role in bringing focus to both quality and patient safety. CMS has partnered with the National Quality Forum (NQF) to establish quality standards and is offering incremental bonus payments to hospitals that excel in meeting those standards. A parallel Medicare pay-for-performance program is also being piloted in the ambulatory care setting with several medical group practices. In recent public comments, Dr. Mark McClellan has forecast the eventual expansion of pay-for-performance methodologies to a substantial percentage of Medicare reimbursement.

At the same time NQF was established, the IOM was launching a three-phase process to assess the quality of care provided across the nation.

The first step in that process was publication of a landmark report, *To Err is Human: Building a Safer Health System* (1999), which concluded that between 44,000 and 98,000 people die annually in American health facilities due to medical errors. That report was followed by *Crossing the Quality Chasm: A New Health System for the 21st Century (2001)*, which made an urgent call to the healthcare industry to institute fundamental change in the healthcare community to improve the overall quality of care. That report stressed that reform around the margins is inadequate to address system ills. Finally, the third report in the IOM series, *Patient Safety, Achieving A New Standard of Care* (2003), offered a systems approach to moving patient safety beyond post-incident event reporting to a *culture of safety* that emphasizes prevention of medical errors through the incorporation of comprehensive patient safety data systems and decision-support tools.

Office of the National Coordinator for Health Information Technology

In an Executive Order issued on April 27, 2004, President George W. Bush called for widespread deployment of health information technology (HIT) within ten years. As part of this announcement, he formed the Office of the National Coordinator for Health Information Technology (ONCHIT) and selected David Brailer, MD, PhD, for this key position.

The president made clear that Dr. Brailer's job is to "move the country toward the broad adoption of an interoperable infrastructure for most Americans within ten years." An important aspect of the president's initiative is the development of a nationwide interoperable HIT infrastructure that can facilitate improvements in safety, quality, efficiency and care coordination. Former HHS Secretary Tommy Thompson made enhancing the quality and safety of healthcare for all Americans through better use and wider application of information technology one of his most important priorities; his successor, Michael Leavitt, has proposed to do the same.

In July 2004, industry interest in HIT and ONCHIT was evident when over 1,200 attendees participated in the launching of the Secretarial Summit on Health Information Technology to accelerate progress toward EHRs and other benefits of HIT for Americans. At the conference, HHS released the Framework for Strategic Action, which outlined the shared responsibilities of the public and private sectors in achieving the benefits of HIT:

- **Goal 1: Inform Clinical Practice:** Incentivize EHR adoption and create tools that ensure successful EHR implementation and use.
- **Goal 2: Interconnect Clinicians:** Identify interoperability as a major milestone for achieving improved healthcare delivery; encourage regional healthcare information exchanges and a national health information network.
- **Goal 3: Personalize Care:** Foster patient-centric care delivery and more informed healthcare consumers.
- **Goal 4: Improve Population Health:** Encourage the collection, analysis, and dissemination of timely and accurate information that impact public health.

In early November 2004, Dr. Brailer released a Request for Information (RFI) on the development of a National Health Information Network (NHIN). The RFI included a series of 24 questions divided into six major areas to assist respondents in their description of an NHIN:

- **General:** Definition and vision of an NHIN; key industry tools and healthcare environment barriers to achieving interoperability.
- **Organizational and Business Framework:** Business construct for developing an NHIN; necessary standards, policies, and organizational parameters.
- **Management and Operational Considerations:** Balancing public and private contributions taking into account competition, public domain, and future innovation.
- **Standards and Policies to Achieve Interoperability:** Outline role of necessary public-, private-, and association-based stakeholders.
- **Financial/Regulatory Incentives and Legal Considerations:** Suggested incentives and legal barriers that need to be addressed to ensure the greatest level of participation across the country.
- **NHIN Design:** Description of necessary technical architecture and success metrics.

The responses, which swelled to nearly 500 responses, were seen as historic in nature for endorsing a "Common Framework" to support improved health information exchange in the U.S. while protecting patient privacy. Word of transferred funds to ONCHIT to fund the projects has received strong support from industry. Funding and timeliness of next steps remain as of the writing of this chapter.

The appointment of Dr. Brailer—and the highly active and visible role he has taken—has greatly enhanced the leadership profile of the federal government in healthcare IT.

Certification Commission for Healthcare Information Technology

The report described above called for a number of key actions, one of which was the private sector certification of HIT products. In response to this call for action, three industry associations in healthcare information management and technology—AHIMA (American Health Information Management Association), HIMSS (Healthcare Information and Management Systems Society) and The Alliance (formerly NAHIT)—joined forces to launch the Certification Commission for Healthcare Information Technology (CCHIT) in the fall of 2004.

The Commission has announced its intent to create an efficient, credible, sustainable mechanism for the certification of HIT products. The goals of product certification are described as follows:

- To reduce the risk of HIT investment by providers;
- To ensure interoperability of HIT products with emerging local and national health information infrastructures;
- To enhance the availability of HIT incentives from public and private purchasers/ payers; and
- To accelerate the adoption of robust, interoperable HIT throughout the U.S. healthcare system.

In his presentations, the National Coordinator has frequently pointed out the existence of an adoption gap in IT utilization between large healthcare organizations and smaller physician practices. Accordingly, the Commission has responded by setting its initial scope to be the certification of EHR products for the physician office and other ambulatory care settings. CCHIT has announced its plans to have the initial certification requirements and processes in place for testing in the summer of 2005. Concurrently, the Commission plans to release a roadmap of certification plans one or more years into the future, to offer standards development organizations a timeline to work against as well as providing vendors a guide for their own development plans.

CONCLUDING COMMENTS

In 2004, President George W. Bush outlined a four-step plan to ensure that most Americans have an electronic, personal health record within the next 10 years. In launching the decade of HIT, the president outlined a plan whose goal is to assure better delivery of healthcare in the U.S.

As the decade of healthcare information technology has certainly begun, and the impact of governmental actions will be great, Ed Larsen, writing in his Standards Insight column, offers this insight:[4]

Computerizing medical records is not the objective; better care more efficiently delivered is. Physicians and other providers deliver care from disparate economic entities. So to create an economically viable market for EHR systems and the NHIN, we really must start at the top of the food chain, not the bottom. To succeed in transforming healthcare we, as individuals, and our intermediaries, albeit the federal government, states, or employers, must provide proper incentives to providers for using EHRs and incorporating EHR system functionality into care delivery. Incentives must be based on the flow of costs and benefits created by an EHR and EHR systems. Providers with a clear economic case will create the sustainable market and will be the economic engine for EHR systems, and ultimately, the NHIN.

References

1 GAO-04-991R. HHS's Efforts to Promote Health Information Technology and Legal Barriers to Its Adoption; August 2004. Available at www.gao.gov/new.items/d04991r.pdf.

2 GAO-04-224. Information Technology: Benefits Realized for Selected Health Care Functions; October 2003. Available at www.gao.gov/new.items/d04224.pdf.

3 GAO-05-309R. Health and Human Services' Estimate of Health Care Cost Savings Resulting from the Use of Information Technology; February 2005. Available at www.gao.gov/new.items/d05309r.pdf.

4 Larsen E. Standards Insight; January 2005. Available at www.himss.org/asp/topics_FocusDynamic.asp?faid=84.

Selected Bibliography

Centers for Medicare and Medicaid. Office of Actuary. National Health Accounts; 2004.

CHAPTER 10

Needed: Performance Sensitive Customers

Arnold Milstein, MD, MPH

Healthcare providers seek to perform well regardless of external reinforcement. However, the behaviors of their payor and consumer "customers" can have a profound influence on their success. This chapter addresses why and how customer behaviors have inhibited excellence in healthcare delivery, and how they must change to achieve quality-reliable, affordable, and personalized health care.

WHY IS HEALTHCARE PERFORMANCE ESPECIALLY PRONE TO FAILURE?

The Land of the Performance-Blind

Quality of care problems are mostly invisible to providers and consumers alike,[1] and most people, whether providers or consumers, will be indifferent to a problem they cannot see. The visibility of healthcare performance failure is dependent upon good moment-to-moment documentation of care processes and their outcomes. In today's antiquated paper record systems, much care is documented inaccurately, incompletely, and in a manner that cannot be deciphered. Gathering data about care quality is also prohibitively expensive because it requires locating paper charts and paying trained staff to search page by page. Because performance assessment is so challenging, most process flaws and preventable suboptimal outcomes remain unrecognized.

Psychological research suggests additional barriers to the visibility of failure. Clinicians may be especially prone to wishful thinking about avoiding bad outcomes. Or, they may be hesitant to acknowledge quality failures because of the "myth of perfect performance." Impediments to failure recognition by patients include an inability to pursue the level of detail needed to assess quality accurately, a bias toward trust of authority conferred by a practitioner's white coat and specialized education, and reduced critical faculties due to illness and its symptoms. Though patients want to trust health professionals, research suggests that active consumer vigilance improves clinical outcomes.

Failure to perceive *longitudinal* clinical outcomes and affordability is another impediment to recognizing performance shortfalls. Results over the course of the entire acute illness, or a year's worth of chronic illness, are much less salient than near-term cause and effect relationships. However, most healthcare outcomes are determined by clinical performance in treating chronic illnesses and ongoing preventive care. Assessing chronic and preventive care requires examination of cumulative processes and outcomes over periods of 12 months and beyond.

Mistaking Low Price for Longitudinal Cost-Efficiency

Not perceiving longitudinal financial outcomes has been equally handicapping. Most cost-efficiency performance judgments rest on the price of an individual visit or hospital day, *not* on the cost for the total stream of healthcare resources utilized over the length of a patient's acute illness or a year of chronic and preventive care.

Assessment of the "cost" of a car illustrates why unit price or other longitudinally narrow frames of reference are an inadequate signal of "cost" in healthcare. Car F (for failure) has a very low sticker price. Car E (for excellence) has a much higher sticker price. However, Car F is poorly built and likely to require "deep pockets" for repairs, gas and insurance throughout its lifetime. Car E is built to minimize longer term "total cost of ownership." In a market focused on "sticker price," substandard performance in cumulative "longitudinal cost-efficiency" is invisible. Waste occurs in four areas:

- ***Overuse of healthcare services:*** Representing a small percentage of total waste, overuse involves the use of treatments where risks have been shown to exceed expected health gains. Expansion of our condition-specific outcomes evidence base may show that the true size of this pool of wasted spending is much larger than the relatively small amount that we can currently pinpoint.
- ***Misuse of healthcare services:*** This also likely represents a relatively small fraction of measured current waste. It is waste as a consequence of failure to follow a best known protocol for treatment administration. The full cost consequences of misuse (for example, necessary surgery applied to the wrong side of the body) are unknown but "guesstimated" to be in the range of 5% of current healthcare spending.
- ***Unwanted "preference-sensitive" services and "supply-sensitive services":***[2] The latter offers no gain in health, quality of care, or patient satisfaction over large populations of patients. Services such as "borderline" admissions to hospitals and ICUs, repeat specialist visits, and lab and imaging studies represent the largest components of such waste. Together these two sources of waste represent a substantial fraction of measured total waste. They likely comprise more than 30% of current spending.
- ***Antiquated clinical work methods:*** These methods include over-reliance on human memory, individual clinician (rather than team) responsibility, paper records, and widespread gaps between most efficient known methods of delivering a service and "average" methods. This waste is estimated by some experts in industrial engineering to approximate 30% of current healthcare spending.

In summary, all stakeholders are mostly in the dark with respect to the level of quality and longitudinal cost-efficiency achieved by particular physicians, hospitals, and most treatment options. Americans have standardized performance measures for automobiles and appliances, but not for the industry that consumes a much greater share of their income and has a much greater impact on the quality of their lives.

PAYOR EFFORTS TO CREATE A PERFORMANCE-SENSITIVE ENVIRONMENT

In the late 1970s, managed care emerged. With the exception of globally capitated payment systems in scattered parts of the U.S., managed care focused on one-fourth of the value equation—low unit price, or longitudinal costs for a narrow service line such as primary care, over a short time frame (Table 10-1).

Table 10-1. Most Managed Care Addressed 25% of the Value Equation

	Single Care Event or Service	Longitudinal Total Stream of Care
Cost-efficiency	X	
Quality		

Stirred by multiple critical Institute of Medicine (IOM) reports, the managed care backlash and a weakened national economy, innovative payors are beginning to better assess and reward performance in all four quadrants of the value equation across all healthcare settings. Data inputs needed to measure and improve performance robustly can only be acquired through the adoption of electronic health records (EHRs). Provider payment methods and patient incentives that increase revenue flows to better performing providers that adopt EHRs and then use them to continuously improve performance must be adequately powered to drive perpetual significant gains. The alternative is that healthcare affordability and quality reliability continue to sag under the weight of increasingly valuable but complex biomedical technology advances.

Why must payors steeply incentivize comparative excellence, either via sharply performance-sensitive pricing or market share shift that favors better providers? No industry in any country has ever undergone dramatic change in work processes without compelling economic incentives. It was only when Japanese car makers brought the industry to death's door that U.S. car makers made fundamental changes in production methods and achieved major progress in quality and "total cost of ownership."

Adopting innovations such as EHRs exemplifies such a fundamental change in work methods. The usual pattern of favorable innovation diffusion can be slow. Speed depends upon the relative advantage offered by the innovation, its compatibility, complexity, trialability, and observability.[3] It can be many years before a third of the possible adopter population makes the change. This suggests that complete redesign of care as prescribed by the IOM[4] will likely happen slowly, absent much more performance-sensitive payor revenue flows to the healthcare industry. How are payors allying with consumers to hasten performance advances? Via *both* consumer-facing and/or provider-facing reforms.

FROM PERFORMANCE-BLIND TO PERFORMANCE-SENSITIVE

Consumer-Facing Reforms

These consist of educating as well as incentivizing consumers to select "better performing" doctors, hospitals, health/disease management programs, and treatment options. A pre-condition is having easily available performance comparisons or "transparency" for each of these four facets of care, and gearing consumer out-of-pocket costs to incentivize selection of better performing options. Informed consumer decision-making will require valid and easily understood performance comparisons among physicians (for example, a surgeon's complication rate), among hospitals by specific service lines (for example, a hospital's average total lung cancer treatment cost), and among treatment options (for example, patient satisfaction ratings from open versus closed biopsy of a suspected breast tumor).[5] Such comparisons generally are lacking. Most payors do not have enough claims experience with individual doctors or individual hospital service lines to allow statistically valid comparisons. Moreover, most plans are hesitant to pool their claims data with other plans for competitive reasons. A legislative solution to this impasse is suggested later in this chapter.

Though currently rudimentary, today's tiered health benefit plans represent a good foundation from which to build. Now small in absolute numbers, but projected to be offered by more than a quarter of employers by 2006,[6] tiered benefit and other consumer-directed health insurance offerings that include provider performance comparisons incentivize consumers to select better performing options, including self care and no care. They also may provide decision-support tools to facilitate such selections. The majority of Americans enrolled in consumer-directed health plans are in tiered models rather than in portable spending account models such as health savings accounts. Most current tiers are determined based on both cost-efficiency and quality measures for providers.

Research led by Meredith Rosenthal notes that decision support in consumer-directed plans, a critical link to help consumers make more informed choices, is still limited: "If (plans) are to succeed in optimizing consumers' utility from health benefit spending, careful attention needs to be paid to how well these models inform consumers about the consequences of their care selections." [7]

Provider-Facing Reforms: Paying More Favorable Unit Prices and/or Bonuses to Those Who Deliver More Quality With Less Spending

More than 90 private sector pay-for-performance or "P4P" programs have arisen in many forms and regions over the past five years. The Centers for Medicare and Medicaid (CMS) and a few state Medicaid agencies have launched several small pilots. Meredith Rosenthal summarized these[8] and derived two essential points. None of the programs approached a rewards potential of the 10% of provider total income widely believed necessary to induce substantial improvement efforts; and, likely as a consequence, no significant performance improvements have been documented. In the American multi-payor environment, the only likely method of exceeding the 10% threshold in most states would be to synchronize private insurer and CMS P4P programs. Since CMS is roughly equal in its spending to all private insurers combined, its P4P policies are widely regarded as leading candidates around which private insurers could most easily synchronize.

GOVERNMENT AS AN ANCHOR FOR MULTI-PAYOR PERFORMANCE SENSITIVITY

Via legislative enhancements, Congress could substantially boost private sector performance sensitivity. These include making its large claims databases available to other health plan sponsors, encouraging their reward of providers for excellence in quality and efficiency, and developing and maintaining a full set of standardized provider performance measures.

Congress could authorize the release of the CMS Medicare & Medicaid claims database to all health benefit plans, subject to strict beneficiary privacy protections via encryption and other methods. This would allow plans to improve their precision in measuring the longitudinal efficiency and quality of individual physicians, hospital departments, health and disease programs, and condition-specific treatment options.

Congress could use tax policy to encourage all health benefits plans to join CMS in rewarding providers for excellence in quality and longitudinal cost-efficiency and for adopting robust, interoperable EHRs. This could occur either by conditioning health benefits plans' tax deductibility on (1) more favorable plan payment for providers and treatment options that offer superior quality and longitudinal efficiency; and/or (2) lower out-of-pocket cost for patients who select them and participate in programs to reduce health risks.

Even in the absence of new legislation, CMS could promote the visibility of performance by funding the National Quality Forum (NQF) to develop and maintain a consensus-endorsed set of nationally standardized performance measures for public reporting of safety, timeliness, effectiveness, equity, patient centeredness, and longitudinal efficiency. Such a set could encompass all care delivery vehicles, including hospitals, individual physicians, health/disease management programs, and major treatment options.

The absence of performance transparency keeps U.S. hospitals, doctors, and consumers in the dark with respect to performance failure, unable to identify opportunities to make healthcare more affordable, and unmotivated to prioritize improvement. Quality measurements paired with longitudinal efficiency measurements would comprise a new navigational system by which consumers, providers, and insurers could improve health and slow per capita increases in healthcare spending.

THE ASPIRATIONS OF PERFORMANCE-SENSITIVE CUSTOMERS

The current U.S. healthcare payment system achieves only weak performance management by professionals, regulators and markets. Because comparative data are lacking, most providers think their performance is acceptable and consumers think their providers are performing acceptably. Performance transparency would enable providers and consumers to become much more aware of performance shortfalls compared with world-class benchmarks. However, transparency is necessary but likely not sufficient to motivate robust performance management.

The use of both types of performance-sensitive incentives (consumer-facing and provider-facing) is needed to speed EHR adoption and then harvest their full potential to facilitate performance improvement. Incentivized consumers will seek providers that offer the highest value. Incentivized providers will be motivated to discover continuously how to deliver more quality more affordably (Figure 10-1).

Incentives to achieve more health with less spending would also send a constructive signal to biomedical technology developers: the market will begin to judge and reward their work products less on their unit prices and more on their contribution to improving health and health care affordability. Such rewards would also emancipate physicians, hospitals and new treatment developers from the tyranny of a market that mostly assesses their value by the lowness of their unit prices.

The IOM has forecasted the form of the prize: a healthcare system that is transformed via continuous application of the six "care redesign imperatives" shown in Figure 10-2. Such a transformation depends on the emergence of "redesigned customers" who are highly sensitive to excellence in provider performance.

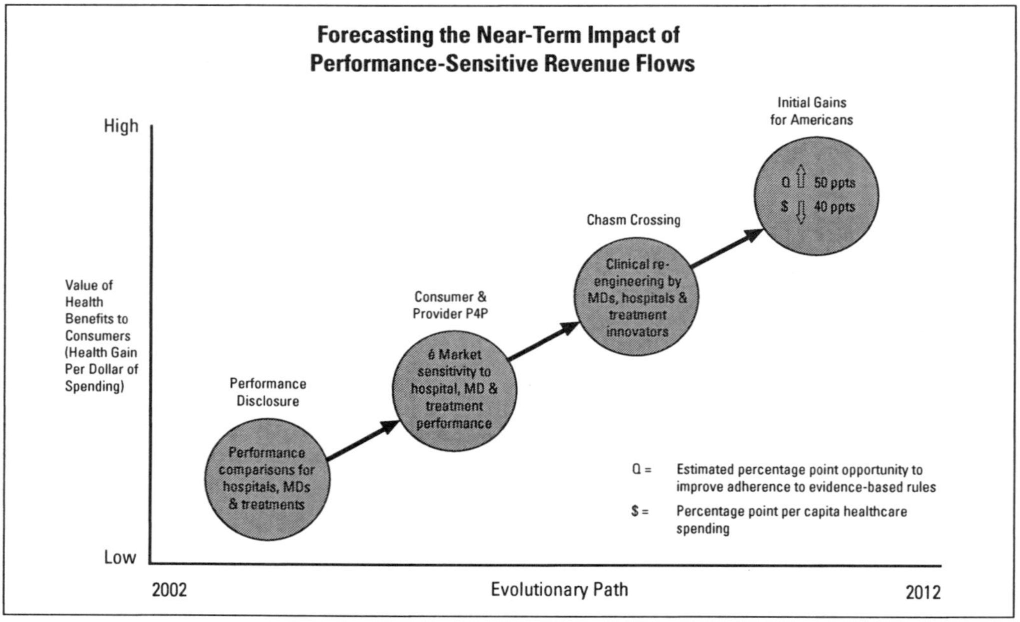

Figure 10-1. **The Critical Path from Performance Disclosure to Performance Breakthrough. Note: "Ppts" is percentage points. Used by permission of Arnold Milstein, MD, MPH.**

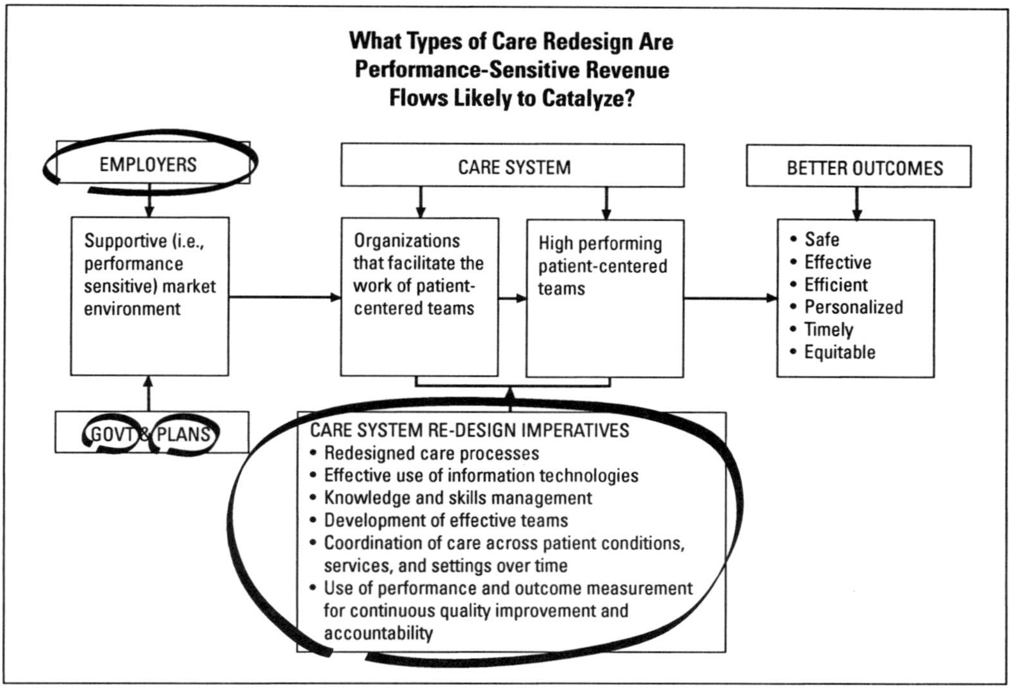

Figure 10-2. Achieving the New Vision of Health Care. Adapted from Institute of Medicine: Crossing the Quality Chasm: A New Health System for the 21st Century. Washington, DC: National Academies Press, 2001.

References

1 Milstein A, Adler NE. Out of sight, out of mind: Why doesn't widespread clinical quality failure command our attention? *Health Aff (Milwood).* March-April 2003; 22(2):119–127.

2 Fisher ES, Wennberg DE, Stukel TA, et al: Variations in the longitudinal efficiency of academic centers. *Health Aff.* October 7, 2004; Web exclusive.

3 Rogers EM. *Diffusion of Innovations, Fifth Edition.* New York: The Free Press; 2003.

4 Institute of Medicine. *Crossing the Quality Chasm: A New Health System for the 21st Century.* Washington, DC: National Academies Press, 2001.

5 Milstein A. Consumer directed health benefits plans could greatly improve the quality of care and health insurance affordability. Testimony before House/Senate Joint Economic Committee, February 25, 2004.

6 Mercer Human Resources Consulting. 2004 Mercer U.S. National Employer-Sponsored Health Plans Survey. November 22, 2004. Available at www.mercerhr.com.

7 Rosenthal M, Milstein A. Consumer-driven plans: What's offered? Who chooses? *Health Services Research.* August 2004; 39:1055–1070.

8 Rosenthal MB, Fernandopulle R, Song HR, et al. Paying for quality: Providers' incentives for quality improvement. *Health Aff.* March/April 2004; 23(2):127–141.

Selected Bibliography

McGlynn EA, Brook RH. Keeping quality on the policy agenda. *Health Aff (Milwood).* May/June 2001; 20(3):82–89.

Milstein A. More health, less spending. Testimony for New America Foundation, Senate Hart Building, November 16, 2004.

Milstein A. Perspective: Hot potato endgame. *Health Aff (Milwood).* November/December 2004; 23(6):32–34.

Milstein A, Adler NE. Out of sight, out of mind. Why doesn't widespread clinical quality failure command our attention? *Health Aff (Milwood).* March/April 2003; 22(2):119–127.

CHAPTER 11

From Vision to Reality: Collaborating to Close the Gap

Mark Leavitt, MD, PhD, FHIMSS, and Charles M. Kilo, MD, MPH

"Out of clutter, find simplicity. From discord, find harmony.
In the middle of difficulty lies opportunity."

Albert Einstein

A GAP THREATENING OUR WELL-BEING

A cavernous gap stretches between the vision articulated in this book and the reality of medical practice today. The gap can no longer simply be ignored, or bemoaned without taking action, because it is has become a direct threat to our nation's economic and social well-being. A great deal of money is being spent, with annual healthcare expenditures of $6167 per capita, an amount that totals $1.8 trillion or 15.5% of the gross domestic product.[1] Yet the delivery of appropriate care—clearly-indicated tests and treatments—is only accomplished about half the time.[2] An even wider gap is felt by those without healthcare coverage, a situation now affecting 45 million Americans.[3] Burgeoning healthcare costs directly impact our competitiveness in global markets, with a resulting loss of jobs they simultaneously threaten our ability to fund the Medicare and Medicaid programs that provide a safety net for those without employment-based coverage.

HOW WE ARRIVED HERE

How did one of our most critical human services come to fall so far short of fulfilling our needs? In Chapter 2, John Wasson and Edward Wagner described the historical backdrop of medical practice, and pointed out that unlike most products and services, office-based care was never consciously "designed"—like Topsy, it just grew. In the primitive days of medical science, when doctors had little to offer besides their comforting presence at the bedside, the basis for compensation centered around the face-to-face visit. But that reimbursement model became a rigid body cast making redesign nearly impossible. Improved delivery models such as the first community-based clinics in Memphis and the Chronic Care Model were developed, but their uptake was limited to those situations where reimbursement was not based on the old fee-for-service paradigm.

A second reason for the gap is the fact that healthcare has barely tapped the potential of modern information technology. Estimates of the penetration of electronic health records (EHRs) vary, but a recent study indicated only 23% of offices with two to nine physicians, and 13% of solo practices, had EHR systems.[4] Three quarters of all office-based physicians practice in those environments. In the midst of an explosion of information, most physician practices continue managing clinical data the way it was done a hundred years ago: with paper files.

In Chapter 3, Blackford Middleton has outlined the adoption barriers that exist, including misaligned incentives, lack of standards and interoperability, and an immature and unstable marketplace. The aggregate benefits of adopting IT in healthcare are enormous: computerized provider order entry (CPOE) in ambulatory care settings could save $44 billion per year,[5] while replacing paper, telephone, and fax with electronic exchange of healthcare information would save $77.8 billion.[6] Yet, for an individual practice, justifying the investment in EHRs is challenging, because under our current reimbursement system 89% of the benefits flow to *other* healthcare entities and do not provide financial return to the practice.[6]

FOUNDATIONS FOR A TRANSFORMED MEDICAL PRACTICE

In Donald Berwick's vision for healthcare, there are "no needless deaths, no needless pain or suffering, no unwanted waiting, no helplessness, and no waste." While this may sound idealistic, that is exactly what a strategic vision should be. To get started on the hard work of transformation, one needs to complement the vision with things that are concrete: concrete principles around which to design, and concrete steps that are individually achievable.

To those who have experience in industries such as manufacturing, retailing, and the nonhealthcare service sector, the principles for a transformed medical practice—relationship, service, and reliability—may sound so obvious as to be derided as "motherhood and apple pie." But the reality is that these concepts are never mentioned in medical school or residency training. Joining an existing practice, the new physician is still unlikely to hear them expressed as goals. Success is measured in visits per day, procedures per month, or levels of complexity when coding. Practicing physicians feel trapped like the proverbial woodcutter who, when asked why he labors so hard felling trees with a dull saw, replies, "I have to work so hard, I don't have time to sharpen it."

In Chapter 4 on Relationship, John Wasson and David Lansky have asserted that a trusting, well-balanced relationship between the patient and his or her healthcare providers is much more than a helpful convenience; it stands independently as a powerful means of caring and healing. They point out in the context of relationship that information technology is a two-edged sword which must be wielded appropriately. At its best, IT can enhance the relationship by improving communication and reducing distractions; less time is spent hunting for results or dealing with minutiae irrelevant to the patient's concerns. When misapplied, however, it can interfere with relationship; for example, a robotic telephone menu system that is poorly programmed will isolate and frustrate the patient who has an urgent, genuine need to speak person-to-person with a caregiver. The potential benefits are well worth the effort and risk. A personal, universal, truly portable health record could be a powerful focus around which relationships and communication in healthcare could be reinvented.

Service is the second foundation of the ideal medical practice. Those who dismiss service as a frill are aptly refuted by Susan Edgman-Levitan's data in Chapter 5: service quality is highly associated with care quality, care outcomes, and staff satisfaction. In the quaint, insular world of medical practice, full waiting rooms and cranky staff were sometimes regarded as the sign of a good doctor. But in today's world of instant gratification—banking, investing, and shopping instantly online, followed by reliable, trackable overnight delivery of goods—the healthcare consumer is becoming increasingly skeptical of that particular myth. Once again, information technology must be regarded as a tool, not an end in itself. However, when the goal of improving service is kept clearly in mind, the IT applications flow readily. Open access scheduling and Web-based appointment request systems can combine to provide a profound improvement. Patients today want to "point and click" for their services, not dial the phone, wait for an answer, and be greeted with "doctor's office, please hold ... click."

Although the concept of patient safety has gained great visibility in the popular and professional press since the Institute of Medicine (IOM) report in 2000,[7] Charles Kilo and Joseph Scherger have appropriately focused on the more comprehensive topic of Reliability in Chapter 6. Safety, or avoiding harm, is only one aspect of reliability. Improving the practice's ability to do the right thing for the patient consistently, efficiently, and safely will deliver the most comprehensive benefits. To practice healthcare today, the provider must gather deep patient-specific information, synthesize an assessment of the situation, and choose from an enormous palette of diagnostic and treatment options, making wise evidence-based choices guided by data accumulating from 10,000 new studies every year.[8] The task is simply beyond the capacity of the unassisted human mind—although our medical school customs continue to encourage such a feat—and here is where information technology truly hits its stride. Computerized assistance can help by retaining and organizing patient-specific information, searching the literature, monitoring for forgotten actions, and guiding the caregiver forward along evidence-based paths. It is just as impossible to practice reliable medicine today without IT as it would be to pilot jetliners sans instrument dashboards, electronic communications, and safety warning systems.

ACHIEVING THE PRINCIPLES IN PRACTICE

The three case studies offered throughout the book illustrate that at least some medical practices are well on their way to achieving new standards of relationship, service, and reliability. These success stories cover a wide range of settings: Thedacare is an example of a large integrated delivery system, Southeast Texas Medical Associates LLP (SETMA) illustrates what is possible in a midsized practice, and the PatientCare Family Clinic case study refutes the argument that solo practices cannot muster the resources to adopt IT and transform themselves. Although their stories prove that new levels of performance are achievable, the difficult task ahead is to make these achievements commonplace rather than unique cases.

The next generation medical practice must combine the best leadership and management techniques along with effective integration of appropriate information technology. In Chapter 7, Charles Kilo, Bruce Bagley, Jill Arena, and Jeff Kegarise reviewed the organizational aspects that must be addressed. While these principles may be familiar to those with management training and experience, they are included here because most physicians have never received such instruction.

Information technology projects are widely regarded as carrying high risks, and experience in the field has confirmed the challenge that faces implementers of healthcare IT. But many lessons have been learned in the past decades, and there is no need to repeat mistakes already made by others in this endeavor. To this end, in Chapter 8 Jane Metzger and Keith MacDonald have distilled their best insights from years of experience in selecting and implementing information systems in clinical settings. The risk of clinical IT projects is manageable when a strong foundation is laid before beginning: development of the business case, agreement on strategy, and creation of a roadmap that outlines all the stages of the project. Also, IT cannot be installed as if it were an end in itself; every feature and function implemented should be tied to a strategic goal of the practice. When this is done, the capabilities of people are continuously enhanced by information technology, and the value received from the technology is continuously increased as part of the practice's quest for self-improvement. Synergy results from the positive, self-reinforcing nature of this feedback cycle.

THE CHANGING ENVIRONMENT: IRRESISTIBLE FORCES

In Chapter 9, David Roberts and Thomas Leary have traced the depth and breadth of governmental activities in healthcare. Besides setting the legal and regulatory boundaries for healthcare providers, government is also the purchaser of roughly half the healthcare services in this country. Finally, some of the largest healthcare delivery systems in the country are public-sector operations, including the Military Health System, the Veterans Health Administration, the Indian Health Service, and networks of Community Health Centers. Although political obstacles make sweeping change difficult to achieve, any movement by the federal government has an immediate and far-reaching effect on the entire healthcare system. Since 2003, the "sleeping giant" of healthcare has awakened and made its powerful presence felt. President Bush has articulated a vision for EHRs and set an ambitious timetable of ten years. The president has also created the new position of National Coordinator for Healthcare Information Technology and appointed Dr. David Brailer, a widely-respected expert in health IT, to the post.

As clearly articulated by Arnold Milstein in Chapter 10, the care we receive is strongly influenced by the healthcare payment systems we employ; in other words, you get what you pay for. The gap between ideal healthcare and the reality of medical practice today can be largely attributed to clumsy reimbursement systems that provide no feedback to correct overuse, misuse, provision of unwanted or discretionary services, and use of antiquated work methods. The managed care of the 1980s and 1990s failed to correct the problem. Paper medical records were unable to provide accurate comparative data on the quality and reliability of medical practices, so attention could only be focused on costs and not value. Meanwhile, consumers perceived little more than an obvious restriction of their choices, and a backlash ensued.

Now, pay-for-performance (P4P) represents a reform movement aiming to finally put the appropriate incentives in place. Driven by large employers, drawing on deep experience in their own quality initiatives in manufacturing or in nonhealthcare services, P4P measures and rewards clinical processes and outcomes rather than volume. When public sector payers such as the Centers for Medicare and Medicaid collaborate with private sector P4P pioneers, there will be sufficient momentum to finally overcome the inertia of antiquated healthcare payment and delivery methods.

COLLABORATING TO EMBRACE CHANGE

The gap between our vision for medical practice and the reality today is huge. The task of transformation is complex, and the barriers to change are strong. But it is the very size of the gap, and the amount of pain being felt by our citizens and our economy, that we believe guarantees that change must now occur. Some infectious illnesses must reach a crisis stage, when invading microbes and the body's immune responses clash dramatically, before resolution. Metaphorically speaking, our healthcare system is spiking a high fever right now, and the drama is about to begin.

All healthcare stakeholders will be affected, but they will have a choice of whether to embrace change and adapt to a new environment or whether to resist it. The HIPAA (Health Insurance Portability and Accountability Act) legislation of 1996 provides a telling example of how the industry may resist external forces. One part of the law had the noble goal of increasing administrative efficiency by standardizing healthcare claims transaction formats, but some organizations, claiming inability to modify their systems in time, were granted delays and exemptions. As a result, good behavior was penalized while intransigence was rewarded. The other part of the law, meant to increase privacy protections for healthcare information, spawned an industry of legal consultation and education, diverting resources from patient care. Then some practice staff, resentful of the intrusion, adopted a passive-aggressive approach and began refusing to provide records-related information to patients and relatives, blaming intrusive new laws. Relationships and service were impacted negatively. By and large, though, healthcare professionals are highly dedicated and caring workers who share the vision but find themselves trapped in a system that prevents them from achieving those idealistic goals.

A more positive path is available when stakeholders work cooperatively, and there are signs that the healthcare industry is becoming more collaborative. Multi-stakeholder groups, led by nonprofit associations and philanthropies, are generating thoughtful landmark reports.[9] A recent Request for Information issued by ONCHIT requesting designs for a National Health Information Network elicited more than 500 responses, with several being notable collaborations between as many as a dozen diverse organizations.[10]

TRANSFORMING MEDICAL PRACTICE: A TEAM EFFORT

With the exception of the large integrated delivery organization—which has its own internal change-management challenges—it is difficult or impossible for a medical practice to transform itself without cooperation from the surrounding healthcare stakeholders. Doing things in a significantly different and better way will require a team effort both within the practice and in the practice's external environment.

The most powerful force affecting the practice is the payment system. Healthcare payers should embrace pay-for-performance models that reward practices for delivering higher levels of relationship, service, and reliability. Government, in its role as a major purchaser of healthcare, should take a leading position alongside P4P pioneers like the Bridges to Excellence program.[11] Although incentives should be based on clinical outcomes in the long run, interim support is needed for incremental steps taken by the practice. In particular, financial support is needed to offset the initial cash outlay in purchasing new information technology systems.

Hospitals also have a major influence on medical practices. Most office-based physicians also care for inpatients at one or more nearby hospitals, and those who do not must coordinate care with a hospital specialist (a "hospitalist") when patients are admitted. Because of their size and sophistication, most hospitals have a substantial IT department, with resources to support applications, workstations, servers and networks. Supporting physician practices would seem to be an efficient and natural extension of those services, but the economic bounds of this activity are tightly controlled by the Stark and anti-kickback laws. While a recent rule offered an exemption for community-wide health information networks, its applicability for most real-world hospital/physician IT collaboration is uncertain. The potential for achieving economies of scale in IT support for physician practices through this mechanism remains an area for active discussion and development.

Academic medical centers and physician training programs are also critical to practice transformation. While a number of training centers have adopted or even built their own cutting-edge clinical IT systems, the majority continue to train new physicians on paper-based paradigms of care. The resistance to IT adoption demonstrated by many mid-career physicians is a legacy of this gap in their training. No academic medical center would train its students on obsolete diagnostic or treatment technology. It is time to extend this aversion to obsolete patient record technology as well. With federal funds playing a major role in supporting these centers, this represents a fertile area for government action, whether through additional funding or by means of incentives to redirect some money away from new buildings and toward information technology.

Of course, the developers and marketers of clinical IT systems have an important contribution to make. The bulk of research and development has been directed toward systems for the large medical center, and for good reason: developing, selling, and supporting systems for small practices simply has not been profitable. For this same reason, vendors dedicating themselves to small and mid-size offices have suffered financial challenges, and the marketplace has been unstable. Because physicians are not trained or experienced with EHR systems, they often pose unreasonable and inconsistent requirements to vendors. Because of past marketplace instability, the confidence of potential buyers is low, and the cost of selling to them is high. Finally, there is a tendency to underestimate the complexity of the implementation project and the ongoing need for technical support, so the failure rate of EHR implementations has been significant. The private sector has recently moved to address these challenges by launching an initiative that will offer voluntary product certification of office EHR systems.[12] The stated goal of that effort is "to accelerate the adoption of robust, interoperable HIT throughout the U.S. healthcare system, by creating an efficient, credible, sustainable mechanism for the certification of HIT products."

Finally, what will be the role of patients, or healthcare consumers, in transforming medical practice? They will be affected more than anyone else, and while the practice redesign movement always seeks to improve their healthcare experiences, there is a risk of oversimplifying their needs and desires. In the pursuit of quality and reliability, we must not make the mistake of turning medical offices into factories, and patients into Toyotas. Guidelines and protocols must always be reconciled with the patient's personal beliefs and preferences. Some defects in our practices are paradoxically regarded by patients as benefits. They may be glad when old records are lost, allowing embarrassing historical data to fade away. And they may be relieved that follow-up is imperfect, eliminating the need for an uncomfortable confrontation with their caregiver about their personal choice not to comply with a recommendation. Information technology and its implementation must always have enough flexibility to accommodate personalization of care.

With due regard for all these challenges and concerns, it is time to move forward decisively. Working together, taking advantage of our new technology tools for informing and communicating, we can begin to transform healthcare by focusing on medical practices—the front lines of healthcare where most preventive intervention and chronic disease management takes place.

References

1 Center for Medicare and Medicaid Services, Office of the Actuary. Available at www.cms.gov/statistics/nhe (accessed April 12, 2005).

2 McGlynn EA, Asch SM, Adams J, et al. The quality of health care delivered to adults in the United States. *New Engl J Med.* June 26, 2003; 348(26): 2635–2645.

3 Kaiser Commission on Medicaid and the Uninsured. *The Uninsured and Their Access to Health Care.* November 2004.

4 Audet AM, Doty M, Peugh J, et al. Information technologies: When will they make it into physicians' black bags? *Medscape General Medicine.* December 7, 2004.

5 Center for Information Technology Leadership. The *Value of Computerized Provider Order Entry in Ambulatory Settings: Executive Preview.* Available at www.citl.org/research/ACPOE_Executive_Preview.pdf (accessed April 12, 2005).

6 Walker J, Pan E, Johnston D, et al. The value of health care information exchange and interoperability: *Health Affairs.* (Web exclusive) January 19, 2005. Available at www.healthaffairs.com.

7 Kohn T, Corrigan J, Donaldson M. *To Err is Human.* Washington, DC: National Academies Press; March 2000.

8 Chassin M. Is health care ready for Six Sigma quality? *Milbank Quarterl.* 1998; 76(4)W5:10–18.

9 Connecting for Health Steering Group. *Achieving Electronic Connectivity in Healthcare, A Preliminary Roadmap from the Nation's Private and Public-Sector Healthcare Leaders.* Published by Markle Foundation and Robert Wood Johnson Foundation; July 2004. Available at www.connectingforhealth.org/resources/cfh_aech_roadmap_072004.pdf (accessed April 12, 2005).

10 The Collaborative ONCHIT RFI Response, submitted by: American Health Information Management Association (AHIMA), American Medical Informatics Association (AMIA), American National Standards Institute-Healthcare Informatics Standards Board (ANSI HISB), Center for Information Technology Leadership (CITL), Connecting for Health (CFH), eHealth Initiative (eHI), HIMSS EHR Vendor Association (EHRVA), Healthcare Information and Management Systems Society (HIMSS), Health Level Seven, Inc. (HL7), Integrating the Healthcare Enterprise (IHE), Internet2, Liberty Alliance, National Alliance for Health Information Technology (NAHIT), January 2005.

11 Bridges to Excellence Program Overview. Available at www.bridgestoexcellence.org/bte/bte_overview.htm (accessed April 12, 2005).

12 Certification Commission for Healthcare Information Technology. www.cchit.org (accessed April 12, 2005).

Case Studies

Large Integrated Network Case Study: ThedaCare Physicians

ABOUT THE PRACTICE

ThedaCare Physicians is a group of more than 140 doctors, physician assistants, and nurse practitioners offering care at 20 clinic locations in north central and northeastern Wisconsin. It is one of three operating divisions of ThedaCare™, a physician-led integrated delivery system which is headquartered in Appleton, Wisconsin. The parent organization was formed by the merger of two community hospitals in 1987 and now provides services across the continuum of care through three hospitals, primary care clinics, occupational health, home health, behavioral health, senior services, and other health programs. ThedaCare employs approximately 5,000 people.

ThedaCare Physicians provides primary care services to approximately 215,000 individuals. Its main focus is primary care, including family practice, internal medicine, and pediatrics. The organization also offers some limited specialty care, such as rheumatology and surgery in very rural clinics. The clinics range in size from those with no doctor and two nurse practitioners to sites with 18 practitioners. Most offer diagnostic radiology, laboratory services, and procedure rooms. Some offer in-clinic physical therapy, behavioral health counseling, mammography, bone densitometry, and pharmacy services. A 24-hour call center staffed by registered nurses, ThedaCare On Call, is also part of the ThedaCare Physician Services Division.

ThedaCare Physicians uses a staff model for physician employment and does not use physician noncompete clauses. Only two groups have left the network in its 12-year history. The division is a profitable one which uses a dyad model of leadership. Each of the 20 clinics is supported by a two-person team consisting of a physician leader and practice administrator. Each of the nine teams oversees two or three clinics.

ThedaCare Physicians has a significant record of IT-enabled excellence in the provision of care quality and safety, and innovation in healthcare practice design. In 2002 and 2003, the organization's physicians were rated best in the nation for quality of care as measured by HEDIS®--the Health Employer Data Information Set. Two ThedaCare clinics were alpha sites for the Institute for Healthcare Improvement's (IHI) Idealized Design of Clinical Office Practices (IDCOP) initiative in early 1999. A description of the organization's IDCOP-led Open Access initiative appears in Chapter 5. In the IT arena, the organization purchased an EHR system from EPIC Systems Corporation and went live in pilot clinics in September of 1999. The EHR system, which is now used enterprise-wide in ThedaCare™, enabled the organization to appear on the list of the "100 most wired hospitals and health systems" for three consecutive recent years, 2002-2004.[1] Patients have complete and secure Web-based access to their health records through MyThedaCare (https://my.thedacare.org).

ENHANCING RELATIONSHIPS THROUGH EHR USE AT THEDACARE CLINICS

The enterprise-wide use of an EHR at ThedaCare has had a significant positive impact on patient/practitioner and primary care/specialty care practitioner interaction. "Through Web-based messaging, we've been able to change the cycle time in getting information from one person to another—from practitioners to patients or patients to practitioners, for example," notes John Barkmeier, MD, the physician champion of the organization's electronic platform. Test results can be communicated to patients the same day the results are obtained. "Through use of the EHR, we're also able to capture a lot more information about patients' preferences, such as how they would like us to communicate with them," says Barkmeier.

ThedaCare primary care doctors can send messages directly to specialists who are connected to the organization's EHR system. By the end of 2005, ThedaCare expects approximately 200 physicians beyond the organization's 140 primary care practitioners to be accessing the system's EHR. Messaging can get information to specialists when they need it. "There are some instances when we still need to talk with specialists, but being able to share the patient's record has changed our relationship. Before the EHR, patients were the conduit for information relayed between primary care physicians and specialists. Because follow-up letters were often so slow in coming to us, patients would have to relate to us what the specialist recommended. Now I can look at the specialists' notes, see what tests they ordered and the results of such tests, and read their recommendations. This has greatly reduced the need to move information physically (whether on paper on in person) around the organization," describes Barkmeier.

ThedaCare is taking steps to ensure that the presence and use of computers by physicians for documentation in exam rooms does not negatively impact patient-provider relationships. "We're looking at best-practice strategies, such as "lean" principles, for how, when, and what physicians should document. Some documentation can be done before the visit and ready for the provider at that time so that he or she can focus on the personal parts of the visit," describes Sally Podoski, Quality Manager of ThedaCare's Physician Services Division.

ThedaCare Physicians views team-based care as central to the enhancement of patient-practitioner relationships and high quality relationships as central to the organization's strategy. The model of care delivery used in the clinics involves teams, consisting of a physician and a nurse practitioner or physician assistant, who each have a counterpart in the clinic. The teams develop long-standing and important relationships with their patients. "Through conjoint market research and analysis conducted in 2000, we learned that, under urgent circumstances, patients want to be able to see their *own* practitioner or a teammate they know. This affirmed our resolve *not* to set up separate urgent care centers, but to improve and assure patients access to their own practitioner or a teammate," describes Jeff Hunter, ThedaCare's Senior Vice President for Planning and Marketing.

Colleague physician teammates see the patient on an alternating basis. "This is most successful when physicians introduce the teammate concept to their patients during initial visits, by saying something like, 'Dr. X and I work together as a team. There will be times when I won't be in the office, so you'll see Dr. X. We'll be partners in your care.' We know from market research that patients are *most* satisfied when they see their own practitioner, *quite* satisfied when they see a teammate, and quite *dissatisfied* when they see anyone else," describes Podoski.

Nurturing the patient/practitioner relationship—one patient at a time, one interaction at a time—is the basis of ThedaCare Physicians' competitive strategy. "Relationship management is the cornerstone of what keeps us successful. We do very little advertising because we believe that word of mouth about the quality of care we provide is what brings patients into our practices, and primary care practices, in general," comments Podoski. The strategy appears to be successful as ThedaCare Physicians enjoys the position of marketplace leader.

PUTTING THE PATIENT IN THE CENTER OF THE RADAR SCREEN AT THEDACARE CLINICS

ThedaCare uses a variety of methods to obtain the patient's perspective on practice design elements that will enhance relationship, service, and quality of care. The organization convenes patient focus groups when it needs to gain knowledge of patient preferences regarding specific issues (e.g., what might be desired in cancer services) and collaborates with Minneapolis-based HealthPartners, which conducts numerous patient forums.

ThedaCare also conducts sophisticated, conjoint analysis-based market research. *Conjoint analysis* is a technique for estimating the value people place on the attributes or features which define products and services. "Patients participate in a computerized market survey that enables them to choose among pairs of options. We can learn quickly about their preferences and the tradeoffs they might make. This methodology simulates a buying situation and has given us insight into which medical practice design changes we should and should not invest in," describes Jeff Hunter.

A recent major research effort, called Transformation 2004, focused on comparative patient satisfaction when patients were offered three different care communication channels—ThedaCare On Call (the 24/7 nurse-staffed telephone service), MyThedaCare (the Web-based system), and in-office visits. "We wanted to identify what patients value most in an electronic, telephone, or in-person interaction with their provider. We also wanted to determine whether we could charge for various pieces of the services, and how to put all that capacity together in a way that created the highest level of patient satisfaction. We learned that the most effective way to increase satisfaction would be to offer ThedaCare On Call and MyThedaCare to *all* patients at no charge," says Hunter.

This ability to provide patients with what they want was echoed by Kathryn Correia, current Senior Vice President, ThedaCare Hospitals, and former Senior Vice President ThedaCare Physicians. Correia believes in the strong connection between patients and their physicians: "We must continuously identify how we can deliver care for patients 24/7/365 in a PROACTIVE way that anticipates their needs. We must be able to deliver that care outside of the walls of the traditional exam room, so that our customers believe we are ESSENTIAL to their healthy, productive lives."

To prevent patients from thinking that the telephone and Web systems were taking them farther away from their primary providers in order to decrease practice costs, clinics are urged to communicate to customers that patients are getting a new personalized provider for their personal care team. This person is a nurse at ThedaCare On Call, who will get to know patients by name. "By encouraging all patients to use ThedaCare On Call and MyThedaCare, we can produce much higher patient satisfaction at lower costs. All calls to the clinics that could be handled by ThedaCare On Call and MyThedaCare will 'go away' and office efficiency will increase," concludes Hunter. Using MyThedaCare, patients can access laboratory results, schedule appointments, send e-mail to their practitioners, obtain educational materials, and conduct many other functions.

ThedaCare Physicians is now studying "lean" principles of eliminating waste and enhancing value from the customer's perspective, modeled on what Toyota has accomplished with its manufacturing processes. "The customer is our primary focus," notes Scott Decker, Vice President of Operational Innovation and Quality. ThedaCare continues to focus on perfecting the patient experience and eliminating barriers to care.

OPEN ACCESS AT THEDACARE CLINICS

In November 1998, a team from ThedaCare participated in an informational meeting on the IHI's Idealized Design of Clinical Office Practices initiative, conducted by Chuck Kilo, MD, then with IHI, and Donald M. Berwick, MD, MPP, IHI's CEO. "Within the first hour, the entire team was convinced that this initiative was ThedaCare's sought-after approach to meeting the next cycle of demands on clinical office practices. Our leadership knew that the service aspects of the care we were delivering could be improved. Open access was to be one component of the redesign," describes Scott Decker.[2]

Selecting two pilot sites with four primary care providers at each site, the organization began the move toward open access scheduling. At that time, patients typically had to wait an average of 40 to 45 days for an appointment that included a full physical exam—a "long appointment"—and 10 days for a "short appointment" for acute care problems. "This situation was not meeting patient access needs. Moreover, we had a competitor that was offering urgent care centers. It was not in our vision to do likewise, but rather, we wanted to provide improved access to the patients' own physicians," says Sally Podoski.

The results at the pilot sites were significant and impressive. Individual practitioners, using means and methods shared through IHI or devised on their own, worked down the backlogs and made other improvements to streamline care and patient flow. By early

1999, same-day access for acute problems and day-of-request or next-day appointments for physical exams could be offered to clinic patients. In 2000, ThedaCare introduced open-access scheduling to all of its clinics. "We provided the results data, and allowed physicians to step up to the plate or take a seat on the sideline. We didn't force any clinics to make the change," describes Decker.

In the early years, some ThedaCare practitioners did not embrace the importance of same-day access. They reasoned that, if a patient were really sick, under the existing system, they would simply "work the patient in" to the day's schedule. "What the practitioners didn't realize is that a patient who had experienced knee pain for a week and finally called his or her physician for an appointment didn't want to have to wait another 10 days to be seen, even if nothing terrible would occur with his or her knee in this interim," describes Podoski.

The lack of competition in some communities also did not foster urgency about redesign of the workflow to improve patient access. "Because we're a financially healthy system, the 'burning platform' for change isn't always present and sometimes it's hard to engender enthusiasm about practice improvements," says Podoski. Access became a system initiative and priority as one important way of differentiating ThedaCare as the healthcare delivery system of choice. At this point in time, all 20 of the clinics use open-access scheduling.

While the work was occurring to allow patients faster and better access to their provider or provider team, changes were also being observed in the visit make-up. Over time, the average number of visits on a per-doctor-per-month basis decreased while the net monthly revenue and net income increased.[3] Since 2000 and particularly in the last three years, profitability has steadily increased in the Physician Services Division of ThedaCare. Although relative value unit (RVU) production in clinic visits essentially has been flat from 2002 to 2004, the coding patterns show a higher complexity of patient visits. Patients are able to get a large number of medical needs met in a single office visit.

PROVIDING CONSISTENT NON-URGENT CARE AT THEDACARE CLINICS

A new triage model, designed to increase the consistency of care quality for minor health issues that do not require an office visit, is being tested at ThedaCare Physicians. "We realized that our clinics do things a certain way Mondays through Fridays from 8 am to 5 pm. They do things a different way weekdays from 5 pm to 8 am, and still another way on weekends," describes Podoski. The organization has invested in a triage model that will be used by nurses in all locations, including the nurse call center ThedaCare On Call.

The model ensures, for example, that if a parent calls about a sick child, every nurse that might interact with that parent in every clinic or the call center at any hour will follow the same process for documenting the child's illness and the instructions provided. Based on the child's condition, the triage nurse can follow standing orders approved by all ThedaCare physicians to order medication, or provide teaching and home care advice in order to save a clinic visit for an exhausted parent. That same nurse can determine if the illness is one that cannot wait for office hours and may page the on-call physician to assure the safest course of action. If an office visit is required, the visit can be scheduled for the next day. The triage model standardizes the triage pathway and documentation to enhance care quality and assure a consistent, high quality experience for the patient and family.

PERFORMANCE IMPROVEMENT AND DISEASE MANAGEMENT/PREVENTION AT THEDACARE CLINICS

Enabled by a robust EHR, data are transparent and performance is data driven for ThedaCare's primary care physicians. "Our system's success relies upon data sharing with providers. We only provided blinded data for a very short period of time; now data are transparent. All of our good results and scores are generated by getting data in front of physicians so that their own desire to improve can enhance those results. What ThedaCare physicians want is world-class performance on identified indicators for all patients," comments Podoski. Performance is impressive. In 2002 and 2003, ThedaCare Physicians was rated best in the nation for quality of care as measured by HEDIS®—the Health Employer Data Information Set. In 2004, the organization wasn't far from the top; it achieved the #2 position.

Since the late 1990s, clinics have used EHR-enabled population management and disease registries for patients covered by the health plan owned by the parent organization. Among many other capabilities, the EHR provides health alerts, so that when a patient with diabetes, who is overdue for a foot check, hemoglobin A1C test, or eye exam calls a clinic, for example, the person answering the phone can alert the patient and schedule the test or check. Registries quickly proved very effective in assuring needed care for patients covered by the health plan. Prevention services increased from 60% of needed services to 90% of such services. Chronic disease patients who achieved agreed-upon goals increased from 30-40% to 70-80%. "We achieve reliability in caring for patients with chronic diseases because we're using our EHR to ensure that patients are getting the services they need. And, we rigorously track how effective we are at delivering these services, thereby leveraging the EHR system to improve population health," notes John Barkmeier, MD.

In 1994, ThedaCare's initial work with the health plan's patients and HEDIS measurements focused on process measures, such as immunizations, mammography and diabetic eye exams. The outcome measures for HEDIS commenced in 1999, and by then, ThedaCare's efforts in disease management were well under way with results that were approaching or reaching the best in the country (Figure 1).

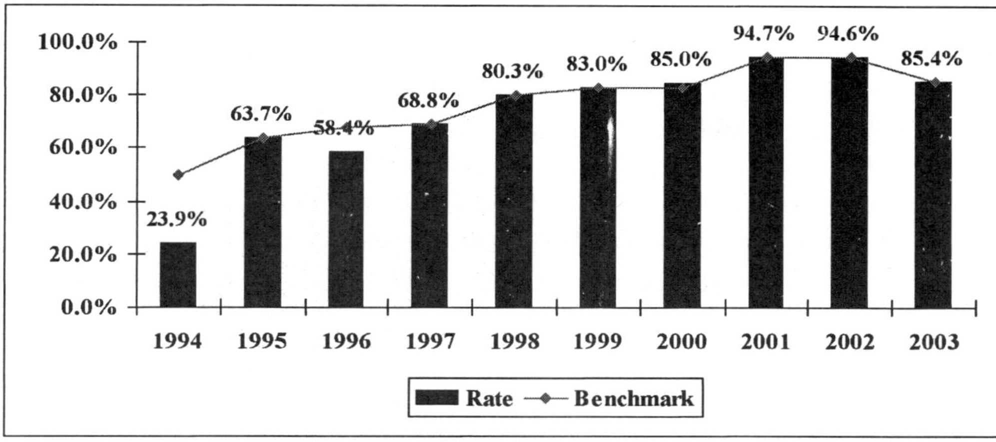

Figure 1. Touchpoint Health Plan's HEDIS Quality Diabetic Eye Exam Rate. From ThedaCare, Appleton, Wisconsin. Used with permission.

Concerned about a double standard of care—one for health plan patients and one for patients covered by Medicare, Medicaid, and other forms of insurance—ThedaCare Physicians expanded the use of registries to improve population health to nonhealth plan patients in 2004. The organization started by conducting a pilot test with all patients with diabetes. The results indicated that although the transition to active management of patients required focus and effort (such as to set up charts), clinics using registry and EHR tools achieved better results. "Organized charts with health maintenance modifiers in effect 'look for results' and prompt action when patients contact the office, thereby reducing the time and effort required to track them down later," describes Barkmeier.

ThedaCare Physicians has expanded population/disease management registries to all patients in all clinics, rolling out in nine clinics in 2004 for either diabetes or coronary artery disease management and fully committed to continuing the implementation with the remaining ThedaCare clinics in 2005. The challenges have not been insignificant. "Organizing registries is time-intensive and requires sorting by each individual factor. Many patients have multiple deficiencies," notes Barkmeier. Strategies for facilitating the transition include the following:

- Assigning an accountable person in each office to make sure the workflows are working;
- Standardizing and simplifying workflow and processes, whenever possible;
- Providing proactive management to improve the patient experience and maximize the value of the office visits. For example, when laboratory tests occur as needed prior to visits, the results can be reviewed at the visit and the need for multiple phone calls to coordinate results review is eliminated. With these kinds of changes, schedules must be actively reviewed and "huddles" with staff must occur when needed; and
- Promoting the use of "MyChart" on the MyThedaCare Web site to involve disease management patients in the proactive management of their health.

"We didn't start actively promoting disease management to clinic practitioners until we could show them the data proving that this approach would help them to be better physicians," says Barkmeier. "I never ask others to do something that I can't prove works. My staff enjoys piloting practices on my patients knowing that, if successful, the results will spur other physicians to adopt them. My numbers and results must prove the point and they did."

Benefits, including improved consistency of care and improved health outcomes, are monitored regularly and are encouraging. For example, a growing body of evidence indicates that low density lipoprotein (LDL) cholesterol levels are an important predictor in determining whether a patient with established coronary artery disease will have a recurrent coronary event. A recent national expert panel[4] recommends an LDL value goal of 100 mg/dl for this high risk population. ThedaCare thus identified the lowering of LDL levels as an early targeted intervention for patients in the coronary artery disease management program. Through use of proactive disease management strategies, ThedaCare significantly increased the percentage of patient with LDL levels "at goal" (Figure 2).

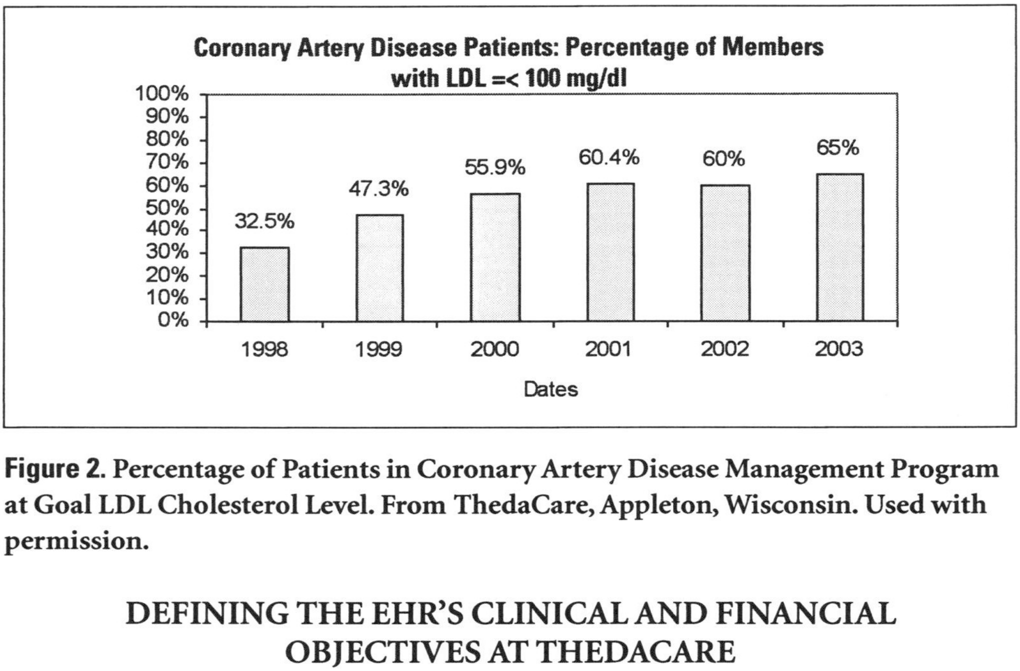

Figure 2. Percentage of Patients in Coronary Artery Disease Management Program at Goal LDL Cholesterol Level. From ThedaCare, Appleton, Wisconsin. Used with permission.

DEFINING THE EHR'S CLINICAL AND FINANCIAL OBJECTIVES AT THEDACARE

In 1998, ThedaCare established the following long-range objective for information technology: To capture and consolidate all pertinent information from across the organization in a central computer system and make the data easily accessible to those who need the information. Major initiatives required to achieve this objective were defined to include the following:

- Implementing a clinical/financial data repository that provides real-time access;
- Implementing an enterprise-wide scheduling system for scheduling all visits and procedures across the organization; and
- Providing clinical management tools that support the patient care process through automation at the bedside.

Figure 3 provides a graphic look at ThedaCare's vision for IT.

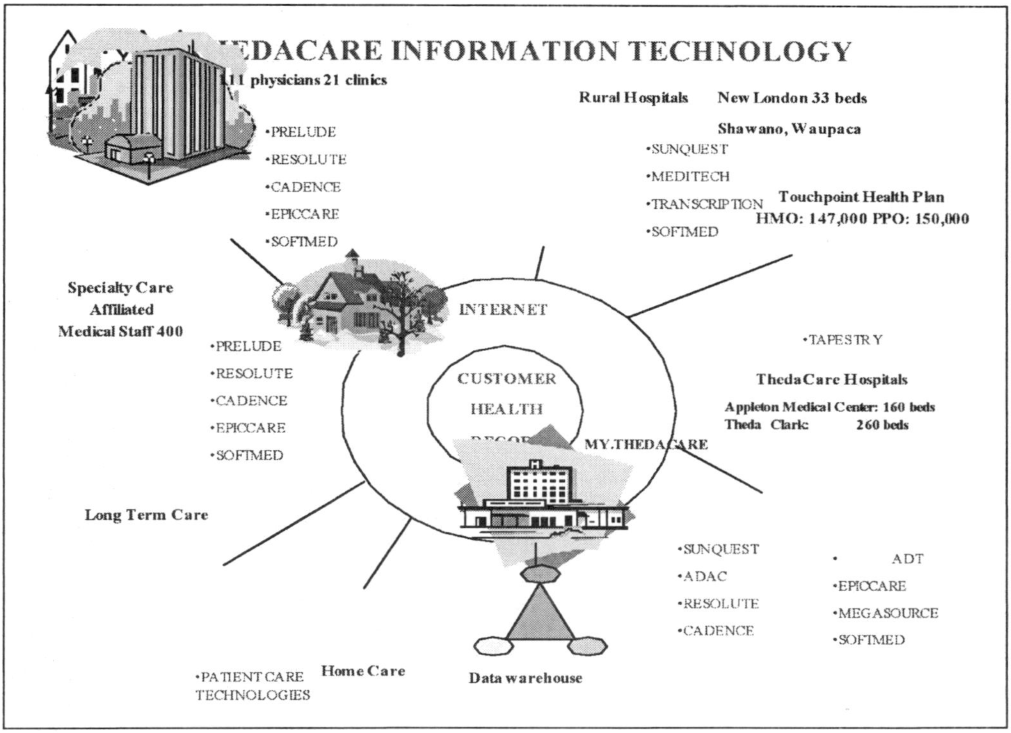

Figure 3. Integration of IT at ThedaCare. From ThedaCare, Appleton, Wisconsin. Used with permission.

ThedaCare defined the clinical objectives of an EHR as follows:

- ***Enhanced Safety:*** Reduced ambiguity in orders and prescriptions, medication alerts, access to information when needed, decision support, and consistency of care through access to best practices at the decision point would increase patient safety.
- ***Improved Health Outcomes:*** Access to information by patient, use of population disease/health management programs, and automation would improve the health of patients while improving productivity.
- ***Improved Care Quality:*** Problem lists would facilitate the monitoring and management of patient care needs, cumulative patient records would avoid duplicate documentation, and organizationwide use of an EHR would ensure continuity of patient care across the care continuum.

Leaders at ThedaCare believe that clinical quality objectives must form one angle of a balanced triangle, consisting of quality, financial performance, and employee satisfaction. John Toussaint, MD, CEO and President of ThedaCare, calls this the "three-legged stool." "Without simultaneous pursuit of financial vitality, world-class quality, and employer-of-choice status which ensures that we're able to recruit and retain the very best people, the stool will not stand," describes Sally Podoski.

LAYING THE GROUNDWORK FOR EHR CONSENSUS, MANAGING CHANGE, AND ALIGNING INCENTIVES AT THEDACARE

In 1996, ThedaCare Physicians' leaders started evolving a vision for IT-enabled ambulatory practice. That vision was to "capture and consolidate all pertinent information from across the organization in a central computer system and make the data easily accessible to those who need the data." ThedaCare's IT staff looked at IT vendors that might offer the ability to achieve that vision. "We chose the EHR system from EPIC Systems Corporation because the company's vision was to develop an integrated sweep of applications around a central database. We wouldn't have to create interfaces every time we brought on-board a new piece of software or equipment," describes John Barkmeier, MD. In addition, the company offered a mature application for ambulatory practices which had been used successfully for a number of years.

Barkmeier served as the physician champion of ThedaCare's electronic platform and provided the liaison between the clinical and IT worlds. "Implementation of an EHR brings many changes to ambulatory practices. Part of my role was to anticipate what some of those changes might be, explain these to practitioners and staff in the clinics, and get their feedback. I also played an active role in informing clinicians and staff what they might do to ensure a more successful EHR implementation, such as organizing chart material and obtaining minimum keyboarding skills," describes Barkmeier. "The transition from paper to electronic is a painful process for some people. To commit to the transition, everyone needs to understand the value offered by an EHR." "Optimization specialists" employed by ThedaCare at the corporate level were later added to work individually with practitioners to help speed the learning curve and spread the best practices.

ThedaCare Physicians has a pay-for-performance type of financial incentive system (called DIMES) that encourages physicians to improve EHR-supported quality of care parameters. Five percent of total physician compensation, or approximately $700,000 dollars a year, is "wrapped around" quality results. "We reward physicians for excellence in achieving clinical quality indicators, such as appropriate antibiotic use, depression and asthma screening, and best-practice medication prescribing. Patients are the real benefactors," comments Scott Decker, Vice President of Operational Innovation and Quality. Performance on defined indicators is tracked closely through the EHR's reporting mechanisms. A sample portion of the DIMES report appears as Figure 4.

Data from 12/1/03 to11/30/04	CLINICAL							
	CAD LDL < 100		DIAB HbA1c <= 7.5		DIABETIC EYE		MAMMOGRAPHY	
	Rates	Points	Rates	Points	Rates	Points	Rates	Points
FAMILY PRACTICE TARGETS:	>= 60%	10	>= 70%	10	>=80%	5	>=85%	5
THEDACARE PHYS NEENAH	62%	10	65%	0	76%	0	84%	0
THEDACARE PHYS NEW LONDON	63%	10	71%	10	88%	5	92%	5
THEDACARE PHYS NORTH	66%	10	69%	0	79%	0	86%	5
THEDACARE PHYS OMM	60%	10	44%	0	78%	0	77%	0
THEDACARE PHYS OSHKOSH	67%	10	63%	0	77%	0	89%	5
THEDACARE PHYS SHAWANO	67%	10	68%	0	83%	5	85%	5
THEDACARE PHYS SOUTH	78%	10	72%	10	83%	5	88%	5
THEDACARE PHYS WAUPACA	76%	10	70%	10	83%	5	86%	5
INTERNAL MEDICINE TARGETS:	>= 60%	10	>= 70%	10	>=80%	5	>=85%	5
THEDACARE PHYS INT MED - APPLETON	62%	10	66%	0	77%	0	87%	5
THEDACARE PHYS INT MED - NEENAH	71%	10	58%	0	74%	0	81%	0
CARE GROUP SUB-TOTAL	68%		67%		79%		86%	
OVERALL TOTAL	65%		67%		77%		86%	

Figure 4. Clinical Quality Indictor Monitoring. From ThedaCare, Appleton, Wisconsin. Used with permission.

References

1 American Hospital Association's *Hospitals & Health Networks Most Wired Magazine.* Available at www.hhnmostwired.com/hhnmostwired/index.jsp.

2 Kilo CM, Triffletti P, Tantau C, et al. Improving access to clinical offices. *J Medical Practice Management.* November/December 2000; 16(3): 126-132.

3 Institute for Healthcare Improvement. A culture of change at ThedaCare. Available at www.ihi.org/IHI/Topics/OfficePractices/Access/ImprovementStories/ThedaCareFeatureStory.htm.

4 National Heart, Lung and Blood Institute's National Cholesterol Education Program. *Third Report of the Expert Panel on Detection, Evaluation, and Treatment of High Blood Cholesterol in Adults (Adult Treatment Panel III),* 2002. Available at: www.nhlbi.nih.gov/guidelines/cholesterol.

Mid-Size Practice Case Study: Southeast Texas Medical Associates, LLP (SETMA)

ABOUT THE PRACTICE

Southeast Texas Medical Associates, LLP (SETMA) is a 20-physician practice in Beaumont, Texas, a city of 115,000 located approximately 90 miles northeast of Houston. Originating in 1995 as a single location, primary care practice with five providers, today SETMA is an integrated delivery system with three clinical locations in Beaumont. It employs 267 personnel, including 16 nurse practitioners, and has a patient base of more than 80,000 patients.

SETMA provides a full range of primary care services and is supported by specialists in rheumatology, general surgery, colorectal surgery, neurology, endocrinology, pulmonology, ophthalmology, radiology, and sports medicine. In addition, the organization has separate locations for billing, physical therapy, hospice, home health, and mobile x-ray, and operates a level two, moderately complex reference laboratory. Annual patient encounters for all services are approximately 263,000.

Believing that its future growth was limited by the paper-based medical record, in 1998 SETMA purchased electronic medical record (EHR) and practice management (EPM) systems from NextGen Healthcare Information Services. The EHR system went "live" in early 1999. The EHR is available across the entire network, providing HIPAA-compliant secure access to patient data at all points of service, including emergency rooms, three hospitals, all clinical locations, providers' residences, and nursing homes.

Chief executive officer James L. Holly, MD, was a driving force behind SETMA's extensive use of IT. He compares the nurturing possible by SETMA's providers with the practice's IT and medical information management to that offered by a gardener "who tends for an acorn until it becomes a mighty oak."

"Due to the complexity of healthcare today, it is impossible for anyone to know all the facts, says Holly. "The knowledge needed to provide excellent healthcare fills multiple libraries. To bring that knowledge to bear on patients' health needs, SETMA has an 'acorn' in every examination room. We call it a computer. The computer places at the provider's fingertips the data needed to guide healthcare decisions. Equipped with this information, the practitioner must still bring his or her experience, judgment, and even intuition to the encounter to provide the very best possible healthcare."

IMPROVED RELIABILITY AND QUALITY OF CARE AT SETMA

Since implementing an EHR in 1998, SETMA has been able to manage patients as individuals and as members of specific populations that can benefit from preventive and continuing healthcare initiatives. For example, prior to implementing the EHR, the practice had a 20% immunization compliance rate; now it exceeds 80%. SETMA has initiatives for preventive healthcare, such as mammograms, pap smears, and PSAs, and patients are contacted when their records reflect a deficiency in their preventive care status. This contributes to increased quality of care, patient satisfaction, and improved outcomes.

SETMA also has implemented the AMA/CMS Physician Consortium for Performance Improvement data sets, covering chronic conditions such as diabetes, congestive heart failure, hypertension, and chronic stable angina. The organization has disease-specific clinics for diabetes, lipid management, renal disease, congestive heart failure, coumadin management, adult weight management, chronic obstructive pulmonary disease and asthma, and headaches. These clinics are supported by template-driven, disease-specific management tools that are based on national standards of care.

Through use of the EHR, SETMA developed hospital order sets for multiple disease states, including diabetes, seizure disorders, pneumonia, congestive heart failure, hyperkalemia, hypokalemia, diabetic ketoacidosis, and numerous others. These order sets make it possible for a provider, regardless of level of training, to initiate care according to national standards of quality care as viewed by specialists in the field.

Through the effective integration of information technology, SETMA has established a continuum of care model of healthcare delivery. "This continuum ties the clinic to the hospital, to the physical therapy clinic, to the home, to the hospice, to the home health agency, and so forth," notes Holly. "This means that when the patient is admitted to the hospital, the hospital-based physician is entering data in the same database as used in the clinic and elsewhere. When discharged, the data are created in the same database. Therefore, when the patient returns to the clinic, the follow-up is done on all issues related to the visit as detailed in the discharge summary, which is already in the EHR. Regardless of the location of service, a common database is used for the encounter, establishing and maintaining the continuity of care. With active interfaces between the EHR and the clinical laboratory, we avoid redundancy and eliminate errors."

The quality of care provided by SETMA has improved dramatically since the implementation of the EHR. Lengths of hospital stays, hospital readmissions, and morbidity have declined, and compliance with national standards of care and the effectiveness of care plans have increased. Since installing its EHR, SETMA has been audited eight times for Health Plan Employer Data and Information Set (HEDIS) compliance. In every case, the practice has been found to be 100% in compliance.

DEFINING BUSINESS AND CLINICAL OBJECTIVES

SETMA leaders, who purchased and implemented an EHR in 1998-1999, realized that the pursuit of excellence in clinical care required EHRs. Their primary objective was to move from paper to electronic patient management in order to ensure clinical care excellence. "We realized that the complexities of 21st century medicine required 'data management' rather than 'document management,' and that the ability to measure provider performance and outcomes of medical decision making processes required 'data manipulation.' These functions were possible only with an EHR," notes Holly.

SETMA's specific clinical and business objectives included the following:

- ***Improved quality of care:*** SETMA wanted to establish a true "continuum of care" delivery model, with continuity of care between the outpatient, inpatient, long-term care, and home care settings. The management of patients as individuals and as members of specific populations with preventive, acute, and chronic health initiatives across all patient care systems, and the ability to infuse national standards of care in complex treatment conditions and settings were also key goals.
- ***Improved patient safety:*** This could be accomplished through electronic drug/drug, allergy, and condition interaction checking, correct medication checking, and the provision to patients of educational materials, including a list of their current medications, dosages, and instructions at every encounter.
- ***Comprehensive clinical documentation:*** Improved integration of clinical documentation with laboratory, radiology, special procedures, consultations, hospital history and physicals and discharge summaries, and specialty care data was a priority.
- ***Increased workflow efficiencies, resulting in improved financial benefits:*** Expected efficiencies included improvement of prescription processes, referral management, online communications, response time to inquiries, drug recall processes, and inquiry documentation.
- ***Increased reporting efficiencies:*** These efficiencies would result in proactive patient management, outcomes management, easier business management, and higher reimbursement.
- ***Increased physician productivity and satisfaction.*** Physicians wanted simplified documentation, more time to spend with patients, access to patient data from any location, and enhanced quality of life.

LAYING THE GROUNDWORK FOR EHR CONSENSUS AT SETMA

Leaders at SETMA advise that successful EHR implementation in any size or type of healthcare organization requires the following consensus-building elements:

- A physician champion who is respected by most of the providers and is totally committed to the project.
- A vendor with a sound financial position and a proven track record of successful implementation, support and continued product development.
- Adequate project management and technical support staffing.
- A determination by the organization that everyone is going to use the EHR and that there will not be a place in the organization for individuals who resist or refuse.

- Proper preparation and training, but a "drop dead" date by which time the project will start. "Many implementations have failed due to poor or inadequate preparation, or because excessive preparation delayed the project so long that everyone just gave up," notes Holly.
- A celebratory attitude characterized by delight in what has been accomplished while recognizing what remains to be done. The approach should be, "See how much we have done," rather than "See how much we still have to do."

ACHIEVING INCREASED WORKFLOW EFFICIENCIES AT SETMA

SETMA's implementation of an EHR in 1998-1999 resulted in the following workflow efficiencies:

- *Improved prescription process.* Prior to implementation of the EHR, physicians had to search for and locate the patient's chart, look up the patient's allergies, check for potential drug interactions, hand write the prescription, and give it to the patient or nurse. With the EHR, physicians have immediate access to the patient's chart and the system automatically performs allergy and drug-to-drug interactions checking. Prescriptions are faxed directly to pharmacies via the system's fax manager.
- *Streamlined referral management.* SETMA now manages the specialist referral process electronically at the point of care from any location, such as a clinic, hospital, office, etc. The referrals initiated during a patient encounter are completed electronically and forwarded to the referral department from the examination room.
- *Enabled online communications.* Patients can now securely e-mail or message their providers, request an appointment, complete forms and questionnaires, or view lab results online via SETMA's Web site. Additionally, the practice now receives referrals, billing information, and laboratory data online.
- *Improved response time to patient inquiries.* The amount of time required to handle telephone inquiries regarding a patient chart was reduced by 73%. The number of associated tasks to process these calls has decreased from 18 to 2. Total annual savings by year 4 following EHR implementation exceeded $103,000.
- *Improved drug recall process.* SETMA's drug recall process was simplified dramatically. With paper charts, there were two options to handle a drug recall: (1) patients would hear about a drug recall and come in for an alternate prescription, or (2) a staff member would scan all paper records, identify which patients were taking the recalled drug, and notify the patients of the recall. Through an EHR database query, SETMA staff can now easily identify which patients are taking the recalled drug, draft a letter to those patients, perform a mail merge, and mail the letter to the patients within a matter of hours.
- *Improved inquiry documentation.* Telephone communications from patients are transmitted to the providers electronically, allowing them to easily access the patient's records with all the necessary elements (lab, allergies and medications). This allows the providers to document their response and automatically and electronically alert the unit clerk or nurse of the proper action to be taken. Through EHR use, SETMA is able to document more than 600,000 phone calls and responses per year.

THE BUSINESS CASE FOR IT AT SETMA

SETMA's leaders recognized that the expense of manipulating and maintaining thorough paper records, of transcribing dictation into those records, and of having them available in a timely fashion made the potential return on investment of an EHR attractive. "Due to shrinking reimbursement, revenue for services performed could only be optimized by having providers 'post charges' using an integrated EHR and electronic practice management system at the point of service," describes Holly.

In considering the business case for IT, SETMA's leaders identified the following administrative benefits of using an integrated EHR and electronic practice management system:

- Reduced medical transcription costs;
- Improved evaluation and management (E&M) coding with a resulting increase in billable charges;
- Lower administrative costs due to the reduced time required for staff to handle charts and telephone inquiries;
- Reduced costs for administrative supplies;
- Decreased claims denial, resulting in reduced days in accounts receivables;
- Improved audits; and
- Revenue enhancement due to all of the above.

SETMA's success in achieving these benefits is described later.

DETERMINING EHR CORE FUNCTIONALITY AT SETMA

SETMA's basic requirements for its EHR were that it be always available, supportive of all clinical processes, minimally intrusive to the patient-physician relationship, and that it improve clinical decision making, workflow efficiency and excellence.

In the clinical domain, the practice's leaders determined that the EHR they purchased should let providers use point-and-click, voice-activated data capture, typing, and/or scanning to capture data related to the history and physical, visit notes, problem list, medications, radiology reports, reports and correspondence from outside the practice, and laboratory results.

The EHR system SETMA implemented provides documentation of the following:

- More than 260,000 patient encounters per year;
- More than 672,000 incoming telephone calls per year and responses to those calls;
- More than 15,000 x-rays and 4,000 EKGs per year;
- Nursing home patient visits;
- Laboratory ordering and reporting for in-house reference laboratory;
- Physical therapy visits;
- Hospital admission history and physical examinations and discharge summaries for more than 40,000 daily hospital visits per year;
- All medications used to treat a patient, including checking for drug/drug interactions and patient/drug allergies;
- Return to work authorizations;
- Waivers of payment of Medicare and Medicaid charges;

- Referrals to specialists at the point of service, whether clinic, hospital, or another setting; and
- Follow-up instructions for additional or future testing.

SETMA's implementation also has resulted in the practice's ability to:

- Fax all prescriptions to pharmacies;
- Communicate via e-mail and e-mail laboratory results to patients with patient authorization and when proper security is in place on both ends of the transaction;
- Receive requests for appointments, referrals, billing information, or laboratory data via SETMA's Web site;
- Use an electronic super bill for association of ICD-9 codes and CPT codes;
- Create a billing event automatically from the patient's examination room;
- Provide patients with personalized educational information automatically at the point of encounter;
- Develop extensive reports on immunizations, disease state management, preventive health issues, practice patterns, provider patterns, payer patterns, and aging of accounts;
- Compare provider performance on dimensions such as quality of records and appropriateness of assessment;
- Incorporate multiple health assessment/prevention questionnaires into the routine office visit; and
- Allow the provider to review information over time, following trends for vital signs, laboratory work and procedures.

EHR COSTS AND FINANCIAL BENEFITS FOR SETMA

The Costs

SETMA's investment for EHR software, hardware, and support for the initial implementation in 1998-99 was approximately $600,000. At that time, the organization had ten healthcare providers, including seven physicians, and one location. Since that time, SETMA has grown to almost 40 providers, including 19.5 FTE physicians in five locations, and has expanded the use of the EHR to the hospital, nursing home, physical therapy, hospice, and home health settings. Additional expenditure for software licenses and hardware, including wiring, routers, and servers (now numbering 22), has been in excess of $1,000,000. The annual IT department budget is $400,000. Capital acquisitions for hardware and depreciable items, without additional location expansion, range between $150,000 and $200,000 annually.

The Financial Benefits

In 2002, four years following implementation of the EHR, SETMA hired an independent agency to conduct an ROI analysis. "While the numbers will be different today, they will be further improved and the cost savings will be magnified because in the interim, SETMA has doubled in size and productivity," notes Holly. Financial benefits include the following:

- ***Increased income due to electronic superbill.*** Because SETMA now bills automatically from the patient's examination room, the overall average charge per patient visit has increased to $206 from $171 (a 20% increase) and the average collection increased to $104 from $80 (a 30% increase). In 2001 alone, total billable charges increased by $2.1 million and overall collections increased by $1.4 million.

- ***Increased revenue.*** Due to lower supply costs, increased billing accuracy, and lower administrative overhead, revenue has increased nearly $3 million annually.
- ***Reduced chart costs.*** The average time required to establish a new chart decreased 85% to 1.2 minutes per chart from 8.0 minutes, resulting in annual savings of more than $22,000.
- ***Reduced transcription costs.*** In one year of EHR use, transcription costs decreased to an average of $0.25 per visit from $5.93 per visit, resulting in an annual savings of more than $340,000.
- ***Increased billable charges.*** Improvements in E&M service coding increased average billable charges for office visits by 4.23%, adding more than $150,000 in billable charges.
- ***Reduced supplies costs.*** Costs for administrative supplies decreased 87% to $0.97 per patient from $8.00 per patient. Based on the number of patients in 2001 (55,000), SETMA saved more than $380,000 in paper and supply costs.
- ***Reduced chart staff.*** The number of administrative staff required to handle patient charts decreased by 76.7% (to $0.62 per visit from $2.65 per visit), for an annual savings of more than $120,000.
- ***Decreased claim denials.*** Denials have decreased by 26%. This has reduced average accounts receivable by seven days, thus increasing actual revenues by $102,000.

SELECTING THE RIGHT IT PRODUCT AT SETMA

Although SETMA's leaders were involved in examining numerous EHR products at a national trade show in October 1997, the responsibility for further investigation and recommendation was assigned to SETMA's chief information officer. The criteria for selecting a vendor and a product included the following:

- Financial stability of the vendor. "The last thing we wanted was a vendor who would go out of business in the middle of our implementation process," says the CIO;
- The commitment of the vendor to research and development. In 1997, most EHR companies were in their infancy. SETMA required a company that had a vision for expanding its capabilities to meet the needs of healthcare data management in the 21st century;
- Availability of support and the company's reputation among existing customers;
- The successful use of the product by an increasing number of medical practices that were committed to excellence;
- Product scalability and flexibility;
- The ability to transition from paper to electronic documentation with the lowest possible interference with patient care and without impeding physicians' abilities to deliver quality care; and
- The ability for successful interaction between the EHR, practice management system, laboratory information systems, scanning solutions, office software, and a number of other functions.

The CIO recommended three vendors who made presentations to the partners and a decision was made in March 1998 to purchase an EHR and practice management system from NextGen Healthcare Information Services.

IMPLEMENTATION PLANNING AT SETMA

An Informatics Committee, comprised of the organization's CEO, CIO, medical director, inpatient medical director, clinical director of laboratory services, network administrator, and template development specialist, designed SETMA's IT strategy based on the goals and objectives for an EHR and practice management system.

A Template Committee guided the customized development of templates to take advantage of the EHR's capabilities. SETMA's leaders decided early in the process that implementation of the EHR and construction of the templates would be by consensus rather than being individualized. This would facilitate standardization and comparison of care and care documentation. "This probably was the most important decision we made and was one that directly impacted our success," notes Holly.

Once the templates were sufficiently developed, an Implementation Team developed an implementation plan. Holly was identified as the principal person responsible for the success of the project, although all SETMA partners, executive management, and staff embraced the project and worked toward its success.

The collaboration between the technical support team, which included four full-time and one part-time person, and SETMA's healthcare providers was close in order to ensure that the system would work and that it would be helpful in the clinical setting. "That collaboration, driven by mutual respect and trust, remains the hallmark of our success in implementing the EHR initially and in keeping the development process moving forward into the future," says Holly.

SYSTEM IMPLEMENTATION AT SETMA

After extensive development of a unique database between April 1998 and December 1998, SETMA went "live" with the EHR on Tuesday, January 22, 1999 with one "pod" at a time. A pod is a self-contained clinical staff team comprised of physicians, nurses, nurse practitioners, and unit clerks.

Holly indicates that although industry standards suggested that the best way to go live was simply to see the last patient of the day on the EHR, SETMA decided to do it differently. The organization began with the first patient of the day and worked with the EHR until it was so far behind that it had to go back to dictation of the records. "That first day, we finished the morning session at exactly the time the afternoon patient session was to start. The IT staff said, 'Of course, you're going to continue to dictate,' to which we said, 'No, we're going back to EHR.' We did and by Friday, only four days later, we saw everyone in that pod on the EHR. Each month thereafter, we took an additional pod live on the EHR. By March 22, 1999, 60 days after we started, every patient was being seen using the EHR," describes Holly. SETMA's leaders also chose not to scan in old data from medical records, but to start data capture from day 1 live.

When SETMA started the EHR implementation, its leaders set a five-year target for being totally paperless. "We prioritized our implementation to maximize the benefit to the patient care side of the practice, even when it meant not immediately gaining all of the financial benefits of the endeavor," says Holly. "While we had to *build* the templates back in 1998, now people can buy systems with templates built in, and in less than 30 days, they can be up and running," notes Holly.

The process redesign was dictated by the design of the workflow, which guided template development. For the first six months, staff used a double system, pulling the charts and having the EHR and the paper chart side-by-side. Very quickly, however, the paper chart became an unnecessary redundancy. Once staff began to use a scanning solution, which had been delayed until October 2003, SETMA was truly and completely paperless, three months ahead of its five-year schedule.

STAFF TRAINING AT SETMA

Staff training at SETMA was conducted initially through tutorials and subsequently in a special training room where new employees and personnel from newly acquired clinics were taught the system and practiced their skills. "Because the EHR is so intuitive, our providers rapidly learned to use the system. In fact, after three to six months with SETMA, all providers commented that they are 'addicted' to EHR," says Holly.

A person who had been through a "train-the-trainer" intensive introduction to the functions of the EHR was assigned to each pod. IT staff was available for troubleshooting, but someone else was on hand who could answer 90% of the questions. "This system continues to work for us, putting experienced people with newly trained people. All of our staff indicates that it takes about two weeks to be very comfortable with the system. Obviously, it takes longer to be expert, but to be productive takes only two weeks," notes Holly.

All members of the healthcare team use the EHR, including physicians, nurse practitioners, nurses, unit clerks, clerical personnel (with access appropriate to their responsibility), management, hospital support team members, physical therapy, home health, and nursing home support staff who work for SETMA.

"Perhaps the greatest lesson we learned was that it's never too late or too early to start implementing an EHR system," Holly concludes. While EHR acceptance by practitioners nationwide is accelerating, it is still early in the process. Now is the time practices should get started. The hurdle is significant but once surmounted, the benefits to the patient, provider, practice, payers, and public are enormous."

Small Practice Case Study: PatientCare Family Clinic

ABOUT THE PRACTICE

PatientCare Family Clinic, a solo practice in Springfield, Missouri, provides family practice outpatient services to approximately 2,500 active patients. The clinic offers the full range of continuing and urgent care services, including laboratory testing, x-ray, spirometry, holter monitor, and EKG. Through use of open-access scheduling, 90% of patients are seen on the same day they call for an appointment. Owned by Thomas F. Landholt, MD, a board-certified family practice physician, the clinic is staffed by two employees—an office manager and a medical assistant. Clinic hours are 7:30 am to 4:30 pm, Monday through Friday. The clinic's Web site is www.yourdoc.net.

Landholt was an early adopter of EHRs and has been involved in testing and demonstrating products from a number of companies for more than a decade. However, Landholt firmly believes that all solo and small practices can implement EHRs quickly and effectively. "It's a misconception that only larger groups have the wherewithal and IT expertise to have an EHR. With lower software and hardware costs, it's no longer so," he says.[1] According to Landholt, practitioners in solo and small group practices are moving toward implementation of EHRs for four reasons: financial viability, enhanced practice efficiencies, better practice quality, and more satisfying lifestyles.[1]

PatientCare Family Clinic currently uses GE Medical Systems' EMR/billing system along with Kryptiq's scanning, secure messaging and Web site solutions. Additionally, devices like Midmark's EKG and spirometry are directly integrated into the other systems, providing seamless access to testing data.

ENHANCING PATIENT-PHYSICIAN INTERACTION AT PATIENTCARE FAMILY CLINIC

Office layout and the integration of technology to enhance patient-physician interaction within the clinic space were key issues considered by Landholt at the PatientCare Family Clinic.

Many medical office-based practices and clinics tend to be designed in what Landholt calls "a physician-centric" manner. In this design, the physician's work flow is most important, so nurses' workstations are close to the physician's office and exam rooms are within steps. Front office staff tends to be isolated in a separate space, making it difficult to communicate with direct patient care staff.

Landholt ensured that his clinic was designed in a process-centric manner more conducive for good patient-staff interaction. "I think for a living—examining patients and making medical decisions. Where I am or where I move within the office is relatively immaterial. Most of the time-and-motion work is done by the nurse and the front office staff. They prepare the patient, process the insurance information, perform the testing, etc. Thus, in my clinic, the front office space, reception area and the nurses' station form a triangle. Everyone can see and communicate with each other. The exam rooms are in the front near the nurse's station; my office is in the back," describes Landholt. "Physicians need to worry less about their own work flow and concentrate instead on how the whole office functions."

Each exam room is equipped with a personal computer and a large-screen monitor placed on a mobile cart. "When in the exam room with a patient and accessing the Internet or the patient's EHR, I'm mindful again about creating a triangle with the patient, myself, and the computer. If I place the computer between myself and the patient, he or she can't see what I see. This physically and interactively separates us. On the other hand, if a patient can see his or her record, for example, which shows an allergy to penicillin, a partnership is created in the exam room. The patient can review the medication list, be reassured by what's there, indicate if anything's missing, and correct any incorrect information," describes Landholt.

While in the exam room with patients, Landholt also frequently accesses Web sites to show patients "pictures worth a thousand words" and guide them to high-quality, peer-reviewed Web-based information resources, such as the National Guidelines Clearinghouse, PDR.net, and others. "If I need to check on a drug dosage or a treatment protocol, I do that right in the exam room with the patient following along. Patients know physicians need to look things up because they can't possibly remember everything, and feel comforted when this occurs right in the exam room where they too can read the information," says Landholt.

The emphasis on high quality interaction between patients and the PatientCare Family Clinic extends to its Web site, which performs three relationship-building information exchange functions. It provides:[2]

- Basic information about the clinic, educational information about medical conditions and procedures, and links to educational Web sites selected by Landholt. By clicking the "Patient Library" button on the Web site, patients can look at educational videos and handouts, download useful forms, and access linked Web pages of interest.

- Access to medical records: patients can log in and obtain secure information from their records. Through the Web site, patients can access summaries of their records and print information related to medications, diagnoses, insurance, laboratory work, and other material.
- Secure e-mail communication to and from Landholt and his staff. Approximately 70% of laboratory tests results are returned to patients via secure messaging. This eliminates the frustrations of telephone tag. Landholt interprets laboratory results for his patients, attaches actual laboratory reports, and recommends Web sites offering additional educational information. Patients can obtain the information and clinical data they need when they need it.

Figure 1 shows the linked functions available to patients when they click the Web site's "MyHealth" button.

MyMedicalRecord
MyMedicalRecord contains my current medical information

Request Appointment
Request an appointment with your physician

Request Referral
Request a referral from your doctor

Renew Medication
Renew a medication

Update Demographic Information
Update your demographic information

Send Message
Send a secure message to your physician

Figure 1. MyHealth. From PatientCare Family Clinic's Web site: https://secure.yourdoc.net/Portal/MyHealth/default.aspx.

ENHANCING CARE COORDINATION AT PATIENTCARE FAMILY CLINIC

Ready access to the patient's complete chart by the solo physician or any member of the staff at PatientCare Family Clinic enhances care coordination. When talking with a specialist about the care of one of his patients, Landholt is looking at the complete EHR for that patient. When calling to schedule an appointment for a patient with a specialist, the certified medical assistant or office manager, who has immediate access to the EHR, can answer specific questions or fax requested data as a chart summary or send it via secure messaging to the specialist's office.

IMPROVING WORK FLOW AT PATIENTCARE FAMILY CLINIC

Solo practitioner Landholt staffs PatientCare Family Clinic with two individuals—an office manager and a medical assistant. Citing Medical Group Management Association data, Landholt notes that the average family practice has more than twice as many (4.5) staff members. Landholt's staff is cross-trained, which reduces the specialization of work flow and enables multiple people to take care of the multiple tasks required in a small office practice.

For example, if a mother of a school-aged child calls the clinic to request her child's shot records, either the office manager or the certified medical assistant can put that package of information together electronically and fax it to the mother while on the phone with her. "With the capabilities offered by technology, my expectations about what staff can and should accomplish have changed. As a result, I need better trained and educated staff that requires better pay, but I need fewer staff members than non-automated practices. Both individuals are well-trained in operating high-end, high-service outpatient clinics with automated work flows. They probably wouldn't last a week in a paper-based clinic based on job satisfaction because they are used to being able to accomplish so much more," says Landholt.

"Automation through a fully integrated EHR at PatientCare Family Clinic provides a better work environment in which staff is empowered to spend more time taking care of patients and less time shuffling paper and making appointments," says Landholt. The use of technology has increased the efficiency of formerly inefficient processes, such as pulling charts and faxing records. Landholt notes that although physicians make the medical decisions, most care is actually delivered by the rest of the office staff.[2] "If I streamline my staff's work flow, I'm going to have the opportunity to see more patients, and they are going to have more rewarding jobs," says Landholt. Landholt indicates that the EHR improves his productivity by enabling him to see more patients in the same amount of time, and allows staff to spend more time on patient care processes.

Landholt methodically streamlined procedures in his office practice *before* he started EHR implementation. "If you automate a bad workflow, it's still a bad workflow," he says. "A good electronic medical record should adapt to the office's improved workflow; it shouldn't make the doctor adapt to it." Efficient work flows are supported by the EHR, not vice versa.

For example, to fax a document to a specialist, most people would accomplish this through a three-step process: preparing a document, printing out that document, walking over to a fax machine and sending the document via fax. A reengineered work process involves only two steps: specifying the format for the document (the EHR fills out the form) and sending it electronically via a fax server. A paper document is never created and time and steps are saved multiple times per day.

The clinic's EHR is fully integrated with its billing system. No paper superbills are created. Rather, when in the exam room, Landholt updates the patient's record, indicates diagnosis codes, and by the time the patient is back up by the front desk, all the necessary information for an electronic superbill has been entered. Front office staff simply collects the appropriate co-payment. "No one has to add up the superbill or re-enter the data into the billing system," notes Landholt.

According to Landholt, the types of technology needed to streamline practice work flow are as follows:

- An electronic medical record: this serves as the data repository into which and out of which data will flow.
- Interface technology: this enables sharing of information between two systems. For example, through interface technology, laboratory data can be delivered to the practice's EMR directly from reference laboratory software.[3] Interface technology includes:
  - Scanning software: This converts paper-based information to electronic information.
  - Fax server and software: This provides inbound and outbound electronic faxing capabilities.
  - Secure messaging: This ensures secure communication between patients and the clinic.

Landholt estimates the initial cost to fully automate a small medical practice to be between $50,000 and $75,000 with annual maintenance costs of $10,000 to $15,000. A three-to-six-month implementation time frame is realistic; another three to six months are required to get completely comfortable with the system.

Landholt cites two challenges in implementing the EHR: incorporating new workflows (which requires staff retraining) and keeping up with the technical environment. "The latter is improving. As vendors better understand practice work flows, they are able to develop improved tools to properly support those work flows," he notes.

References

1. Reece RL. E Pluribus E-Unum. Available at www.HealthLeaders.com (accessed December 23, 2004).
2. Goodwin J. Medical influencial: family clinic embraces technology. *Springfield, Missouri News Leader.* November 16, 2004.
3. Landholdt TF (and The Coker Group). *Managing the Outpatient Medical Practice: Strategies for a Changing Environment.* Chicago: AHA Press; 1999, 104.

Index

D

E

I

K

L

M

Q

R

S

T

V

W